The Murderous History of Bible Translations

The Murderous History of Bible Translations

Power, Conflict and the Quest for Meaning

Harry Freedman

BLOOMSBURY PRESS

NEW YORK · LONDON · OXFORD · NEW DELHI · SYDNEY

Bloomsbury Press
An imprint of Bloomsbury Publishing Plc

1385 Broadway	50 Bedford Square
New York	London
NY 10018	WC1B 3DP
USA	UK

www.bloomsbury.com

Bloomsbury and the Diana logo are trademarks of Bloomsbury Publishing Plc

First published in Great Britain 2016
First U.S. edition 2016

ISBN: HB: 978-1-63286-601-1
ePub: 978-1-63286-603-5

Library of Congress Cataloging-in-Publication Data is available.

2 4 6 8 10 9 7 5 3 1

Printed and bound in USA by Berryville Graphics Inc., Berryville, Virginia

To find out more about our authors and books visit www.bloomsbury.com. Here you will
find extracts, author interviews, details of forthcoming events and the option to sign up for
our newsletters.

Bloomsbury books may be purchased for business or promotional use.
For information on bulk purchases please contact Macmillan Corporate and
Premium Sales Department at specialmarkets@macmillan.com.

For Eli. Already gifted in several tongues.

Contents

Introduction

Most of us take the Bible for granted. That is to say, irrespective of our religious beliefs we assume that the Bible in our hands, or the one we never take off the shelf, or the copy in the hotel drawer, has always been the way we see it now. Like any other book, it was written, printed, bound, published and is sometimes read. It may or may not be, depending on our views, sacred or divine. But that's not the point. It is what it is; it's the Bible.

The Bible that most of us are familiar with is not printed in its original languages. It's a translation. Translators tend to be anonymous people; when we read a foreign book in our own language we know who wrote it; we don't think much about who translated it. But the people who translated the Bible, many of them anyway, were not just ordinary translators commissioned to render a piece of literature into a different language. Almost without exception, they had a story. And for many of them, their story is every bit as illuminating, and frequently as violent, as the Bible itself.

In 1535, William Tyndale, the first man to produce an English version of the Bible in print, was captured and imprisoned in Belgium. A year later he was strangled and then burned at the stake. A co-translator, John Rogers, was also burned. In the same year, the translator of the first Dutch Bible, Jacob van Liesveldt, was arrested and beheaded. They weren't the only Bible translators to meet a grizzly end, they just happen to be among the best known.

The history of Bible translation has not always been murderous, but it has rarely been lacking in contention. Even in our own time the controversies have rarely gone away. The politics of modern Bible translation is peppered with arguments and disputes about how to read the Good Book, and what it really says. The violence has dissipated but, given the history of religious conflict, it is not unthinkable that it may one day return. Religion generates extreme emotions. Unlikely as it may seem, there is only a fine line between Bible translation and sectarian conflict.

The translated Bible lends itself well to polemic and religious manipulation. The sixteenth-century translators of the Geneva Bible harnessed it to promote their anti-monarchist views. The medieval Church used it as a whipping boy, prohibiting its use to ensure that people believed what they were told, not what they read, or had others read to them. Missionaries and evangelists throughout history have relied upon it to promote their message among non-believers.

The Bible is central to Western civilization and the Judeo-Christian tradition. One doesn't need to be a believer to recognize that many of the principles we hold dear come straight from its pages. Can we imagine a world in which it had not been translated? If the Bible had remained exclusively in the hands of the priests, would science, education and freedom have prospered? Alternatively, had the hallmarks of civilization developed wholly independently of religion, is it conceivable that someone would not have translated the Bible?

The translated Bible was intended to be radical, liberating and inspirational. Yet in the hands of religious conservatism it became a negative force, a barrier to social evolution. In its earliest narrative, the story of the translated Bible reflects the separation of early Christianity from its Jewish ancestry. Centuries later, it became a paradigm for the battle between medievalism and modernity. And in modern times the experiences of the translated Bible encapsulate all the uncertainties afflicting formal religion in an open and secular age. But at no time has the translated Bible been free from violence; even now, when there is little physical threat, the turbulence a new translation engenders is palpable. The translated Bible's history is truly murderous.

Nobody ever sat down with the intention of writing a Bible. How could they? The concept didn't exist. Over the course of many centuries, individuals under varying degrees of inspiration wrote accounts of revelations, histories, prophecies and myths. The Bible is a collection of some of these accounts, or more accurately, three collections. The earliest collection is known colloquially as the Old Testament, the Bible of the Jews. The most recent is the Christian New Testament. A third, slightly less revered compendium is known to the Catholics as the Deuterocanon and to everyone else as the Apocrypha.

The process of translating the Bible, of bringing it to the masses, began even before the collections, or canon, were complete. Parts of the Bible were being translated even as it was being written. The Book of Nehemiah, one of the later volumes in the Old Testament, relates how Ezra the Scribe translated the Five Books of Moses for the benefit of Aramaic-speaking, Jewish refugees returning home from Babylon. Acts of the Apostles describes how the Bible was miraculously translated into many languages simultaneously.[1] But the first Bible translation controversy did not erupt until much later, early in the second century of the Common Era. The cycle of controversies took several hundred years to reach a climax. Things moved more slowly in those days.

This book tells the story of those for whom the idea of a Bible that ordinary people could read was so important that they were willing to give up their time, their security, often even their lives. It tells the story of the translated Bible, but it does not pretend to be a comprehensive history of the translated Bible. Too many books on the Bible are overlong and full of dry facts; that is fine for an academic work but it can wear down readers who are not looking to become experts in the field. So, in this eclectic account, many translations, and many seminal characters in the translated Bible's history, get scarcely a mention, either because they managed to remain free from controversy, or because their story adds little to what has already been said. For similar reasons we do not delve into the technicalities of translation techniques, nor fret over contentious interpretations. The Bibliography lists many of the good books available on these and other subjects, for those who are interested.

Just a word on terminology. No designation of the Bible or its various constituents will satisfy everybody. For Jews the Bible is only the Old Testament, but the name itself is inappropriate because it implies that their Bible has been superseded. For Christians the Bible means both Old and New Testaments, together with the Deuterocanon, or Apocrypha, for Catholics and Orthodox, and without it for many Protestants. The order of the books in the so-called Old Testament is different for Jews, Protestants and Catholics. To keep things simple I have used the traditional terms of Old and New Testament throughout and tried not to dwell overmuch on the various definitions of what actually constitutes the Bible.

Part One

Before The Violence

1

The Legacy of Alexandria

The Legend of the Septuagint

The story begins, as many good stories do, as a shard of truth, deeply buried within a legend. We are unlikely ever to uncover the whole story but the legend is as good a place to start as any.

The only indisputable fact in the legend is that the history of Bible translation began in the ancient world's most important city, in the vibrant, dazzling heart of Greek culture, science, architecture and scholarship. A city bearing the name of its recently deceased founder, Alexander Macedon, known to the world as Alexander the Great: the city of Alexandria, capital of Egypt.

The lighthouse, which sat at the tip of the Alexandrian island of Pharos, was one of the Seven Wonders of the ancient world. But wonders do not last for ever; everyone knew that the lighthouse was an impermanent edifice – in time it would crumble and fall. The Macedonian general Ptolemy I, King of Egypt and ruler of Alexandria, believed that his city deserved more than this. The majesty of Greek culture was worthy of an enduring testament, an eternal monument unshackled by the transient world. The monument would contain that which men craved but could never destroy; a sanctuary for the ephemeral virtue of Wisdom.

Demetrius of Phalerum was an adviser to Ptolemy. A renowned public speaker and former pupil of Aristotle, Demetrius had spent ten years as the governor of Athens. There, among other things, he had supervised the erection of countless statues to himself. His authority in Athens had been prematurely ruptured when the city was besieged and conquered by his enemies. Demetrius fled, first to Thebes, near the modern Egyptian town of Luxor, and from there to Alexandria where he joined King Ptolemy's court.[1] According to the Greek historian Plutarch, it was he who advised the king to 'collect together books on kingship and the exercise of power, and to read them'.[2] The king accepted Demetrius's counsel, and, round about 288 BCE, the Library of Alexandria was born. It would serve as a testament to the supremacy of Greek culture, to demonstrate that even here on the northern shores of Africa, at the mouth of the River Nile, the Greeks could contemplate no better use of their wealth than the acquisition of knowledge and learning.

Ptolemy gave the order to build the library within Alexandria's magnificent royal complex, a vast, palatial area of the city, just a little way inland from the lighthouse. Unlike a modern library, it was not housed within a room, nor did it contain books in the form we know. Instead the Library was woven into the fabric of the Temple to the Muses, hence its name, Museum, a vast scholarly establishment where Euclid wrote his *Elements of Geometry* and, almost two millennia before Copernicus, Aristarchus proved that the earth revolved around the sun. The library itself seems to have been a vast bookshelf that ran along one side of a long, covered walkway, snaking and slithering into recesses and cubicles as it progressed.

Papyrus scrolls from every corner of the world were stacked in lidded boxes on the shelf. They included lists of names, catalogues of gods, heroes and adventurers, chronologies of great events. But the subject that dominated, the one which every Alexandrian librarian and reader gravitated towards whenever they had the opportunity, was Greek drama; the plays of Sophocles, Aeschylus, Euripides and all those whose names have no longer survived.[3] Ptolemy had sent letters throughout the world, to every known king, prince, baron and demagogue, asking them to send him copies of the books in their possession. Few dared to disobey. The king had further ordered that every ship which docked in Alexandria's harbour was to surrender for copying any books that it carried. The library would keep the originals; the copies were to be returned to the mariners. When finished, the library would contain works by every conceivable manner of author; 'poets and prose-writers, rhetoricians and sophists, doctors and soothsayers and historians, and all the others too'.[4]

The library differed in another way from our modern, rather tame image of a place where books are stored and quietly read. According to Peter Stothard's entertaining book *Alexandria: The Last Nights of Cleopatra*, the concepts of library and laboratory were, in those ancient times, closely related. A place of learning was just that, whether the learning came about through the use of books or whether by practical experimentation. The royal palaces, which sat on the eastern flank of the Great Harbour, were well endowed with dungeons. Some of the unhappy captives, who no doubt thought their lives could get no worse, found themselves at the mercy of librarians keen to advance the cause of Ptolemaic science through the practice of live dissection.[5]

According to the earliest version of the legend, Ptolemy's adviser, Demetrius of Phalerum, was awarded the position of founding librarian, charged with compiling the fledgling library's ambitious collection. He thought his work was well in hand, and he had already amassed two hundred thousand books, when he was summoned by a disgruntled Ptolemy. The king, who had placed every conceivable resource at his librarian's disposal, was concerned that the acquisition programme was not moving fast enough. He was impatient to hear Demetrius's plans to increase the library's holdings to an acceptable level.

The king had set Demetrius a target for the finished library of half a million books. The two hundred thousand in his vault when the monarch summoned him was clearly nothing like enough. Demetrius assured Ptolemy that he was taking urgent steps to expand the library's stock. He reminded the king that neither of them would be satisfied with merely the largest library in the world. Size wasn't everything. Quality was essential too. As was the imperative that every book be rendered into Greek. After all, the library was a testament to Greek culture; it would be unthinkable for it to contain works written in a foreign language.

A swarm of scholars had been hired and set to work, translating the swelling pile of foreign books. They'd breezed their way through complicated, alien works like the two million verses attributed to the Persian philosopher Zoroaster (a work which would later be indexed in its entirety by Hermippus, the pupil of one of Demetrius's successors). But Demetrius had a problem, one which threatened to undermine the library's status as the unchallenged repository for the whole of the world's literature. According to the earliest source of our legend, a letter sent in the second century BCE by Aristeas, an Alexandrian Jew, to his brother Philocrates, one text in particular stumped the translators. It was the Hebrew Bible, the sacred literature of the Jews.

This is just the first of several instances which lead us to suspect there is something not quite right about Aristeas's account. He wants us to believe that nobody in Alexandria could understand Hebrew. Yet there was a large Jewish community in Alexandria, probably the world's most numerous outside of the land of Israel. Even if none of Alexandria's Jews were able to read and understand Hebrew, which is highly improbable, Egypt and Israel shared a border; traders and merchants went back and forth all the time. And yet Aristeas implies that nobody in Alexandria was literate in Hebrew; none could decipher the strange characters in which the language was written, nor understand the words the characters formed. Demetrius was insistent that the Hebrew Bible be included in his library. Aristeas tells us that there was nobody among his impressive body of scholars who could translate it.

The king didn't think that Alexandria's lack of Hebrew translators was much of a problem. Visionary thinking was his forte; that's why he had risen to be King of Egypt while Demetrius was a sad, failed ruler of Athens. To Ptolemy the answer was quite clear. He instructed Demetrius to despatch a delegation across the border, to the Temple in Jerusalem. The envoys were to carry gifts; silver and gold for the Temple treasury, first fruits to be presented upon the altar. They were instructed to seek out Eleazar, the High Priest of the Jews. He would be presented with a letter in the king's name, requesting him to send a delegation of Jewish scholars. This delegation would be treated with honour and highly rewarded. In return their task was to be no more than to translate their holy writings into Greek. They would write the first translation of the Bible.

This is the point at which Aristeas, whose letter was written a century or so after the events he purports to recount,[6] chooses to write himself into the story. He tells us that he advised Ptolemy of the presence in Egypt of one hundred thousand Jewish slaves, whom the king's father had taken into forced labour during a campaign he had waged in Judea. Aristeas claims to have suggested to the king that the slaves be freed, and that Demetrius should make mention of this benevolent, selfless and gracious act when making his request to the

High Priest in Jerusalem. Ptolemy, we are assured, duly followed suit. He also appointed the yet-to-be-born Aristeas as one of the envoys despatched to Jerusalem.

The letter begins to sounds even more contrived when Aristeas describes the delegation that the High Priest sent from Jerusalem. He tells us that the delegation of translators consisted of seventy-two men, six from each Israelite tribe. It sounds neat but it was too tidy. The ancient, Israelite tribal system had long since broken down; most people no longer knew which clan their ancestors had belonged to, and they certainly didn't identify themselves by tribal affiliation. Only the priestly caste had retained its distinctive identity.

Aristeas's account, and his predilection for the number seventy-two, becomes even more fanciful when he describes a week-long banquet that Ptolemy allegedly held in the delegation's honour. Over the course of the feast the king posed seventy-two, profound, metaphysical and philosophical questions to the delegates. Aristeas ponderously records each and every question, along with the delegates' responses. The account of this symposium takes up far more room in Aristeas's letter than anything else.

Finally, when all the questions are turgidly disposed of, Aristeas returns to his original theme. He recounts how the delegation was conducted to well-appointed quarters on the seashore of the island of Pharos.[7] The Jerusalem scholars were given all the materials they needed to collaborate on their translation and, exactly seventy-two days later, the seventy-two men proudly presented Demetrius with a copy of their work.

Demetrius summoned the Jews who lived in Alexandria and, despite its great length, read the translation to them. It must have taken hours. The crowd, whom we had been given to understand had no knowledge of Hebrew, gave an ovation to the translators and to Demetrius, voicing their uncritical approval of the new work. Their enthusiasm was so great that all agreed this magnificent translation of the Hebrew Bible into Greek should become an official, unalterable version. Great curses would descend upon anyone who dared tamper with it.

Aristeas's letter is considered by most scholars to be a fanciful account of how the Bible was translated into Greek.[8] It's not just that it contains fantastical elements like the recurring number seventy-two. It is also historically inaccurate; Aristeas has Demetrius working for Ptolemy II whereas he actually worked for his father, Ptolemy I. Indeed, Demetrius was no friend of Ptolemy II. He had badly miscalculated when caught up in a political intrigue that had sought to prevent Ptolemy's accession to the throne. Demetrius backed the wrong side, the intrigue failed and one of Ptolemy II's first acts when crowned king was to arrange for his assassination, poisoned by the bite of an asp.[9] It is inconceivable that Demetrius would have been Ptolemy II's librarian.

The account written by Aristeas is the first, but not the only source to suggest that a translation of the Hebrew Bible was undertaken in Alexandria in the second or third century BCE. It is possible that the underlying facts are true, that the translation was commissioned, or at least endorsed, by one of the Greek-Egyptian monarchs. The general view today is that the translation was conceived and carried out by a Greek-speaking Jew, for members of the large and flourishing Alexandrian, Jewish community whose grasp of their ancestral Hebrew tongue was diminishing. One reason for this theory is the dialect of Greek used in the translation. Known as *koine*, it is similar to that found in other Egyptian documents from the same period. The translation even contains a few Egyptian words. All this suggests that the translation was made by Greek-speaking Egyptians. Not by Hebrew-speaking foreigners from Jerusalem.[10]

The legend was popular in its day. It crops up a second time in the writings of Philo,[11] a Jewish philosopher who lived in Alexandria from about 25 BCE to 50 CE. Aristeas had neglected to mention which books of the Hebrew Bible had been translated in Alexandria. But Philo tells us. He declares that the translation commissioned by Ptolemy was just the first part of the Hebrew Bible; the Five Books of Moses, known in Greek as the Pentateuch and in the language of the Jews as the Torah. Modern scholars agree. Although the translation was eventually expanded to include the whole Hebrew Bible, the style in which the Pentateuch has been translated is noticeably different from, and considerably earlier than, that of the later books.[12]

Philo doesn't agree with every detail of Aristeas's account. He still believes that the translation was commissioned by Ptolemy II and he relates the arrival of envoys from Jerusalem, the lavish banquet and the symposium instigated by the king.[13] He doesn't mention Demetrius, and there is no reference to the ancient tribes of Israel, nor the recurring number seventy-two. However he does add new information. Whereas Aristeas has his seventy-two translators collaborating to produce the best possible version, Philo's delegates (he doesn't tell us how many there were) each produce their own version. And every version they produce is identical, each translation corresponds with the other, word for word, 'as if guided by an unseen prompter'.[14] In Philo's version a miracle seems to have taken place.

The miracle that Philo hints at becomes more pronounced as the legend develops over the coming centuries. In later versions, the translators do not simply produce identical Greek versions of the Pentateuch; they do so despite being locked into separate cells, unable to communicate with each other. Towards the end of the second century, the Church Father, Irenaeus of Lyons, wrote that Ptolemy 'wishing to test (the translators) individually, and fearing lest they might perchance, by taking counsel together, conceal the truth in the Scriptures...separated them from each other'.[15] In making this statement, Irenaeus is not just naively alerting us to a slightly different version of the legend that he has heard. For reasons which will become clear, he wants to emphasize the miraculous, ineffable nature of this translation, and to stress that even if the translators had wanted to 'conceal the truth' they were not able to do so. In Irenaeus's eyes, the miracle stopped the Jewish translators from falsifying the Bible, from eliminating prophesies which he believed foretold the coming of Jesus. The legend was evolving into polemic. And the translated Bible was on the brink of its first foray into religious politics.

Jewish sources of the same period agree that the translators, although separated, produced identical works. Their reasons for stressing this are different. The Jews were not afraid that the translators might conceal doctrinal truths. Their concern was about possible ambiguities, ways of translating the text that might give rise to theological problems. What was miraculous for the Jews was that in the version the translators produced, passages which were potentially ambiguous or misleading had been elucidated. The Talmud cites several amendments to verses which might otherwise have been misunderstood. One occurs in the Creation narrative when, in the Hebrew text, God states 'Let us make man in our image.'[16] This could suggest that God collaborated with others in the world's creation. The Jewish sources tell us that the translators all came up with the far more straightforward, 'I shall make man in an image.' Similarly, in the account of the Tower of Babel, God's 'We will go down and confuse their speech'[17] becomes 'I will go down...'[18]

By the second century CE, the legend that Aristeas composed had become a miraculous fable. It told of a team of scholars, each shut away incommunicado in his own cell, each working on his own, and each translating the Five Books of Moses in identical fashion. The legend had become a miracle and the Greek translation of the Bible was turning into a battleground.

Although both the Jewish and Christian sources affirmed the miraculous nature of the translation, they did so for very different reasons. Irenaeus had said that it was so the Jewish translators couldn't collude and falsify the Bible. The Jewish sources claimed it was to eliminate the possibility of people reading ideas into the Hebrew text that weren't there. It was these two different ways of interpreting the legend and its miracle which generated the first Bible translation controversy. It would be the first of many, and they would grow more violent with time.

The Septuagint Controversies

Four hundred years or more after the original translation, the Greek Bible was complete. The Alexandrian translation of the Pentateuch had been supplemented by Greek renditions of the other Old Testament books. The translation had also acquired a name. The versions of the legend now in circulation had deducted a couple of translators from Aristeas's mythical seventy-two, and the work had become known as the Septuagint, meaning seventy in Latin.

The Septuagint's impact on history has been colossal. It is far more than just an ancient Greek translation of the Old Testament. Alexander the Great's conquests had led to the dialect of Greek known as *koine* becoming the language of trade, law and culture throughout the ancient Middle East and Asia Minor. The completion of the Septuagint meant that, for the first time, everybody in the Greek-speaking world had access to the foundational texts both of the Jews and of the new, rapidly expanding Christian faith, which were also circulating in Greek. The Septuagint brought Hebrew ideas and beliefs to the attention of the world.[19] It explained the background to Christianity. It even introduced the one word which has probably changed the course of human history more than any other. It gave the world the word Christ, which is Greek for Messiah. And by extension, the terms Christian and Christianity.[20] Without the Septuagint, London and Rome would still be heathen and the scriptures would be no better known than the Egyptian *Book of the Dead*.[21]

Aristeas's account of how the Septuagint came into being is nothing more than a fable. But it is still of value. Even if there were not six men from each of twelve tribes, even if the delegation didn't consist of seventy-two envoys, even if there was no delegation from Jerusalem at all, the legend nevertheless provides several important pieces of information. It establishes the probability that the earliest translation of the Bible was made in Alexandria. It implies that this particular translation of the Bible was of such cultural significance that, even a century later, Aristeas felt it worthy of glorification.[22] Perhaps most importantly, for the future history of the translated Bible, it tells us that, even in the earliest days, there were important differences between the Hebrew and Greek versions.[23] It was these differences which the account of the miracle attempted to explain away.

By the second century the details of the miracle were no longer able to account for all the differences between the Hebrew and Greek texts. The Septuagint's popularity meant that there were now many copies in existence. They had all been written by hand; this was long before the invention of printing. But scribes can, and do, make mistakes. When a manuscript is copied, so are its errors. And the copying scribe may well introduce further errors of his own. So the inaccuracies multiply. Once the manuscript leaves the scriptorium it falls upon the mercy of assiduous scholars, who may decide to erase and replace something they suspect is incorrect or with which they disagree. Other readers may scribble notes in the margin, which the next copyist can easily mistake for the main body of text. It is not hard to see how hand-written documents, once they have been copied a few times, can end up very different from the original.

Like all frequently copied manuscripts, the Septuagint went through this process of continual corruption. The result was that the Hebrew and Greek bibles diverged ever more widely from each other. The Jews, who had access to the Hebrew text as well as the Greek version, would have spotted the differences sooner; the Christians, who in the main didn't speak Hebrew, had no base text to assess their manuscripts against. It was the differences between the two versions that caused the first round of Septuagint controversies.

For the Jews the Septuagint would always be a translation, an adjunct to the Hebrew original. To the emerging Church, however, the Septuagint represented the essential text of the Old Testament. It was written in a familiar tongue, the very language in which the New Testament had been transcribed. It was natural for the Church to vest the same degree of sanctity in the Septuagint, the Greek Old Testament, as they did in the New.

Significantly, the Church's adoption of the Septuagint underlined the essential difference, in those early days, between Christianity and the Jewish faith out of which it had been born. Judaism had become an inward-looking religion, demoralized by centuries of Roman occupation, declining economic fortunes and ongoing emigration. Paul's Christianity, in contrast, had a universal ambition; it aspired to bring salvation to the world. It made absolute sense for Christianity to reject the old representation of Scripture, written in the obscure, provincial tongue that only the Jews spoke, and to proclaim the universality of the miraculous new revelation that was the Septuagint, the eternal Bible reincarnated into a language that everyone understood. Throughout history the translated Bible has found itself tangled up in the politics of religion.

One theological dispute in particular cemented the Jews' rejection of the Septuagint and confirmed its authoritative status within the Church. It concerned Isaiah's prophecy about the birth of a child to be named Immanuel.[24] Isaiah had described the child's mother using a Hebrew word, *almah*, which is usually translated as 'young woman'. The Septuagint translated it as *parthenos*, or 'virgin'.[25] Of course, the Septuagint, written two or three hundred years before Jesus's birth was completely oblivious to the implications of its choice of word. Nevertheless, the apostle Matthew took it as proof that Isaiah had foreseen that a virgin would give birth and that the child she bore would turn out to be the Messiah.[26] Matthew, when he quotes this prophecy from

Isaiah, delivers the Septuagint translation, not the original Hebrew. The Jewish religious leaders, who paid little attention to the Septuagint, knew nothing of this. Until they were confronted by Christians seeking to prove that the Hebrew Bible foretold the birth of Jesus. The Septuagint's translation of Isaiah's prophecy led to possibly the most contentious of all interpretative disputes between Christianity and Judaism, one which still reverberates today.

Challenging the Septuagint

From the second century onwards both Jews and Christians became increasingly aware of the discrepancies between the Septuagint and the Hebrew text. Even though each faith regarded its own version as sacred, nobody denied that the Old Testament had originally been written in Hebrew. The Jewish Bible was rooted in antiquity; in debates over authenticity the Septuagint was naturally at a disadvantage. When the Jews challenged its accuracy, the Church robustly rose to its defence. When defence proved ineffective, they went on the attack.

Leading the charge was the Church Father Justin. Writing a century or so after Jesus, Justin was the first to claim the superiority of the Septuagint over the Hebrew version.[27] In his *Dialogue with Trypho*, a polemical work in which he disputes Christianity with an imaginary Jewish opponent,[28] Justin argues that the discrepancies between the two versions were the result of the Jews doctoring the Hebrew text. He would place no reliance, he insisted, on Trypho's teachers, who had 'taken away many Scriptures from the translations effected by those seventy elders who were with Ptolemy'.[29] Justin's attack was a seminal moment, the first occasion in which the still-developing Church expressly distanced itself from the Hebrew Old Testament. Justin's argument set a precedent for theologians of the early Church to maintain that, in all cases of conflict with the Hebrew, it was the Septuagint that ought to be followed.[30]

Justin was aiming far higher than simply making a point about the mechanics of textual transmission. His argument was that the Jews had 'taken away' scriptures because they had deliberately set out to refute Christianity. Denying the accuracy of the Septuagint was, in Justin's eyes, a Jewish tactic to undermine Christian belief. As far as he was concerned, the Septuagint was the authentic translation of the original Bible, while the Hebrew version that the Jews of his day were using had been tampered with, so as to erase evidence that supported the Christian view. The 'miracle' which resulted in all seventy translators producing identical versions restored the Bible to its primitive state, eliminating all the errors and falsifications that, so he claimed, the Jews had inserted into the Hebrew text. Justin was so persuaded of this view that he even asserted that when he was in Alexandria he saw the very cells in which the translators carried out their work.[31]

The Jews rejected Justin's allegations, but they too believed the legend of the miracle. Nevertheless, as their theological disputes with Christianity became more strident, their attitude towards the alleged events in Alexandria changed. Jewish sources began to describe the moment that the Septuagint was completed as an occurrence as tragic 'as the day the golden calf was made',[32] a misfortune which caused darkness to fall upon the earth for three days.[33] This rejection of a translation that had in all likelihood been carried out for Jews, by Jews, was, at least in some part, the consequence of what the twentieth-century Anglican theologian C. F. D. Moule called 'one of the most remarkable takeover bids in history'.[34] When Christianity adopted the Jewish Septuagint as the authoritative text of the Old Testament, the Jews turned their backs on it.

Abandoning the Septuagint was not an option for the many Jews who were unable to read the Hebrew Bible. Greece may have ceased to be a world power but the Greek language was still widely spoken across the Eastern Roman Empire. A Greek Bible was still needed and, if the Septuagint was not up to the task, an alternative would have to be composed, one which reflected more accurately the meaning of the Hebrew text. During the second century, at least three, maybe more, of these works were made.[35]

The best known of these new translations, although the least well preserved, was made by Aquila. We know very little about him; he lived during the first or second century and some of the early Jewish sources describe him as a convert to Judaism. His name in Hebrew is Aquilas, which frequently led him to become confused with the similar-sounding Onkelos, another Jewish convert who also translated the Bible, but into Aramaic. The early Jewish sources tended to muddle the two of them up, sometimes treating them as the same person, sometimes not.[36] The Christian sources are no more helpful; they either assume that Aquila was a relative of the emperor Hadrian or they equate him with the Aquila in the Acts of the Apostles who was married to Priscilla. There doesn't seem to be any basis for either of these views.

Aquila set out to translate the Hebrew text into Greek as literally as he could. When he finished his translation he made a revised version, to improve its accuracy.[37] He'd intended it as a simple Greek alternative to the Septuagint, an everyday Bible for Greek-speaking Jews, but in the febrile religious environment which marked the divergence of Christianity from Judaism, an alternative to the Septuagint could be nothing other than controversial. Aquila's translation offered too easy a way to spot errors in the Septuagint, to give its Jewish critics an opportunity to condemn the accuracy and validity of the Alexandrian text. It became even more controversial in the fourth century when the Christian theologian and Bible commentator Jerome harnessed it to argue for the supremacy of the Hebrew text.[38]

The second of the three translations was attributed to a man with the relatively common name of Symmachus. Again, his biography is obscure. One theory is that he was based in Caesarea, a cosmopolitan, Roman garrison town on the Mediterranean coast of Israel. The city was populated by Christians, Samaritans and a hellenized Jewish community. Alison Salvesen, in a rigorous and thorough study of the work of this man of whom we know virtually nothing, suggests that his translation may have been made for the benefit of the Greek-speaking Jewish community of that city.[39]

The third translation is attributed to a man named Theodotion, of whom we know still less, to the point that we are not sure if he really existed.[40] Like Symmachus, Theodotion was a common name, which has led to a jumble of theories about who he may or may not be. The translation attributed to Theodotion may even have been the work of more than one person. We just don't know.

All three of these translations were made by Jews for Jews, but that didn't stop one senior Christian theologian from feeling deeply offended by them. Epiphanius, the fourth-century Bishop of Salamis in Cyprus, attacked them with as much ire as he could muster. He was convinced that each of the three translators had wanted to supersede the Septuagint out of nothing more than spite and personal ambition.[41] He attacked the character and integrity of the individual translators personally; he may well have known more about them than we do now. Or he may simply have made up his pejoratives.

Epiphanius described Aquila as a convert to Christianity who was unable to let go of his former idolatrous leanings. Expelled by the Church he became a Jew and wrote his translation with the intention of distorting the words of the Septuagint. As for Symmachus, he had a different, yet equally disruptive agenda. Born and circumcised as a Samaritan, he lusted for power and was enraged by his failure to succeed. He reversed his circumcision (Epiphanius furnishes us with the technical details of how this was done), converted to Judaism, and was re-circumcised. He decided to write his translation in order to pervert the version of the Bible the Samaritans used.[42] Theodotion on the other hand had been a follower of Marcion, a heretical quasi-Christian. Theodotion eventually grew angry with Marcion's heretical views but instead of turning to Christianity, had himself circumcised and became a Jew.

With the translators' reputations abased, Epiphanius constructed a slippery argument to play what he imagined to be his trump card. Implying that the three translators were collaborating (an assertion for which he had no evidence), he pointed out that each of them came up with a different translation. How, he asked, can their versions be regarded as accurate, when there were only three of them yet they couldn't even agree among themselves? Compare this, he demanded, with the seventy-two Septuagint translators, all of whom came up with identical versions. As far as Epiphanius was concerned, the three Jewish translations offered nothing of value when compared to the Septuagint. Their work was nothing more than the consequence of personal vendettas; hardly even worth bothering about.

Epiphanius lived long after the new Greek translations had been completed. They had been challenging the Septuagint even before he was born. His concern was not whether or not the new translations were accurate; his only interest was to restore the reputation of the Septuagint, to reassert its inerrancy and protect its sanctity. In the eyes of the emerging Church, the Septuagint surpassed the Hebrew original as the truly inspired word of God. Its supremacy over the three Jewish translations was, for Epiphanius, never in doubt. That did not prevent him from considering the alternative translations offensive.

There was a second factor, nothing at all to do with their theological differences with Christianity, which led the Jews to reject the Septuagint. It is easy for us, living at a time in which the demarcation lines between different religions are more or less clear, to overlook the complexity of a world still struggling to differentiate between the competing claims of different, and not yet fully formed, beliefs. The Jews had a separate complaint against the Septuagint, nothing at all to do with Christianity. It was an internal matter, a difference of outlook between different types of Jews. The argument was a direct consequence of the relationship, or lack of it, between Jewish and Greek society, and consequently, between rabbinic and hellenized Jews.

Once, Greek thought and culture had been instrumental in shaping the way Jews saw the world. It even influenced parts of the Bible itself. The inclusion in the Bible of the so-called 'Wisdom' books, which include Ecclesiastes and Proverbs, is attributed to Hellenistic influences flowing from Alexandria to Jerusalem. But when the Jerusalem Temple was destroyed by the Romans in the year 70, the character of Judaism changed. The priests who had run the Sanctuary were now redundant, and it was the rabbis who were laying the foundations of the new, post-Temple Jewish faith. For them the whole purpose of existence was to obey the divine commandments through closely prescribed modes of behaviour. They took a dim view of Hellenistic life, with its emphasis on art and physical beauty. The Talmud rebukes those Jews who reversed their circumcision in order to compete naked in competitions in the gymnasium.[43] Such acts represented the antithesis of everything the rabbis stood for. The Alexandrian Septuagint, created by and for such Greek Jews, was an affront, a perpetual reminder of the Hellenism which rabbinic Judaism was desperate to erase. That is another reason why, as far as the rabbis were concerned, the moment of the Septuagint's composition was a tragedy as great as the day the golden calf was made.

There is yet a third reason, nothing to do with Hellenism; the alleged falsification of texts or the accuracy of translations, which led the Jewish religious authorities to reject the Septuagint. The rise of the rabbis had been the consequence of the first-century victory of the populist Pharisees over the aristocratic, patrician Sadducees. But although acknowledged by the majority of the Jewish population as their legitimate religious authority, the rabbis feared what might happen should their sacred texts be democratized through translation into other languages. They were concerned at the possibility of the Jews in foreign lands, away from centres of rabbinic teaching, studying the Bible in their own language, not understanding it properly and introducing new, possibly heretical ideas. They worried even more about new, poorly educated translators emerging, who didn't have the skills or knowledge to make accurate translations. Because they hadn't yet come to terms with the idea of the Bible being translated into foreign languages, the rabbis were insistent that, if it was to happen, it was only to take place under their control. That's why there are so few references to the Greek Bible in rabbinic writings. The rabbis' concern was one which surfaces time and again in the controversies over Bible translation; a fear that seizes all ideologues when they sense a threat to their grip on doctrine. It is equally a paranoia that can easily grip autocrats and unelected leaders.

As we will see time and again, religious establishments, which tend to be conservative by nature, dread losing control of the educational agenda, fearing that they will not be able to maintain correct forms of belief and practice as the masses gain access to, and understanding of, the sacred texts.

The First Bible Critic

Epiphanius was not the only one to rise to the Septuagint's defence. As the Church grew in size and influence, the vulnerability of the ancient Alexandrian translation to its new Greek rivals became a matter of concern. By the fourth century, the works of 'the Three'; Aquila, Symmachus and Theodotion; were subjected to attack by some of the most prominent Christian thinkers of the age.

John, Archbishop of Constantinople, was nicknamed Chrysostom, or Golden Mouth, because of his formidable and outspoken oratory. He was not the only person of his era to be awarded the sobriquet[44] but, as the foremost exponent of macrologia or long-winded rhetoric, it is he to whom the name has stuck. John Chrysostom cast scorn upon the 'Three', comparing what he considered to be their impure intentions with the integrity of the earlier translators in Alexandria. The Septuagint, he argued, had been written before

Christianity; it therefore was, of necessity, free from anti-Christian bias. On the other hand, Aquila, Symmachus and Theodotion had all produced their translations after the birth of Christianity, and they had done so as a reaction to the alleged inadequacies of the Septuagint. They had set out, said Chrysostom, to deliberately discredit Christianity.[45]

At the other end of the Mediterranean, in the town of Hippo in Algeria, the theologian Augustine was advancing similar views. St Augustine, as he would become, felt that the translators' isolation from each other in Alexandria was sufficient proof of the Septuagint's infallibility. He asserted that the Jews had falsified their Hebrew original to prevent the truth being known to other nations. However, he claimed, they didn't get away with it because the Spirit which rested on the seventy translators restored the text to its original meaning, to the sense it had been imbued with before the Jews tampered with it.[46] This, Augustine asserted, had happened in order to offer salvation to the nations.[47]

We have seen that the Jews' rejection of the Septuagint was not exclusively due to Christian accusations. Similarly, the robustness with which Augustine and Chrysostom defended it was not solely because of the Jews. A debate was hotting up within the Church itself, between those who upheld the inerrancy of the Septuagint and those who were prepared to accept the argument that it had indeed become corrupted over time.

The argument had started a century earlier, shortly after the year 230. Once again, the seeds were sown in Alexandria where the Roman emperor Severus had launched a wave of persecution against Christians. On hearing that his father had been captured and imprisoned, Origen, a pious, teenage ascetic, decided that his only viable recourse was to consecrate himself as a martyr. We don't know what heroics he had in mind, we only have the story from the fourth-century historian Eusebius of Caesarea. We do know that his plans were thwarted when his mother hid his clothes. The prospect of naked self-sacrifice brought Origen to his senses. But not for long. When he read the verse in Matthew about 'those who choose to live like eunuchs for the sake of the kingdom of heaven'[48] his religious zeal got the better of him. He castrated himself, or at least that is what Eusebius tells us he did.[49]

The local bishop, Demetrius, heard about the pious young ascetic and took him under his wing. But as Origen's reputation and popularity grew, Demetrius, a man of far lesser status, grew ever more jealous. Matters came to a head when Origen was invited to preach in Caesarea, the Roman garrison town in Judea. While he was there the local bishop ordained him into the priesthood. This further piqued Demetrius, who considered that Caesarea had hijacked his own local talent. He rounded on Origen, accused him of heretical preaching and had him condemned by a synod, fatally damaging his career prospects in Alexandria. Fortunately for Origen the condemnation fell on deaf ears everywhere else. He gave up any hope of returning home and continued his career in Caesarea.

Origen's great passion was the Bible. He wrote commentaries on much of it and, although most of what he wrote is now lost, we know that he occasionally wrote more than one commentary on certain books. Unusually for his time, he didn't cocoon himself in his own religious environment; third-century Caesarea was a centre of vibrant Jewish as well as Christian scholarship and Origen was more than willing to engage with rabbinic scholars, even incorporating some of their ideas into his own thinking. He even learned Hebrew, although perhaps not as successfully as he may have wished. He spotted differences between the Septuagint and the Hebrew text. He also noticed discrepancies between the various Septuagint manuscripts that he had.[50] But although he was aware of the new translations by the 'Three' he was not prepared to reject the Septuagint in favour of any one of them. Discrepancies or not, he was an orthodox thinker who accepted the Septuagint as the Church's authoritative text. He was also an Alexandrian. Unlike his bishop, he wouldn't turn his back on the product of his home town. He wasn't prepared to abandon the Septuagint. He did, however, want to get rid of its errors.

Origen embarked on a major project of literary analysis. Nowadays, when scholars try to get back to the original version of an ancient text that exists in various recensions, they reproduce the edition they consider the most reliable and at the bottom of the page they note the variations found in other manuscripts. Origen went one better than this. He drew six vertical columns and placed a version of the Old Testament in each. The left-hand column contained the original Hebrew text. The next was the same, written in Greek characters rather than Hebrew. In the adjoining two columns he inscribed the translations of Aquila and Symmachus. The Septuagint was in the fifth column and finally the translation attributed to Theodotion. He devised a series of symbols which he added to the Septuagint column, highlighting where it differed from the Hebrew original. Origen called his whole work the *Hexapla*.

The *Hexapla*'s structure made it easy to use. Its six columns were arranged so that each horizontal line contained only one or two Hebrew words together with their various Greek equivalents. This made cross-referencing very easy. Anyone who wanted to clarify the reading in the Septuagint, or to find the best Greek word to represent the Hebrew, could scan across the columns to compare the different versions.

The *Hexapla* was a phenomenal work. It had one serious drawback. The Old Testament is a lengthy document. The *Hexapla* was six times as long. Origen's work was so vast that it could only realistically be used as a reference work in a library. The idea of having a personal copy, even for those few people who could both read and afford one, was completely unrealistic. Origen did make a smaller, four-column version containing the versions most likely to be used by Christians. But the complete *Hexapla* itself was hardly ever copied, indeed it may never even have been copied at all.

Origen's original manuscript was stored in the library of Pamphilus in Caesarea. It was destroyed in 638 when the city fell to Saracen invaders. Only a few fragments have survived.[51]

Origen was a controversial theologian; he was condemned as a heretic long after his death. Even before then, while his reputation remained relatively intact, Origen's rigorous scholarship was not universally appreciated. Those who believed that the Septuagint was a divinely inspired text resented his attempts to compare or harmonize it with the Hebrew. Both John Chrysostom and Augustine, each born a century after Origen had carried out his work, continued to defend the Septuagint. Despite its academic value, the *Hexapla* never seriously challenged the status of the Alexandrian translation as the Church's official text. But the version of the Septuagint which Origen placed in his first column was used as the master copy when the emperor Constantine commissioned his scribes to provide fifty major churches in the Roman Empire with their own copy of the Bible.[52]

In the end it wasn't so much scholarship that did for the Septuagint, rather the vagaries of passing time. Greek's dominance as an international language was drawing to an end; in the Western Empire Latin had taken over as the new standard. The Septuagint may have been revered, but it was used less and less. By the time Christianity had spread across Europe the Septuagint was, in all but name, effectively redundant. No Christian denied its divine inspiration. Still, they preferred to read the Bible in a language they understood: Latin.

But the Latin Bible was not yet on the stage. While the Septuagint was declining in popularity, the belief in one God was nevertheless spreading rapidly. Across the East, both Christianity and Judaism were putting down roots in locations where neither Greek, Hebrew nor even Latin were the vernacular. New translations of the Bible were appearing in these places. Unlike the Septuagint they were not the cause of controversy. Yet, when we look at them carefully we can see that they often emerged from communities which were deeply split and traumatized.

The new levantine translations symbolized the essential differences between East and West. They mark the moment when monotheistic belief began to evolve separately in Europe and Asia along divergent trajectories.

2

A Wandering Aramean

The Old Testament *Peshitta*

The Silk Road was the name given to the ancient trade route that linked India and China with the West. Caravans brought gems, spices and of course silk from the Orient, seeking markets in Mediterranean and Byzantine lands. On their return they carried wool, gold and silver. Few traders made the complete journey from the Great Wall of China to Antioch in Syria, and fewer still once the itinerary expanded to Egypt, Greece and eventually Rome itself. Staging posts and entrepôts along the route enabled the merchants to meet, barter and exchange the goods they carried, and to return home sooner with their new wares.

But although the route had grown up through trade, precious goods and exotic items were merely its visible cargo, the traffic which bore a monetary value. Far more precious, from the point of view of a world still in its infancy, were the free, yet priceless goods which found their way along the Silk Road: the ideas, stories, information and beliefs that circulated among the wayfarers. The Silk Road was a cauldron into which merchants, holy men, soldiers, camel drivers, thespians and bandits poured their skills, science and knowledge, barely conscious of the impact they were making on the rapidly connecting globe, one that was newly encountering and hungrily soaking up a huge and diverse range of cultural influences.

The city of Edessa, now known as Urfa in Turkey, sits on the Silk Road. It was the last major staging post before Antioch, the first important centre the traveller reached after leaving Nisibis. Fifty miles east of the river Euphrates, the city was located on the border between the vast Parthian Empire, and the eastern fringes of Rome's territory. Frequent border skirmishes resulted in the city veering from one dominion to the other until finally, in August 116, it fell permanently under Roman control.

Edessa is said to have been where Nimrod, the builder of the Tower of Babel, had his capital. It also claims to have been the home town of Job and even the birthplace of Abraham (although Genesis places his home town at Haran, 25 miles to the south). Visitors to the city can still see the cave that, local legend has it, was once Abraham's home. A short distance away lies the site of the furnace into which, according to Jewish and Muslim folklore, Nimrod is said to have cast him.

More reliably, Edessa is known as the birthplace of Eastern Christianity. This is not disputed even though the events surrounding the city's conversion to its new faith are unclear. A legend recorded by Eusebius, who gave us information about Origen, tells of an Edessan king writing to Jesus asking him to cure him of a disease with which he was afflicted, and of Jesus sending an emissary to do just that.[1] If nothing else this legend indicates that Christianity reached Edessa at a very early period, perhaps even at the very dawn of the faith's foundation. The city became a hub for the spread of Christianity across the region, and eventually a place of pilgrimage in its own right. Sadly, Urfa today retains little of its former glory. In 1146 a futile attempt by a Crusader force to recapture the city from the Turks led to its destruction and the end of its life as a major Christian centre.

One factor in the rapid spread of Christianity during the second and third centuries was the belief in monotheism, an idea which, even before Paul, had taken root in many localities. The Roman occupation of the Mediterranean lands and much of the area we now call the Middle East had led to widespread dispersal of populations. Among the many émigrés were Jews who were settling more widely across the region. Their monotheistic beliefs began to resonate among those they came into contact with. And although the people the Jews settled among were not thrilled by the idea of taking on the rigours of the Mosaic religion, they were attracted to the idea of a single God instead of the local deities they had worshipped for generations. They were ready for a monotheistic faith and they bought into the beliefs, if not the daily practices, of Judaism. The Jews called these people 'fearers of heaven'.[2] They, and many of the Jews who lived among them, were the earliest communities to accept the message of Christianity, the new faith which offered monotheistic belief without covenantal stringencies. Edessa in the second century was one of the places where 'fearers of heaven' could be found.

During the first century CE Izates, king of neighbouring Adiabene, converted to Judaism, as did his mother Helena, his sons and many of their subjects. The early Jewish law code records gifts sent by Helena to the Jerusalem Temple; among them a golden plaque which bore the biblical injunction against a woman accused by her husband of infidelity.[3] It's not the sort of gift we'd expect a queen to send today.

When one of Izates's sons became King of Edessa, he encouraged its inhabitants to adopt his Jewish faith, or at least to subscribe to monotheistic principles. By the time the Christian apostle Addai visited Edessa, early in the third century, he found a receptive audience of Jews and 'fearers of heaven'. Already won over to the belief in one God, they responded to his message with enthusiasm.

They spoke a dialect of Aramaic in Edessa, known today as Syriac. Aramaic and Syriac are Semitic tongues, related to Arabic, Hebrew and the Ethiopian language Amharic. There were once many other languages in the Semitic family, but names like Ugaritic, Akkadian and Phoenician are now only found in universities and history books. Aramaic is still spoken in scattered communities across Iraq, Syria, Iran and Turkey, although there are fears that it will disappear altogether within the course of the next generation.[4]

It was in Edessa that one of the most intriguing Old Testament translations was composed, one which seems to conceal a devastating and highly charged communal disintegration. The translation itself, as its name implies, is relatively straightforward; it is known as the *Peshitta*, which means 'plain' or 'simple', as in the 'plain' or 'simple' translation. Historians are perplexed by its background, by who translated it, and why. There is a Syriac translation of the New Testament with the same name but the Old and New Testament *Peshittas* are completely different compositions. It's the Old Testament version which seems to mask the occurrence of some deeply traumatic events.

Exactly what happened is by no means certain; the background to the composition has been argued over by scholars for decades. There's little doubt that the Old Testament *Peshitta* was composed in or near Edessa during the third century or the early part of the fourth.[5] The translator wrote in a local Syriac dialect, which bears similarities to inscriptions discovered by archaeologists in the region. He has substituted local place names, such as Nisibis and Haran, for some of the names in the Hebrew text, presumably to stoke the interest of his local readers.

Like the Septuagint, the *Peshitta*'s translator seems to have been a Jew. The way he writes suggests that he identified himself as part of an exiled Jewish community, experiencing all the hardships that such a status entailed. When deciding how to translate a phrase or word, he seems to have relied on earlier Jewish commentaries and explanations to guide him.

And yet the Old Testament *Peshitta* has never surfaced anywhere in the Jewish world. It was preserved by the Assyrian Church. Unlike the Septuagint, there is no evidence that the Jews ever used it, or even knew of it. Indeed, if the Church had not adopted and treasured it, we may never have known of this Jewish translation.

The reason why historians think that the *Peshitta* was written on the back of some great communal tragedy or upheaval is because of the way it handles the book of Chronicles. Unlike the rest of the *Peshitta,* which is generally a fairly direct translation from the Hebrew, Chronicles contains passages which the translator seems to have written himself. We find passages into which he weaves his own desperate feelings. At one point, in the middle of a prophecy eschewing idolatry, he complains, '*we had forsaken the Lord our God and refused to hearken to his servants the prophets and he too has requited us for our deeds*'.[6] Quite what these deeds were, or how they were requited, we don't know.

Although he identifies himself with the Jewish community, the *Peshitta* translator is not typical of the Jews of his day. He seems ignorant of certain basic practices, and yet he is assiduous, if idiosyncratic, about others. He doesn't seem to subscribe to rabbinic Judaism, the mainstream religion which has survived to the present day. All in all he seems more interested in ideas of faith and belief than in religious practice and it appears he knows quite a lot less than we would expect about the way the Jewish religion was observed.

Michael Weitzman's detailed analysis leads him to the conclusion that the *Peshitta* was translated by one or more Jews who had either never practised ritual Judaism or had long given it up. The obvious distress which the translator displays in Chronicles is probably the result of large-scale defections by members of the Jewish community to Christianity, an exodus he could not countenance and which caused him much heartache. It isn't possible, without further evidence, to be more specific, but the fact that the *Peshitta* was preserved by the Church not by the Jews adds weight to the theory that the lapsed Jews brought their Syriac Old Testament with them when they converted.

Just like the Septuagint, the *Peshitta* was rejected by the Jews despite its Jewish origins. Maybe those Jews who did not convert had no use for it; it's possible that they took a greater interest in their cultural heritage and could read the Bible in Hebrew, which was after all a sister language. Or perhaps they could understand the other Aramaic versions that were now in circulation. Known as *Targum*, these versions were to become the next battleground for the Bible. A battle which, this time, had nothing to do with the widening gulf between Judaism and Christianity, but which was fought between different camps within the Jewish world.

The *Targum*

Although Hebrew has always been the language of the Jews, it was not always the one they spoke. In much of the region in which the ancient Jews lived, the dominant language was Aramaic, the vernacular of the Babylonian and Assyrian empires. Following the destruction of Jerusalem and the exile of the Judeans to Babylon in the sixth century BCE, Aramaic began to overtake Hebrew as the day-to-day speech of the Jews. It has been suggested that by the year 300 BCE every Jew who had acquired the skills to read was proficient in Aramaic.[7] Three hundred years later, when Jesus walked the streets of

Jerusalem and preached to the villagers in Galilee, Aramaic had become the vernacular in Israel. Hebrew had been elevated to the status of a literary language; reserved for the Jewish religion, its scriptures, law and scholarship.

The Aramaic translation of the Bible developed in the Jerusalem Temple and the synagogue.[8] It was originally declaimed alongside the reading of the Hebrew Bible, part of the regular prayer service. During the course of the year the Pentateuch, also known as the Five Books of Moses or Torah, was recited in its entirety, section by section, week by week. The cycle was completed in Israel every three years. In Jewish communities in Babylon and elsewhere the sequence of recitations were condensed into a year. Alongside the weekly reading of the Pentateuch there would also be a shorter reading on an associated theme from one of the books of the Prophets.

The biblical readings always took place in the original Hebrew.[9] While Hebrew remained the language that people spoke, the readings were understood. Once Aramaic began to take over as the everyday language, fewer and fewer people in the synagogue were able to understand what was being read to them.

We don't know when the first translator stood up in a synagogue and delivered an Aramaic rendering of the piece that had just been read in Hebrew. The Babylonian Talmud, the encyclopaedic record of discussions in Jewish religious academies during the third to fifth centuries, attributes the first translation to Ezra. He was one of the leaders of the Jewish community which resettled in Israel in the fifth century BCE, freshly liberated from the exile into which the Babylonian king Nebuchadnezzar had driven them a century earlier.

The Bible recounts how Ezra and his colleagues assembled the returnees in front of the Water Gate in the newly rebuilt Jerusalem and read to them from the Five Books of Moses. We are told that they read the Torah, 'with an interpretation, giving the meaning, so that they would understand the reading'.[10] The phrase 'with an interpretation', says the Talmud, means that they read it together with the *Targum*.[11] The *Targum* is what Aramaic translations of the Bible are called; the word is Aramaic for 'translation'. The person who called out the translation in the synagogue was the *meturgeman*.[12] A corruption of the word exists in English; an interpreter in an oriental country is often referred to as a dragoman.

If Ezra did read a translation of the Torah to the assembled masses it is pretty certain that he didn't read from any of the various Aramaic translations that have come down to us through the ages. The oldest known *Targum* is attributed to Onkelos. We encountered him when discussing Aquila's Greek translation; the two names sound similar in Hebrew and the early sources tended to muddle the two translators up. Although Onkelos is the earliest *Targum* that we know of, it probably wasn't the first ever. Scholars believe that an earlier *Targum* existed, traces of which can still be seen in the translations which have survived till today.[13]

Onkelos lived in the late first, or early second century of the Christian era. He is frequently referred to in early Jewish sources as Onkelos the convert. Jewish tradition holds that he was a nephew of the Roman emperor Titus.[14] It's a quaint idea, but unlikely; there is no mention of Onkelos in any Roman source and it would be odd for a native speaker of Latin, however well educated, to compose an Aramaic translation of a Hebrew text. Titus did however have a cousin, Flavius Clemens, who, according to the Roman historian Dio Cassius, was executed for flirting with, and possibly even converting to Judaism.[15] It is quite possible that, in an age when social standing was all-important, and great literature was produced by people of high birth, Onkelos the convert was repackaged by his followers as a pseudonym for Flavius Clemens the convert. This would make his Aramaic translation of the Old Testament far more significant and prestigious, in much the same way as the Septuagint had been lionized through its association in legend with the Alexandrian king Ptolemy.

The ancient Jewish religious authorities were not particularly keen on the *Targum*, but they were far less hostile towards it than they had been to the Septuagint. Unlike the Septuagint, the *Targum* hadn't become the authoritative text of another religion. Nor was there an Aramaic equivalent of a sectarian, Hellenistic Judaism that claimed the *Targum* as its own.

That's not to say that the rabbis didn't try to control the *Targum*, to ensure it remained well within the fold. The danger we highlighted earlier, that the ability to understand a sacred text can lead people who are not members of the religious hierarchy to develop their own ideas, was as real in the case of the *Targums* as it had been for the Septuagint. And so the rabbis instituted, or at least tried to institute, measures to keep the *meturgeman*, and his *Targum*, under their control.

The earliest Jewish law codes specify various requirements to which the *meturgeman* was expected to adhere. Certain ignominious passages were not to be translated.[16] Nor was the translation to be written down; there should be no possibility of people confusing it with the written Bible.[17] The reader from the Bible in the synagogue was to pause after each sentence to allow the translation to be delivered; this minimized the risk of the *meturgeman* making mistakes because he had memorized too much all at once.[18] All this was because the early Jewish legislators did not want the *Targum* to become a competing source of biblical interpretation, or of religious authority.

But of course this is exactly what happened. All the rules were ignored; written copies of the *Targum* have circulated since the earliest times, and they all translate the 'forbidden' passages. It seems that the constraints into which the rabbis tried to lever the Aramaic translations made little or no impression upon the translators themselves. Once again, the translated Bible was enmeshed in the politics of religious authority.

The rabbis' rules about what could and could not be translated were not the only things to be ignored. Just as the rabbis had feared, the translators sometimes interpreted the biblical text in an unorthodox manner. Occasionally the rabbis would derive one practical ruling from a particular biblical text, and the *meturgeman* would derive another.[19] This doesn't mean that the translators were competing with the rabbis as legislators, but it does suggest that they weren't too bothered about falling in line with the religious establishment. They even wrote in their own, unique dialect of 'Late Jewish Literary Aramaic',[20] a form of the language that is unknown in any of the rabbinic writings.

Several different *Targums* have survived to our time. They include three full translations of the Pentateuch and at least one of every other book. For a long time they faded from popular view, with the exception of Onkelos, which is read in some oriental synagogues and by many religious Jews as part of their weekly study cycle.[21]

In the early twentieth century the *Targums* caught the interest of a small band of Christian scholars who were captivated by the apparent connection between the Aramaic of the *Targum* and the language that Jesus spoke.

They assumed that the *Targums* and the New Testament were roughly contemporaneous, that Jesus and his disciples may have used them to read and understand the Bible, and that therefore the content of the *Targums* may throw light on the theology and background of the New Testament.[22] The Harvard theologian George Foot Moore profoundly disagreed. He believed that the early *Targum* scholars had 'very much overworked them...in consequence of the erroneous notion that they antedated the Christian era.'[23]

In the 1930s Paul Kahle, a Polish-German Lutheran pastor, published *Targumic* fragments that had been discovered in the Cairo Genizah. A Genizah is a place where Jews store worn-out, sacred documents, which may not be thrown away or burned. Instead they are either buried, or in many cases, simply piled up in an out-of-the-way place. The discovery of the Cairo Genizah had been one of the most fortuitous archival discoveries of the nineteenth century, the result of a visit to the Middle East in 1896 by two erudite Scottish adventurers, Mrs Agnes Smith Lewis and Mrs Margaret Dunlop Gibson.

The twin sisters were regular visitors to the Middle East and had already acquired a reputation for themselves as experts in ancient biblical manuscripts. During their 1896 journey, a dealer in antiquities turned up at their hotel room with some evidently ancient documents. Among them the sisters recognized Hebrew manuscripts of the Bible. They bought the collection and took them home. Sorting through the manuscripts on their return, the two ladies found they were unable to identify some of the fragments. They called in their friend Solomon Schechter, reader in Rabbinics at Cambridge University, and asked him to take a look.

Schechter could hardly believe what he saw. Among the documents that the women brought back was a Hebrew manuscript of part of the Book of Ecclesiasticus, a work which is not included in the Hebrew Bible but which the Talmud refers to, and even quotes, in several places. Nobody had ever seen a Hebrew original; all the contemporary evidence suggested that it had been written in Greek. Schechter however had always held that Ecclesiasticus, or Ben Sira as the Jews called it, was originally a Hebrew work; astonishingly he was at that very moment in the middle of an academic dispute with a colleague in Oxford who insisted that the work was originally Greek. In support of his contention Schechter had already pointed to a statement by the fourth-century Church Father Jerome that he possessed a Hebrew version, and the book's own introduction, dated to around 132 BCE, in which the author's grandson claims to have translated it into Greek.

The document that the sisters showed him contained passages identical to those quoted in Hebrew in the Talmud. Taken together with the other evidence, Schechter's position was vindicated. Ecclesiasticus was a Hebrew work after all, and the authoritative Greek version that had survived for centuries in the Apocrypha, the collection of biblical-era books that did not make it into the Jewish scriptures, turned out to be a translation.

This wasn't the end of the story. Schechter, who had already heard rumours of ancient documents circulating in the back streets of Cairo, suspected that someone must have got hold of the contents of a Genizah. Furthermore he had a pretty good idea of where this Genizah was sited. He organized a trip to Cairo, made enquiries of the local Jewish community and was confirmed in his suspicions that a medieval Genizah still existed at the back of the ancient synagogue in Fostat, Old Cairo. Schechter visited the synagogue. He discovered an ancient storage chamber in a windowless and doorless bricked-up area, with one, solitary opening high in the wall through which documents could be posted. He climbed a ladder, crawled inside and discovered what turned out to be 193,000 Hebrew and Arabic documents, dating back to the year 870. Although some were crumbling, many had been preserved in the dry Egyptian air. It was a treasure trove documenting a thousand years of Egyptian and Jewish life. Alongside sacred texts it contained seemingly unimportant ephemera, shopping lists, bills of sale and personal correspondence.[24]

Kahle's publication of fragments of Aramaic Bible translations found on scraps of parchment in the Genizah triggered a fresh wave of academic interest in the study of the *Targums*. The subject received a further boost in 1949 when a complete copy of a previously unknown version of the *Targum* of the Pentateuch was discovered in the Vatican's archive. Suddenly, *Targumic* study was back on the agenda.

One of the key areas of focus for *Targum* scholars has been the way in which the Aramaic translations strive to eliminate any suggestion that God has a body or a physical presence. The Old Testament is full of phrases like

'God said', 'the hand of God' and 'God came down'. Virtually without exception every *Targum* rephrases the Bible text to imply that God is not acting in a physical manner. They frequently use the Aramaic word *Memra* to do this. *Memra* literally means 'speech' or 'utterance';[25] it is used in the *Targums* as an intermediary between an apparently physical action carried out by God and the purely spiritual deity. For example, Genesis says that 'God planted a garden in Eden'. One of the *Targums* rephrases this into 'a garden had been planted in Eden by the *Memra* (i.e. utterance) of God'.[26]

Some scholars saw a parallel between the *Targum's* use of *Memra* and the first verse of the Gospel of John: 'In the beginning was the Word and the Word was with God and the Word was God.' They argued that the *Memra* was the background to John's concept of the Word, or *Logos* as it is more correctly phrased in Greek. If so, this made the *Targums* almost essential for understanding the Gospel of John. However this theory has been thrown into disarray by the realization that the *Targums*, at least in the form we know them, are generally later than the New Testament. The idea of the Logos is much more complex than a simple transplant of *Memra* from the *Targum*. There are other equally good theories as to where the idea of the Logos came from[27] and if there are any apparent similarities between the *Targum* and the New Testament, this is probably because both are drawing on common, earlier Jewish traditions.

But scholarly investigation into the *Targums* hasn't subsided and other, sometimes extreme, theories have emerged. Such as the one which takes a seventh-century *Targum* (easy to date since it mentions people and places which didn't exist before then), and claims that it was written in the fourth century. Apparently it was written for Jewish priests to use.[28] The fact that, by the fourth century, the Jerusalem Temple had been in ruins for three hundred years and its priests no longer had any significant religious role, doesn't seem to matter for this academic viewpoint. Unwilling to take the *Targum* at face value, this particular school of thought prefers to read into the text things that aren't really there.

Although the history of the *Targum* has had its contentious side, they have an especial significance. The Aramaic *Targums* were composed to be read out in the synagogue, for those who could not understand the reading from the Hebrew Bible. The Jews have lived in very many places, and have translated their Bible into scores of languages. Yet no other translation was ever considered sufficiently important to be given a formal role in the religious liturgy. All other Jewish translations of the Bible, in whatever language, were made solely for educational or personal purposes; never for use in the formal synagogue service. In the history of Bible translation the *Targums* are quite unique.

3

Old Words, New Tongues

The Language of the New Testament

The earliest known New Testament manuscripts are written in the Greek dialect spoken in Alexandria and across most of the Middle East. It is known as *koine* or 'common' Greek. The general consensus is that the language of these manuscripts is the very tongue in which the Christian Bible was originally written. This consensus is not without its detractors, because there is almost certainly a difference between the language of these early manuscripts, and that which Jesus and his disciples spoke.

Jesus and his followers spoke Aramaic. Yet the earliest New Testament manuscripts are in *koine* Greek. But there are Aramaic phrases in the Gospels[1] and all the direct speech, the things Jesus and his followers actually said, would originally have been in Aramaic. This has led scholars to believe that an Aramaic layer lies beneath the written Greek of the New Testament, one which may never have been written down; it only circulated orally, gradually being translated into Greek and then transcribed.[2]

If that is right, then the written Greek text is itself a translation, while any renderings of it into another language are themselves translations of a translation. This of course raises questions about the inerrancy of the text. Since every translation requires a judgement on the part of the translator as to the best word to use, when the chosen word is itself then translated it becomes easy for a text to drift further and further from the original.

A good example of how this process works can be seen in the Lord's Prayer, which is based on the Gospels. In the Book of Common Prayer it includes the words 'forgive us our sins' or 'forgive us our trespasses'. The Greek text of Matthew reads 'forgive us our debts' and in Luke it says 'forgive us our failings'. Debts are not the same as sins, and sins are much more severe than failings. But there is an Aramaic word, with a root sense of 'obligation', which can also mean debt, legal liability or even guilt. Matthew and Luke are likely to be translating this Aramaic word, giving it different nuances; 'debts' in Matthew and 'failings' in Luke. The Aramaic word does not mean sin; the language expresses that concept using a different noun.[3] So, although the English version of the Lord's Prayer is clearly derived from the language of the Gospels, its phrase 'forgive us our sins' does not accurately translate the Aramaic which underlies the Greek Matthew and Luke. Translations are rarely straightforward.

Nearly everyone agrees that the earliest written versions of the New Testament were in Greek. But there is one version which some people argue was translated directly from the oral Aramaic. It is the New Testament *Peshitta*, the Syriac sibling of the Old Testament translation that we came across earlier. Some people in the Church of the East believe that their *Peshitta* was transmitted to them in its original Aramaic language. And although this claim has long been dismissed by Western Bible scholars, the advocates of so-called *Peshitta* Primacy feel strongly that the Greek New Testament is not the authentic version.[4] It is not a disagreement that has hit the headlines, as many later translation controversies did. Nevertheless, it is another example of the powerful emotions that translating the Bible generates.

The New Testament *Peshitta*

Like its earlier, Old Testament cousin, the New Testament *Peshitta* also originated in Edessa and is written in the Syriac dialect of Aramaic. Those who don't accept the claims of *Peshitta* Primacy argue that it is by no means the earliest Syriac version; they point to an earlier work in the same language known as the *Diatessaron*, a Greek word meaning 'From Four'. The *Diatessaron* is a condensed version of all four Gospels woven together into one text. It was an ambitious exercise that seems to have been quite unique for its time.

The *Diatessaron* is traditionally thought to have been compiled by Tatian, a second-century convert to Christianity who described himself as having been born in the 'land of the Assyrians'.[5] As a young man he travelled to Rome where he studied under Justin and then went back East. His peregrinations have generated some doubt about whether he wrote the *Diatessaron* in Greek before it was translated into Syriac, or whether Syriac was its original language. Although the prevailing view is that it was translated from Greek,[6] the debate is not helped by nobody having seen a full copy for over a thousand years. The *Diatessaron* started to vanish from view early in the fifth century when the Bishop of Edessa decreed that his congregants were to use the four separate Gospels in its place. A few years later another decree by a local bishop resulted in the destruction of over two hundred copies.[7]

Fortunately, we know quite a bit more about the early history of the New Testament *Peshitta*. Our knowledge comes courtesy of the dogged efforts of a small number of nineteenth-century treasure hunters and archaeologists.

In 1843 the British Museum 'acquired' a collection of manuscripts that had been preserved in the Syrian monastery of St Mary Deipara, to the south of Alexandria. It's interesting how often Alexandria crops up in our story! The manuscripts were obtained by Henry Tattam, the Archdeacon of Bedford, during a visit to Egypt. Quite how Tattam came across the manuscripts is a matter of conjecture. The church architectural journal *The Ecclesiologist*, in its 1849 edition, suggested that by plying him with sweet raisin wine, the Archdeacon had managed to so inebriate the abbot of the monastery that he willingly gave up treasures that the monastery had steadfastly guarded for a millennium and a half. *The Ecclesiologist*, quite understandably, frowns upon this, declaring with all the severe pomposity of its age that 'We must say that when such manoeuvres are practised on the poor monks, and their success boastfully recorded, not only by worldly laymen but by grave divines... morality must be at a very low ebb amongst us.'[8]

But Tattam also brought many other manuscripts back from Egypt. It's quite possible that he acquired his collection legitimately. The assistant keeper of manuscripts at the Museum, William Cureton, must have thought so; he seems to have had no qualms about examining the Archdeacon's finds. He recognized one of the manuscripts as an ancient Syriac text of the Gospels made up of three separate documents, 'taken as it would appear, almost by hazard, without any other consideration than that of their being of the same size, and then arranged so as to form a complete copy of the Four Gospels'.[9] A note on the first leaf records that the book originally belonged to a monk named Habibai, who presented it to the monastery.

Cureton, who describes the manuscripts as 'Venerable Remains of Christian Antiquity',[10] transcribed the text and published it in 1858. He dedicated it to Queen Victoria's husband, Prince Albert. It briefly flourished as the oldest known Old Syriac, Gospel manuscript. It didn't keep the title for long.

Later that century the twin sisters, Mrs Agnes Smith Lewis and Mrs Margaret Dunlop Gibson, who would in due course lead Solomon Schechter to the Cairo Genizah, were on one of their several trips to Egypt. They were carrying out research in St Catherine's monastery on Mount Sinai when they came across an ancient parchment, the original writing of which had been scraped away and a new text superimposed. This technique, designed to make the best use of scarce and expensive parchment, was not uncommon; a manuscript overwritten in this way is known as a palimpsest.[11] The top layer of the palimpsest they found was venerable in its own right; it dated from the eighth century. But the original layer, which as a result of the ageing process had become just about visible again, was far older. Although this was long before digital photography, or even rolls of film, the sisters took four hundred photographs which they sent back to Cambridge. When the photos were deciphered, it became clear that the original layer was similar to the manuscript that the British Museum had acquired, although somewhat older. It dated from the fourth or fifth century, and contained most of the text of the four Gospels.

The dialect and style of Syriac in the palimpsest suggested that it had been translated from the Greek in the late second century, making it the earliest known text of the Gospels. It differed in some significant ways from the versions of the Gospels that are known today. Most notably, the palimpsest did not contain the last twelve verses of the book of Mark which narrate Jesus's resurrection. These verses were also missing from the two oldest, surviving Greek Gospel manuscripts but up to this point nobody had been sure whether this was because they were never there, or whether a page had just fallen away. The Old Syriac Palimpsest, as it is often known, helped confirm that these verses were indeed a later addition to Mark, probably copied across from one of the other Gospels.

From the third century onwards the Old Syriac version underwent frequent revision.[12] By the fifth century, after it had gone through several incarnations, the work had become known as the *Peshitta*. It is the name by which it is still known today, giving it an affinity with the earlier Syriac translation of the Old Testament, even though they are completely different works. The Old Syriac versions are the first known translations of the New Testament into any language. Their considerable scholarly value lies in the fact that they are the earliest snapshot of the original text.

The *Peshitta* continued to be reworked by succeeding generations, bringing it closer all the time to the Greek. In 615, Thomas of Harqel wrote that the text had been revised 'with much care by me, the poor Thomas, on [the basis of] three Greek manuscripts... to keep the profitable accuracy of divine books.'[13] Poor Thomas's version did not prevail. His translation technique was so literal, imposing Greek nuances, style and word order into the Syriac text, that what he wrote, while accurate, was virtually unintelligible. Despite his efforts, the earlier version of the *Peshitta* remained the popular choice for Syriac speakers; it became the standard text for the Eastern churches, and remains so today.[14]

Meanwhile, back in the West, the ubiquity of Greek as an international language was fading. The Septuagint and the Greek New Testament were both maturing into little more than venerable curiosities, revered but generally impenetrable. There was an urgent need for a new standard translation of both the Old and New Testaments into the language most educated people understood: Latin.

Jerome's Vulgate

The ancient Syrian city of Antioch, where the Spice Road originally terminated, had been a Christian centre since the earliest days. The apostle Peter is said to have evangelized there, happily eating at the same table as the pagans, until he received a message from Jesus's brother James which shamed him into withdrawing from heathen society. Paul travelled to Antioch during his first missionary journey. He preached to the city's large, independent community of hellenized Jews, converting many of them to his new faith and establishing Antioch's reputation as the pre-eminent theological and spiritual capital of Christianity.

In the year 374 a young man, not yet thirty years old, had a dream in Antioch. His name was Jerome. He was one of the few Bible translators to leave enough of a legacy for us to be able to trace large chunks of his life story and personality.

Jerome was born into a well-off, Christian family in Stridon near Aquileia, which lies at the head of the Adriatic, seventy miles north-east of Venice. His parents sent him to Rome for his education. There, under the tutelage of the best teachers in the city, he immersed himself in the study of classical writers and poets. He also started to take an active interest in his religion. On his return home he joined together with some friends and formed a small monastic community.

The monastic ideal didn't last too long. A quarrel with his friends in the community coupled with a falling out with his family, led to his abrupt departure from his homeland. It was to be a pattern of behaviour he would repeat throughout his life. In a tirade against his birthplace he wrote, 'Men's only god is their belly. People live only for the day and the richer you are the more saintly you are held to be.'[15] Such grumblings are the earliest evidence of a developing character trait; Jerome's acerbic nature comes across frequently in his many writings.

Jerome travelled east, on a long and exhausting journey, eventually arriving in Antioch, where he fell sick. It was there, possibly while he was fevered from his sickness, that Jerome had his famous dream. He saw himself standing in front of a heavenly court. The judge asked him his religion. 'I am a Christian,' replied Jerome. 'You're a liar,' replied the heavenly judge. 'You are not a Christian, you are a devotee of Cicero.' Jerome was mortified. It was his love of classics that he feared defined him in the eyes of heaven, rather than his Christianity.

The dream was the kick that Jerome needed to start him off on his life's work. As soon as his strength had sufficiently recovered he journeyed to a monastery in the desert of Chalcis, a little way south-east of Antioch, where he tried to return to an ascetic life. It seems however that his asceticism was not all-consuming; he tells us in his writings that he was 'often present at dances with girls'.[16]

During his stay in Rome, Jerome had accumulated a library of classical works. They didn't sit well with his renunciation of Cicero and his new ascetic lifestyle. He disposed of his books in Chalcis, throwing himself instead into the study of the Bible and the writings of the Church Fathers. He learned Hebrew, under the guidance of a converted Jew named Baraninas. It was a name which would return to haunt him later in life when he was castigated for Jewish sympathies. Rufinus, a former friend now turned critic, sneeringly called Jerome a disciple of 'Barabbas'.[17]

Jerome's stay in Chalcis did not last long. Theological differences with his fellow monks and hermits made life intolerable for him. Once again he stormed out of a monastery, echoing his earlier intemperance, this time complaining that 'It is preferable to live among wild beasts rather than with Christians such as these'.[18] He left the desert and settled for a second time in Antioch.

Jerome was a prolific writer. He developed a reputation as a Bible commentator, penning introductions and commentaries to many of its books. When not commenting on the Bible he wrote biographies, polemics and letters, dozens of which have survived. And even though he had given up his classical studies, his youthful education started to prove its worth. He started receiving commissions to correct Greek manuscripts of the New Testament. On one occasion he translated an Aramaic gospel known as pseudo-Matthew into Greek. Neither language was his native tongue.

By the year 382 Jerome's reputation as a scholar and biblical commentator had spread far beyond Antioch. He travelled as part of a delegation to Rome, a city which he knew well from his youth, and where he still had influential contacts. He was spotted by Pope Damasus, who took him under his wing, hoping to benefit from Jerome's knowledge of the politics of the Eastern Church. The Pope soon found that Jerome's scholarship was an even greater asset; he effectively became Damasus's secretary, helping him with his correspondence and answering questions on his behalf.[19] It turned out to be the most important engagement of his life; building up to the moment when

Jerome was asked to undertake his greatest work, the one for which, despite everything else he did, he is best known today.

By now there were various Latin translations of the Greek Gospels already in circulation. They varied greatly in quality and differed significantly from each other, the result of careless translation and mistakes made by copyists. Not the least of their inaccuracies was the accidental appearance of parts of one Gospel in the middle of another.[20] The confusion was so great that discerning readers didn't know which versions to trust.

Jerome wasn't at all happy when the Pope asked him to review the existing translations and produce a more reliable Latin version. He complained that he was being asked to sit in judgement upon Scripture, that those who were comfortable with the old versions would be unsettled by his revisions. He feared they would revile him for having the audacity to tamper with the sacred, ancient texts.[21]

Of course the Pope's request was not something that Jerome could ignore. Nor could he be self-effacing about the opportunity to bring some clarity to the Bible text, to help people be certain about what it really said. Grudgingly coming to terms with the request, he mused, in his usual truculent manner, why should he not 'correct the mistakes introduced by inaccurate translators, and the blundering alterations of confident but ignorant critics, and all that has been inserted or changed by copyists more asleep than awake?'[22]

To begin his task Jerome gathered together the oldest Greek manuscripts he could lay his hands on and compared them with the Old Latin versions. Within a year, he had revised the Latin translations, coming up with a new, coherent rendition. He acknowledged the affection that many people retained for the Old Latin versions and tried to remain sensitive to their feelings. Striving to keep his new version as close as possible to the original meaning, retaining wherever he could the old phraseology even at the expense of consistency, he described his translation as 'sense for sense, and not word for word'.[23] Bruce Metzger points out that Jerome translated the words 'High Priest' in three different ways, depending upon how it had been rendered in the Old Latin versions.[24]

Once the Gospels were complete, Jerome turned to the remaining books of the New Testament. Not all of them though; the translations of Acts,

Revelation and the Pauline Epistles, which were once attributed to him, are now assumed to have been made by someone else. It may have been his one-time friend Rufinus,[25] with whom he was destined to fall out very badly over their respective interpretations of Origen's theology. Stefan Rebenich suggests that Jerome's claim, in his treatise *On Famous Men*, that he had translated the whole of the Greek New Testament into Latin 'might at best be understood as an intention that was never fully realized, unless one is prepared to explain it as another testimony to his amazing showmanship'.[26]

His translation of the New Testament was only the first part of Jerome's greatest achievement. The second part came in no small measure due to his astonishing ability to offend. Alongside his scholarly work in Rome, he waged an aggressive campaign encouraging ascetic, devout behaviour. He consorted with wealthy, attractive young women, nobly encouraging them to remain chaste and preserve their virginity. He warned them sternly to avoid long-haired, bearded men and instead to make their companions 'those who are pale of face and thin with fasting'.[27] Unsurprisingly, this relentless piety made him unpopular in Rome, particularly with long-haired, bearded men. He also did his best to offend wealthy widows: 'Look at them as they ride in their capacious litters, a row of eunuchs walking in front of them, look at their red lips and their plump bodies, you would not think that they had lost a husband, you would fancy they were seeking one.' Nor did he mince his words about 'the very clergy, who...kiss these ladies on the forehead, and then stretch out their hands...to take wages for their visit'.[28]

As long as Pope Damasus lived, Jerome managed to get away with this behaviour. When the Pope died in 384, Jerome's star plummeted. His sojourn in Rome came to a hasty end. He set off on his travels again, finally settling in Bethlehem.

Jerome's new home was only a two-day journey from the library in Caesarea where Origen's *Hexapla* was stored. This gave him the opportunity to study the mammoth, six-columned work. Never one to miss an opportunity, Jerome decided to use it to produce a new Latin translation of the Old Testament, one which would throw light upon all 'those passages in it which are obscure, or those which have been omitted, or at all events, through the fault of copyists have been corrupted'.[29] This time, he did not intend to use the Septuagint, or any other of the Greek versions, as his starting point. Instead he determined to produce a radical, new translation, directly from the Hebrew. He was certain that the Hebrew studies he had undertaken during his time in the desert would be more than adequate to equip him for this task. If he got stuck with a difficult passage, he knew he could always seek the assistance of local, Jewish scholars. He even had a strategy for pre-empting those critics who were bound to accuse him of producing an inaccurate translation; he would highlight the changes he had introduced by marking every place where his rendition differed from the Septuagint. He called his technique of reliance on the Hebrew text *Hebraica Veritas*.

Jerome's recourse to Hebrew was not popular. As ever, he defended himself robustly. He compared himself to Origen, whose name he said was even more reviled than his own. He wrote that he would gladly have Origen's knowledge 'even if accompanied with all the ill-will which clings to his name...I do not care a straw for these shades and spectral ghosts, whose nature is said to be to chatter in dark corners and be a terror to babies'.[30] Elsewhere he reminds his 'barking critics' that his motive was not to censure the existing Latin translations but to 'recover what is lost, to correct what is corrupt'.[31]

We don't just have Jerome's word for the unpopularity of his work. Augustine, who as we have seen was a fierce defender of the Septuagint, wrote to Jerome in 403. He told him, peevishly, that a riot had broken out in a church in Tripoli, because a bishop had read the Book of Jonah from Jerome's translation. When deciding how to translate the Hebrew name of the plant which had sprung up overnight to provide shade for Jonah, Jerome had opted for the Latin *hedera* meaning 'ivy'. The congregation had expected to hear the word *cucurbita*, or 'gourd'. The idea that the plant which sheltered Jonah from the sun was no longer a sturdy, large-leaved squash, but a flimsy, creeping ivy, did not go down well. Augustine, no doubt feeling that his defence of the Septuagint was vindicated, reported that it was all the bishop could do to stop the congregation from abandoning him.[32]

Jerome's translation from the Hebrew was no less controversial than any of its predecessors. It attracted opprobrium from many quarters. He had long been accused of stirring up theological controversy, and now heresy was all but added to the charge sheet. His critics censured him, not only for departing from Christian tradition, but for denying the divine sanctity of the Septuagint and the Old Latin versions. True to form, he defended himself with a venom-tipped quill. There is little doubt that the people he upset and the enemies he had made throughout his career impeded the reception of his work. Despite its superior quality, it took four hundred years or more for his translation to become fully accepted as the Roman Church's official Bible.

In the sixteenth century, by which time much of Jerome's translation had been revised, his translation became known as the Vulgate. It has had a profound impact, not just on the Church but on non-Christian religions too. Jerome's original Latin terminology became the basis for much of today's religious lexicon; words like *salvation, sanctification, Scripture* and *sacrament* all derive from his translation.[33] Just like its author, the Vulgate did not have an easy ride. As we will see, its superiority was seriously challenged when it became one of the most closely contested battlegrounds in the sixteenth-century Protestant Reformation.

Jerome divided his life between the pampered nobility of Rome, and the ascetic intellectuals of the early Church. He courted controversy in both environments and upset people with his writings. Even the reception of his Vulgate was contentious. Despite all this he has gone down in history as a member of the theological elite of the early Church, one of its four Doctors.

Jerome was raised in a privileged environment and educated well. The opportunities that came his way were in large measure an accident of where and when he was born, and his social standing. In the wilder, less developed regions of Christian Europe, not so far to the north of Jerome's homeland, there was far less opportunity to have one's name lauded by future generations. The challenges of a life of religious leadership were much harder, and a place in history far less easy to achieve.

Little Wolf and Mesrop

The emperor Constantine's fourth-century adoption of Christianity as Rome's official religion transformed the faith's prospects. Christianity was soon pushing northwards, and wherever the Bible put down roots it needed to be taught in the local tongue. Unlike Jerome, not every Bible translator had the opportunity to divide their lives between the indulgent patricians of Rome and the ascetic monks of the early Church. Nor were they able to soak up the rich, intellectual currents that, although operating in diametrically opposed domains, marked the age of the Talmud and Church Fathers. In the wilder, less developed regions of Europe, not so far to the north of where Jerome was born, two men in particular faced almost insurmountable hurdles.

Ulfilas – his name meant 'Little Wolf' – was a Visigoth, a member of the Western tribe of the Gothic nation which had once hailed from the eastern regions of Germany. A century or so after his birth, his compatriots would rampage through Southern Europe, sacking once-mighty Rome as they went. Hastening the end of the Latin Empire they disappeared from world view almost as quickly as they had appeared, overrunning Spain and assimilating into the native population.

Christianity had started to reach the Goths during the third century. Their first Christians had, so it is said, been converted by captives from neighbouring Cappadocia, seized by a Gothic raiding party in Northern Turkey. Among the captives were a number of Christian monks. The holy men turned the tables on their captors, preaching religion to them and wooing the Goths from their ancestral ways. By the time Ulfilas was born, some of his tribe had adopted Christianity.

It is not easy for us to conjure up an image of life among the Goths. Unlike the Greeks or Romans they produced no great monuments or literature. We know a few limited historical facts; they provide us with a picture of a primitive tribe, dwelling in basic, unsophisticated huts, going about their daily business with a minimum of tools and artefacts. Until our attention is caught by one of the most remarkable works of calligraphy of the Dark Ages, the sixth-century, Eastern Gothic *Codex Argenteus*. A codex is the forerunner of the modern book, its contents contained in pages rather than on a scroll. This codex's silver lettering, implied by the name *Argenteus*, is inscribed upon a purple dyed parchment. It can still be seen in the library of Uppsala University, in Sweden.[34] The Goths may have been a primitive, warlike nation, but at least one of their number had a fine eye when it came to writing manuscripts.

The sparse information we have about Little Wolf's life comes from two extremely old sources. One is a ninth-century summary of an even earlier, fifth-century, chronicle written by the church historian Philostorgius.[35] The other comes from a manuscript written by one of Little Wolf's pupils, a bishop called Auxentius, which was discovered in 1840 in the Louvre.[36] From these documents we learn that Ulfilas was born in or around 311, was ordained as a bishop at the age of thirty and spent seven years preaching to the Goths. He was not made welcome. The Goth's leaders resisted the spread of Christianity, which they saw as a political ploy by the Roman Empire to extend their influence in the region.[37] Ulfilas was driven out of the Gothic lands in the late 340s, fleeing with his supporters to Moesia in what is now Bulgaria.

At the age of seventy Ulfilas travelled to Constantinople to take part in a disputation. Jerome was in the city around the same time, taking part in a theological showdown between warring Antiochan churches.[38] The two men may have met; if so it would have been one of the last encounters of Little Wolf's life. He fell ill in the city and died shortly afterwards.

Ulfilas's great achievement was to translate the Bible into his native Gothic tongue. The only books he omitted were those of Samuel and Kings. He left them out because he feared that their tales of battle between the early Israelites and their neighbours might stimulate the warlike tendencies of the Goths.[39]

Translating the Bible presented Ulfilas with a far greater challenge than just transposing the words from one language to another – even though that itself is no easy task. Not every word in the Greek Bible which he used as his source existed in Gothic. There was no Gothic word to convey the act of abstaining from food. There was a word however, *fastan*, which meant 'to endure'. Ulfilas adapted it for his Gothic translation. It later passed into German. It is the source of our word 'to fast'.[40]

The problem was not just one of adapting old words to new uses. Ulfilas didn't even have the tools at his disposal to write his translation down. The Goths didn't have an alphabet; the language they spoke had no direct written equivalent. Until Ulfilas came along, the only way for Goths to communicate in writing was by using runes, a primitive technique which was hardly practical for the Bible.

So, before he could begin his translation Ulfilas had to create an alphabet. He broke the Gothic tongue into its component sounds and allocated symbols to each, using Latin and Greek characters. At least, that is what we surmise from the historian Philostorgius, who sums up the whole enterprise with the words 'he reduced their language to a written form'.[41] It was probably a bit more complicated than Philostorgius implies. One suggestion was that the alphabet and translation were composed collaboratively by Ulfilas and his followers, some time after they had been expelled from the Gothic lands.[42]

Of course, a society which has no written alphabet is a society that cannot read. Equally, there is no point in inventing an alphabet unless people are given the skills to read it. And although creating an alphabet and translating the Bible are accomplishments in their own right, the greatest of Little Wolf's achievements must have been providing the Goths with the skills to read his work. We don't know how many people Ulfilas and his collaborators taught to read from his new Gothic Bible, nor how he managed to disseminate the art of reading. But we do know how another translator solved a very similar problem elsewhere.

The Goths were not unusual in not having an alphabet. This was the fourth century after all; most of the human race was still coming to terms with its capacity for learning. Half a century later, in Armenia, it fell to the intriguingly named Mesrop Mashtots to emulate what Little Wolf had earlier done.

Mesrop was a monk blessed with the gift of language. He spoke Greek, Persian, Syriac and Armenian. Like the *meturgeman* who translated the Pentateuch into Hebrew in the Jewish synagogues, he was skilled at rendering the Bible on the hoof to Armenian-speaking, Christian congregations. He was, in the Armenian language, a *targmanitch*[43] (we can see that the two job titles derive from the same root). But although he was a skilled translator, Armenian wasn't his first language and he didn't always find it easy to declaim the Bible in that language without a written translation to hand.

Mesrop, and his collaborator Shahak, the patriarch of the Armenian Church, knew that it was essential for the Armenian people to have a Bible written in their own language. But they recognized that there was no point in embarking on a translation until people could read it. They determined to devise a nation-wide programme with the aim of teaching literacy to young children. Only then, when they had raised a generation with the skills to read, would Mesrop present them with an Armenian translation of the Bible.

It didn't occur to them that the lack of an Armenian alphabet would present a problem; they assumed that they could just as easily teach the children to read using an Aramaic script. They were wrong. When the programme finally got going they discovered that the Aramaic alphabet was not adequate for reproducing Armenian sounds accurately. The kids found it impossible to understand the calligraphy in front of them. After two years, Mesrop and Shahak deemed the experiment a failure.

Mesrop didn't give up. He saddled his donkey and travelled the country, listening to the way people spoke and cataloguing the various phonemes they used. He engaged the services of a calligrapher, who took the Greek alphabet as his base and adapted it to represent Mesrop's phonemes. They ended up with a thirty-six letter, exclusively Armenian, alphabet.

Once they were satisfied that the alphabet they had devised was fit for the task, Mesrop and Shahak began the most innovative part of their project. They persuaded the country's rulers to help them create a national network of schools. The plan was to build a literate, cultured population, with a strong enough sense of national identity to resist the pressures of assimilation that were already buffeting them from the neighbouring Persians and Byzantines. Once the schools were up and running, Mesrop and his students were finally able to get on with translating the Bible.

Mesrop is still remembered in Armenia today. A national holiday in his honour marks the start of the school year and is dedicated to the accomplishments of translators, teachers and writers. His picture can be found on the cover of many school books.[44]

We cannot know if Ulfilas's educational strategy was as ambitious as Mesrop's. He lived a little earlier, his country was more remote and he may not have had the resources to match those available to Mesrop. Still, it is safe to assume that he did more than just invent the Gothic alphabet. For his alphabet to succeed, and for his Bible to become known, Ulfilas or one of his collaborators must have laid the foundations for some sort of educational system, even if it was confined only to the most learned segments of Gothic society.

Ulfilas's translation was almost certainly made from the Greek. All that survives from his Old Testament are a few fragments of the Book of Nehemiah. Although about half the New Testament is extant, the only complete book is the Second Epistle to the Corinthians. It is quite possible that the task that confronted Ulfilas was more challenging than that faced by any other biblical translator, before or after. Yet, like the nation for whom it was made, most of the Gothic Bible is now lost.

Mesrop's Bible did survive, albeit greatly revised. Mesrop had used both the Syriac and Greek versions for his sources but when the thirteenth-century Armenian king Het'um became a vassal of the Pope, the Bible was revised, to bring it in line with Jerome's Latin text.

Mesrop and Ulfilas stand out as the most innovative of early Bible translators. Many others also rose to the task. By the early Middle Ages the Christian Bible had been translated into nearly every language where a church had put down roots. The Jews, scattered by now across the world, held fast to their Hebrew version; they had little need of any other, their ancestral language was integral to their faith. But everything was about to change. In twenty-seven campaigns and ten short years, Mohammed and his followers changed the religious landscape of the East. By the year 632, as Tom Holland puts it in his entertaining book *In the Shadow of the Sword,* 'paganism in Arabia had everywhere been put in shadow'.[45] The Jews and Christians were no longer the only proponents of monotheism, nor the only faiths which laid claim to the messages of the Bible. A new culture, a new world force, had emerged. And a new language into which the Bible would be translated.

4

The Sublime Bible

Hunayn Ibn Ishāq

Islam's rapid spread across the Middle East propelled the Bible into areas it had never previously reached. Not that the Mohammedan forces carried Bibles with them; far from it, they had their own holy text, the divine revelation mediated to Mohammed through the agency of the angel Jibril. But the Bible is 'everywhere and nowhere'[1] in the Qur'an, rarely quoted yet frequently acknowledged, its divine origin taken for granted.[2] From the Bible's point of view the emergence of the Qur'an, almost certainly the first book to be produced in Arabic,[3] provided the stimulus for Arabic-speaking Christians and Jews in the new Muslim lands to create vernacular copies of their own scriptures. Thus the Arabic Bible was born, and a new controversy opened in the story of the translated Bible.

Up to now, the Bible had only been translated by people who wanted to use it for the sake of their religion. The Jews had made translations into Greek or Syriac for educational purposes and into Aramaic for the benefit of those in the synagogue who needed help in understanding the Hebrew readings. Christians who didn't speak Greek used Latin or vernacular versions of the Old and New Testaments in their churches. But the Bible rarely extended beyond Jewish and Christian places of study or worship. Very few people outside of Judaism or Christianity were aware of it, and even those who were, paid little attention to it. The founding of Islam changed all that.

The Qur'an is familiar with both the Bible and with many of the stories, fables and folklore which the Jews and Christians span out of its narratives. It frequently refers to biblical personalities and it believes in the divine revelations afforded, among others, to Abraham, Moses and Jesus.[4] But despite its frequent allusions to biblical topics, the Qur'an never quotes from the Bible directly, neither the Old nor the New Testament. The Qur'an takes it for granted that its readers are familiar enough with the biblical narratives not to have them recounted word for word. It retells, rather than repeats, the Bible's stories. Sidney Griffith notes that the manner in which the Qur'an presents the Bible is similar to the style of 'interpreted' bibles that circulated among Arabic-speaking Jews and Christians prior to the birth of Islam.[5]

Although the Qur'an knows the Bible, and accepts that its key personalities were gifted with the spirit of prophecy, it does not slavishly accept everything that the Bible says. It subordinates the Bible to its own world view, insisting that what the early Jews and Christians believed needs to be reinterpreted in the new light of Islam. It frequently seeks to correct, or even polemicize against the Bible and at times it accuses the 'People of Scripture', by which it means the Jews and Christians, of deliberately falsifying their account.

Of course, this didn't go down too well with the Jews and Christians. They may not have been concerned that the Qur'an had its own, idiosyncratic way of interpreting the Bible. But once they'd found themselves accused of deliberately falsifying the scriptures they held sacred, it's more than likely that Arabic-speaking Jews and Christians would have wanted to set the record straight. One can imagine some very difficult conversations taking place between the adherents of the Bible and those of the Qur'an (although, since there was neither an Arabic Bible nor a Qur'an in any other tongue, such conversations would have been restricted to those few who could understand the language of each Scripture). The Pact of Umar, an early agreement that non-Muslims would be protected in Islamic lands in return for certain conditions, stipulates that Christians and Jews will neither learn the Qur'an, nor teach it to their children.[6] Given that the Muslims were the conquerors and the Jews and Christians their subordinates, this restriction could have been imposed by decree. The fact that it forms part of a pact to which both parties assented implies that the Islamic conquerors were more than keen to protect the Qur'an from examination.

Alternatively, the Pact of Umar's ban on Jews and Christians studying the Qur'an may have been a defensive measure, to deter missionary activity. Muslim rulers would not have relished the idea of preachers from other faiths trying to destabilize Islamic belief by constructing arguments against the Qur'an. Far better to worry the non-Muslims by denying them access to it. The Jews and Christians knew that the Qur'an accused them of falsifying the Bible. They worried that their own people, living in an Islamic environment, might start to believe the accusation. But they could only deal with this if they could read the Qur'an, to find out what it actually said. It wasn't as if the members of the different religions lived in isolation from each other. Contact between the communities was frequent, not least in the markets, streets and bathhouses. If adherents to the conquered religions couldn't study the Qur'an there was only one thing they could do to protect adherence to their own faiths. Jews and Christians both needed to set up effective, educational programmes that would prop up their own religions in Muslim lands. And religious education begins with an understanding of the Bible.

With the exception of a few Jews who could still read Hebrew, and far fewer Christians with a command of Greek, everybody in the first lands that fell to the Arab armies read their scriptures in Aramaic or Syriac. But as Arabic became the dominant tongue in the conquered lands, the old languages turned out to be less and less useful. A Bible that Arabic-speaking Jews and Christians could read became an imperative. It didn't take long for the translators to get to work.

The first parts of the Bible to be rendered in Arabic were probably the Gospels. They were most likely translated in monasteries in Syria and Judea during the seventh and eighth centuries. The earliest surviving example, dating from around the year 800, resides in the Vatican.[7] We know little of the story behind this translation, other than that it was probably inscribed in the Mar Saba monastery in the Judean desert, that it seems to have been copied from an earlier manuscript, and that it was translated from the Syriac, not from the Greek.[8] The history of this particular translation is, however, so shrouded in the fog of time that we have no idea how widely it circulated, or what impact it had.

By the time we are able to pick up the main thrust of the Arabic Bible's story there had been a fresh impetus for its translation. It was now the eighth century and times were changing. Islam was established and confident, and a new age was dawning. It was an age which placed ideas, art, science and literature at its pinnacle, rather than the ideological quarrels of different belief systems.

The change began in the aspirational city of Baghdad, Islam's pioneering capital founded by the Abbasid dynasty's second caliph, al-Mansur. The Abbasids had come to power in 750, overthrowing the previous Umayyad dynasty. To mark the transition of power, al-Mansur built himself a new city with the ambition of making it the greatest the world had ever known. It was here in Baghdad that the process of translating the Bible into Arabic would flourish, as an offshoot of a project to make all the great mathematical, philosophical and scientific works of the Greeks available in Arabic.

The project was the brainchild of the caliph Harun al-Rashid. His influence on Islam's emergence as the leading civilization of the early Middle Ages was profound. It extends far beyond his legendary cameos in the *Thousand and One Nights*.

Baghdad at the end of the eighth century assaulted the senses of its visitors as no city had ever done before. In its markets one could find every known herb, fruit and spice. The mingling of their rich scents all but neutralized the heavy odours steaming off the laden camels and donkeys reluctantly pressing their way along the thoroughfares. Bejewelled wives and daughters of wealthy merchants, decked in coloured satins and gold-embroidered silks, on rare excursions from the luxurious palaces in which their menfolk confined them, picked their way delicately over prone, pleading beggars, some maimed, some mad, some simply malingering. Important men in coloured turbans bestrode the streets, their servants hurrying behind, urging along porters weighed down by their burdens. Noise filled the air, the cries of merchants proclaiming their wares, of dogs fighting, children screaming, of masons hammering on the stones from which the House of Wisdom was being constructed.

Bayt al-Hikma, the House of Wisdom, was the flagship institution of what we now call the Translation Movement. Its seeds were sown by al-Mansur when he founded the city but it attained its greatest prominence during the reign of Harun al-Rashid's son, al-Ma'amun. Inspired by his father's vision of a Baghdad unmatched by any other in architectural, cultural and scientific grandeur, al-Ma'amun turned the dream into reality. The House of Wisdom was to be the city's library, the place where all the books in the civilized world, now available in Arabic, were to be stored. The echoes of Alexandria a millennium earlier are not hard to discern.

The project to translate everything worth knowing into Arabic, realizing the caliphate's ambition to elevate Islamic knowledge, culture and civilization above anything that had gone before, was greatly assisted by new paper-making technology from China. It made the manufacture of books cheaper and easier, allowed authors and scribes to work faster, and elevated the written word above memory as the medium in which to store knowledge.[9]

The Translation Movement lasted for over two centuries. It was made possible by generous subsidies and endowments from both public and private funds, and was supported by the elite of Baghdadi society.[10] It underpinned the Golden Age of Islamic philosophy and medicine. But on the face of it, it wasn't about the Bible at all. Its declared aim was to render Greek philosophical and scientific works into Arabic. The translation of the Bible into Arabic was little more than a spin-off. Who could have dreamed that it would outlive all its secular rivals?

Dozens, probably hundreds of translators worked in the House of Wisdom during the lifespan of the project. None was more famous, nor more influential, than the man whose name has come to symbolize the entire Translation Movement; Hunayn ibn Ishāq.

Hunayn's speciality was the translation of Greek and Syriac medical and logical texts into Arabic. But according to the tenth-century historian al-Masudi, he also translated some of the Septuagint. al-Masudi was nearly correct: Hunayn did translate some of the Bible, but from the Syriac, not from the Greek.[11] That is what we would expect; Hunayn was a Nestorian Christian, he spoke Syriac and had grown up reading the Bible in that language. But he wasn't recognized as a theologian or scriptural expert; he was a doctor by profession. He translated Galen's anatomical writings and is said to have authored over a hundred works himself, including ten treatises on ophthalmology.[12] When he chose to turn his hand to translating the Bible it was almost certainly a labour of love, not a career move.

Hunayn doesn't get the credit for the first Arabic Bibles; that went to the anonymous monks in the Syrian and Palestinian monasteries a century or so earlier. But by admitting the Arabic Bible into the House of Wisdom, the translation scholar par excellence threw down a gauntlet to its detractors. As a Christian living in an Islamic city he had a point to make. The Bible, he implied, should no longer be seen in Islamic eyes as the old, corrupted text belonging to two decaying religious faiths which the new faith declared had been superseded. In the House of Wisdom the Bible ranked as equal to every other classical literary work. Hunayn took the Bible out of the monasteries, churches and synagogues, and planted it firmly within the Islamic secular corpus, on the pinnacle of world civilization.

Nothing remains of Hunayn's biblical translations, although it is likely that subsequent Arabic Bible manuscripts were based on his. His personality too is obscured from us, dwarfed by his tremendous scholarly achievements. In that respect he differs from a certain Egyptian Jew who, a century later, not only produced a new Arabic recension of the Bible, but also left us with a very clear impression of his character, his passions and his fierce commitment to the many principles for which he fought.

Saadia Gaon

Saadia ben Yosef's life was colourful, controversial and subversive. Colourful and controversial as a result of the many arguments and disputes he involved himself in; subversive because, steeped in the Islamic, theological science of *Kalām*, he was the first major Jewish thinker to try to demonstrate the validity of his faith through reason and logic.[13] In subjecting the pronouncements of Scripture and the ruminations of the rabbis to the tools of epistemology and philology, Saadia ushered in centuries of Jewish philosophical speculation.

Saadia was born in Egypt in 882. His birthplace was, at that time, a stronghold of the Karaite sect; a Jewish faction which differed forcefully from the rabbinic mainstream. The rabbis and their followers believed that the Bible's injunctions could only be understood through the traditional interpretations of the

Talmud. The Karaites took the Bible at face value; they weren't interested in Talmudic reasoning. The gulf between the two camps is thrown into sharpest contrast by the biblical stricture not to kindle a fire on the Sabbath.[14] The rabbis took it to mean that it was acceptable to bask in the heat and light of a fire kindled before the holy day began. The Karaites on the other hand took the injunction literally. They spent the day in the dark and cold.

Saadia spent much of his life battling Karaite ideology. He started the fight as a young man in Egypt, writing polemics against the sect's founder, Anan ben David. The Karaites responded in kind; accusations, refutations and personal attacks were hurled around liberally. The atmosphere became so vituperative that it eventually forced him to leave the country.[15] He spent some years in Israel, studying and teaching in the lakeside city of Tiberias, before finally packing his bags once more and journeying to Baghdad.

The rabbinic academies in Baghdad, where the Babylonian Talmud had been given its final form,[16] were regarded by most of the Jewish world as the pre-eminent centre of religious scholarship. They were rivalled only by the scholarly centres in Israel, where Saadia had studied. Because they were situated in the ancient Jewish homeland, the Israeli academies traditionally had the last word in matters of Jewish law. Once Saadia established himself in Baghdad, that all changed.

Despite Jewish Baghdad's traditional deference to Israel's legal authority, the scholarly rivalry between the two centres was undisguised and growing. Baghdad was blossoming as a cosmopolitan hub of intellectual, cultural and mercantile activity, while conditions in Israel were disintegrating after years of political and economic neglect. As the disparity between the centres grew, the Babylonian school became increasingly assertive. Matters came to a head in 921, the year Saadia arrived in Baghdad, with a dispute between the two centres over the fixing of the calendar for the coming year, and the dates on which the major festivals would fall.[17]

Had Saadia not involved himself in this dispute, the Baghdadi scholars may well have capitulated, if for no other reason than respect for the fading glory of their rivals in the West. But Saadia was not a man to turn a blind eye when it came to a matter of principle. He was convinced that the calculation on the calendar that had been performed in Israel was wrong. He embarked upon a furious correspondence, in which he displayed his legal, mathematical and literary skill with such passion and energy that his opponents barely stood a chance. The head of the scholarly community in Israel backed down, the Babylonian calculation was vindicated and, as long as Baghdad continued to remain a centre of Jewish scholarship (which wasn't that long), the authority of its scholars was never again disputed.

Saadia's battles were personal as well as institutional. Shortly after being appointed as the head of the foremost Jewish college in Baghdad, which effectively made him the rabbinic leader of the Jewish world, he got himself excommunicated. It came about because he refused to countersign a will in which the Exilarch, the secular head of the Babylonian Jewish community, stood to make a lot of money. The Exilarch of course was furious but Saadia, as always, stood on principle. He'd smelt a rat and nobody could make him compromise. Even the caliph's vizier, Ali ibn Isa, got involved, convening a council in which judges and scholars attempted to adjudicate between the parties. But although Saadia had his principles he didn't have the Exilarch's wealth or influence. He was drummed out of town and despite an extravagantly publicized reconciliation five years later, when Saadia was nearing the end of his life, he never truly regained his former vigour.

Saadia's Old Testament translation bears all the hallmarks of his personality. There was no obvious need for another Arabic translation of the Bible; several existed already. But Saadia deemed that there was a need, and not just because the style of earlier translations left much to be desired. In his youth he had dreamed of producing a grammatically correct, stylistically attractive Arabic version of the Bible that conformed both to Jewish tradition and to current philosophical thinking.[18] But as he grew older, and more disputatious, he perceived a more urgent need. A new translation was essential, Saadia believed, to address the twin challenges that the Bible faced: the Muslim charge that the Jews had falsified its text, and the Karaite rejection of traditional biblical interpretation.

Saadia's first translation, which he probably commenced while living in Tiberias,[19] began as a series of annotations on the Pentateuch. The annotations evolved into a commentary and eventually metamorphosed into a full-blown translation. It covered the whole of the Pentateuch and several other books of the Bible.[20]

It was important to Saadia that his work became known to Muslims. It would have little polemical value if it simply remained a text used by the Jews. He had been educated in a Muslim environment and spent his life surrounded by Islamic culture; he knew how to make his translation acceptable to the aesthetic refinements of literary Arabic. His purpose may have been to rebut Muslim criticism of the Bible but he deferred to Islamic grammarians and philologists when it came to matters of style.

Islamic writers and intellectuals of the time placed great emphasis on the literary economy of language. They frowned on the use of unnecessary words or phrases and on superfluous repetition. That the Hebrew Bible contained such, apparently unnecessary, material offered ammunition for the Muslim accusation that the Jews had falsified the Bible. The literary critic and philologist ibn-Qutayba had transfigured the classic translation by the non-Muslim Hunayn ibn-Ishāq by converting repeated names into pronouns and deleting phrases that seemed redundant. Saadia's *Tafsir*, as his translation came to be known, displays similar stylistic alterations.

The similarities between his amendments and those of ibn-Qutayba, and his echoes of Hunayn's phraseology, have led Richard Steiner to suggest that Saadia may also have made use of Hunayn Ibn-Ishāq's translation when composing his own.[21] Both men translate the opening words of Genesis as 'the first of what God created was heaven and earth'. To our minds this is little different from the standard rendering of 'In the beginning God created'. But as Sidney Griffiths points out, the prevailing view at the time was the Aristotelean notion that time had always existed. 'In the beginning' suggests that the world was created within pre-existent time. Saadia is at pains to stress that nothing, not even time, existed before the creation of the world.[22]

Saadia went to great lengths to eliminate every biblical suggestion that God might have a body or a voice, worrying that the mention of a divine hand, arm, heart or speech might lead uneducated people to believe that God had a physical presence. Nor was this just a matter of education; Saadia's pugnacity displayed itself in every aspect of his life, even his Bible translation. The Muslim theologian al-Jāḥiẓ had attacked the Hebrew Bible for its portrayal of God as a physical being. He had taken particular exception to the reference in Deuteronomy 4.24 in which the deity is described as a 'consuming fire'. Saadia had no qualms about meeting such criticisms head on. The consuming fire, according to Saadia, is a metaphor for heavenly punishment.

In his preface to the translation Saadia made it clear that he wanted to produce a work that would not be 'rebutted by tradition'.[23] He meant rabbinic tradition, the very system that the Karaites opposed. Throughout his translation Saadia was at pains to reflect the mainstream rabbinic interpretation; no unnuanced Karaite literalism would grace his endeavour. He'd dreamed, as a young man, of producing a sublime, literarily immaculate Arabic rendition of the Hebrew Bible. By the time he reached middle age he'd become equally concerned to refute and silence his two great intellectual enemies, Islamic and Karaite theologians. The great polemicist never left a battle unfought.

Saadia's ideological fervour didn't go down well with everyone. He probably enjoyed some success in deflecting Muslim and Karaite attacks but the Jews themselves, long used to their traditional way of reading the Bible, weren't well pleased. He was criticized by his own followers for artlessness; for transforming metaphysical ideas like God's heart in Genesis 6.6 into 'his prophet', a substitution which made little sense and did not fit the context. The Jews had long accepted the principle that the Bible speaks in human terms, using language that people understand to express complex theological ideas. Many felt that in his zeal to rebut external criticism, Saadia had gone too far in abandoning this principle.

Saadia did listen to his critics – up to a point. He accepted some of what they said and revised a number of his translated phrases. But he stuck to his guns as far as the bigger picture was concerned; he had set out to write a polemical work, and that is exactly what it was. Saadia wasn't the sort of person to hand ammunition to his opponents just to appease critics who were not as willing to stick their necks out as was he.

Perhaps this is why, despite all the criticism, Saadia's translation endured. It may not have been a word-for-word literal rendition, it may have replaced poetic anthropomorphisms with somewhat clumsy alternatives, but it was a readable and ideologically clear text. It became the most well-known and popular of all Arabic Bible translations, widely used by Jews, Copts and Arabic-speaking Christians. In the sixteenth century, when multi-lingual, polyglot Bibles became briefly fashionable in Europe, Saadia's translation was the most likely Arabic version to be found on the page. It is still in use today.

Sword and Bible in Hand

The first stage in the translated Bible's history was nearly complete. It could be read in Latin across Western Europe, in Arabic and Aramaic in the East, or in one of several languages in Armenia, the Balkans and the further reaches of Byzantium. It had even been given a home in cosmopolitan Baghdad's erudite House of Wisdom. But its story was about to take a different turn. As Christianity began to spread across Northern Europe, the translated Bible turned out to be an extremely useful weapon of war.

The first king to appreciate the bellicose potential of the translated Bible was probably Charlemagne, king of the Franks and future Holy Roman Emperor. When he came to power in 771, not only were large tracts of Europe ungoverned and pagan, but even his own Frankish lands were backsliding towards barbarism, undermining the alliance that his father Pepin had made with Rome. Charlemagne (his name is a contraction of Charles Magnus or Charles the Great), aspired to unite Europe into a single, Christian empire. He purposed to achieve this by uniting the Germanic tribes. The translated Bible would form part of his armoury.

Philip Schaff, whose nineteenth-century, eight-volume *History of the Christian Church* remains a monumental work of reference, compares Charlemagne's conquest of the Saxons to that which would be pursued in the future USA towards the Native Americans. 'Treaties were broken, and shocking cruelties were committed on both sides, by the Saxons from revenge and for independence, by Christians for punishment in the name of religion and civilization. Prominent among these atrocities is the massacre of four thousand, five hundred captives at Verden in one day. As soon as the French army was gone, the Saxons destroyed the churches and murdered the priests, for which they were in turn put to death.'[24]

Charlemagne's policy of conversion by conquest had a second dimension; one which transcended sheer brute force. While in Italy, the emperor had met, and been won over by, Alcuin, an Anglo-Saxon monk from York. Struck by the monk's faith and ability, the king recruited him to devise an educational curriculum for his clergy. He soon found that he had engaged more than just an educator; the man he employed turned out to be a skilled manipulator of the king's conscience.

Alcuin didn't like Charlemagne's forced imposition of Christianity upon his conquered subjects. Shrewdly playing upon the emperor's known affection for the German language, he persuaded him to temper his aggression towards his new subjects with a sprinkling of religious education; to encourage them to appreciate the higher aims of Christianity. Top of the agenda, of course, was a translation of the Bible into German. One of the few documents to survive from Charlemagne's German campaign is a Bavarian rendition of passages from Matthew,[25] carried out, or at least supervised, by Alcuin. Alcuin's enlightened strategy of education as a corollary of conquest stands in marked contrast to the policy favoured by church leaders in subsequent centuries, who, as we will see, resorted to extreme measures to keep the Bible well away from the languages spoken by ordinary people.

Charlemagne's use of the translated Bible in conquest was relatively benign. Less so in the Slav lands, where, in an example as good as any of medieval double-dealing, deceit and treachery, it was sucked into a power struggle between the Byzantine and Roman Churches. The two hierocracies, representing the Western and Eastern expressions of Christianity, were engaged in a perpetual struggle for authority; particularly in territories where their spheres of influence overlapped.

Some little while after Charlemagne had imposed Roman Christianity on the Saxons, his grandson Louis the German installed an acolyte, Rastislav, as Prince of Moravia. Little is known about Rastislav's early career; it is thought that he may have been a relative of Moravia's rebel leader, taken as a hostage by Louis during one of the many wars he fought in the course of his fifty-year reign.[26] Conflict, territory and dynastic power were very much the theme of what passed for ninth-century Central European diplomacy.

Whatever the origins of their relationship, Louis obviously thought Rastislav the right candidate to keep the lid on Moravia's rebellious tendencies; in return for power and protection Louis expected him to keep Moravia subdued. And, in virtue of Louis' status as Holy Roman Empire, he charged Rastislav with maintaining the Pope's authority in his lands. But Rastislav turned out to be of a more independent mind than Louis had bargained for.

In the ninth century the Church, reflecting earlier divisions in the Roman Empire, was headquartered in both Constantinople and Rome. The two churches would soon irreversibly split into Eastern and Latin denominations, but in Rastislav's time the divisions were only just becoming apparent; in theory Constantinople and Rome still formed one united Church. There was, however, already enough tension between the two centres for Rastislav to spot an advantage. He could free himself from Louis' yoke. He wrote to Michael the Drunkard, the Byzantine emperor in Constantinople, asking him to send missionaries to Moravia. It was a shrewd political move; Rastislav was effectively seeking to align himself with the Byzantine Empire, thereby freeing himself from Louis' Holy Roman dominion.

The Byzantine emperor was happy to oblige. He despatched two Greek brothers, Cyril, a linguist and philosopher, and Methodius, a former governor of a Byzantine principality. The two brothers were born in the Greek city of Thessalonica. They could already speak Slavic, which gave them a considerable advantage over the incumbent German bishops, who had only a limited grasp of the local tongue. Rastislav endowed Cyril and Methodius with the rights to teach in Moravia and the two brothers set about converting the country to the Byzantine rite.

As part of their endeavours the two brothers instituted a programme of translating the Bible into the Slavic language. Like Ulfilas and Mesrop before them, they first had to create an alphabet, one of two which appeared in Moravia at the same time. Cyril's alphabet was named Glagolitic, but his name survives today in the one he didn't write: the Cyrillic script that is used across Russia, Central Asia and parts of Eastern Europe.[27]

Unsurprisingly, the German bishops fiercely resented the brothers' success in introducing the Byzantine liturgy. They tried to ban the rite, together with the brothers' Slavonic Bible. That they failed to impose the ban was due in part to Rastislav's protection of the two brothers and, just as significantly, because the key player in the inter-denominational dispute, the local bishop Hartwig of Passau, had suffered a stroke and could not speak.

Even so, things did not work out for Rastislav as planned. Louis, angry at his former client's treachery, gathered his forces. He invaded Moravia and took Rastislav prisoner. The archbishop of Salzburg travelled to the region to reassert the Latin rite, and the use of the Latin Bible. Methodius was thrown into prison.

Seven years later the tables turned. Rastislav's nephew Svatopluk became ruler of Moravia. He reached an accommodation with the Pope, set Methodius free and appointed him archbishop. Methodius was instructed to work under the Pope's auspices and remain loyal to the Roman rite and Latin Bible. But like everyone else, Methodius too was his own man. He reinstated the Byzantine rite and brought back his own Slavonic Bible.

Svatopluk bided his time. Methodius was an old man. When he died a few years later Svatopluk expelled all his followers, selling many of them into slavery. Those who managed to escape carried Methodius's Bible with them.[28] It had been the translated Bible's first encounter with temporal politics. It would not be the last.

Part Two

The Violence Begins

5

Medieval Conflict

Moses' Horns

The vernacular Bible made a brief appearance in Britain in the so-called Dark Ages. It didn't last long, Following William the Conqueror's Norman invasion of 1066, which brought French to the people and reinvigorated Latin in the English Church, the Anglo-Saxon Bible retreated to the shadows. Only one complete manuscript survived; it is, however, quite exceptional.

Known as the Lindisfarne Gospels, and written in the monastery of that name during the seventh century by Bishop Eadfrith, the manuscript ranks among the world's most important religious artefacts. Its rich colours and elaborate designs, a fusion of knotwork, key patterns and the Celtic decorative style known as La Tène, still have the power to take our breath away today; we can only guess at the impact they had when first created. But the importance of the beautifully illuminated Lindisfarne Gospels to the story of Bible translation has little to do with their aesthetic qualities. It's more about what we can read between the lines.

The Lindisfarne Gospels were written in the Latin of Jerome's Vulgate. Towards the end of the tenth century, three hundred years after the manuscript was first emblazoned, by which time it resided in the Minster of Chester-le-Street, Aldred, the Minster's Provost, added a word-for-word, Anglo-Saxon translation. He composed it in the Northumbrian dialect and inscribed it in the gaps between the lines of the Latin.

Why he did this is a mystery. Maybe it was an act of homage to the majestic splendour of the Lindisfarne manuscript; maybe this was the only copy of the

Bible he had available. Fortunately history considers his interpolation to be an enhancement of the original text, not an act of cultural vandalism. Compared to the original calligraphy, Aldred's handwriting is relatively unobtrusive, if somewhat scratchy.

Aldred's translation in the Lindisfarne manuscript is the oldest Saxon Bible to have survived.[1] Others were made but no longer exist; the Venerable Bede, the most important of all early English theologians, is said to have dictated a translation of the Gospel of John while lying on his eighth-century deathbed. The Psalms too were translated, in Canterbury, at around the same time. But only Lindisfarne has come down through the ages intact. It is now in the British Library.[2] There are also early copies of the manuscript in Oxford's Bodleian Library and in Cambridge.[3]

Illuminated Anglo-Saxon translations were produced during a period of remarkable creativity and originality in English art. They were highly influential, but not always in the manner that the artist or translator had intended. Aelfric, a learned Anglo-Saxon monk, translated the first seven books of the Old Testament, known as the Heptateuch, towards the end of the tenth century. We know very little about Aelfric other than his reputation as one of the most skilful writers and translators of his time. He translated a series of Latin sermons, the *Catholic Homilies*, into Old English and composed a biographical treatise, *Lives of the Saints*. He was spurred on to translate the Old Testament by his patron, Aethelweard, a historian best remembered for his Anglo-Saxon chronicles.

Although considered a translation, Aelfric's Heptateuch is really little more than a paraphrase. It takes the credit for possibly the most misleading, and culturally significant, of all vernacular Bible mishaps. It wasn't really Aelfric's fault, the error was the illustrator's. Aelfric was simply rendering the Latin Vulgate into Anglo-Saxon. He would surely have been astonished had he foreseen the consequences of his translation.[4]

In the Book of Exodus, when Moses descends from Mount Sinai his face beams with a radiant, spiritual glow; so powerful that he has to put on a veil before anyone can look at him. The Hebrew word used to describe this glow has a number of other possible meanings. In the Exodus narrative it means a beam of light, as in 'Moses' face beamed', but it can also depict a ray, horn or even a corner; the meanings are all connected, they have the underlying sense of something which projects. Although the Septuagint follows the Hebrew in referring to Moses' glowing face,[5] Jerome's Vulgate, seemingly confused by the various possible meanings of the Hebrew word, chooses to translate 'beamed' as *cornuta*, which literally means 'horned'.

Jerome's choice of words doesn't seem to have caused much of a stir at the time. Horns had been used for centuries on idols and icons to denote power; gods and kings, including Alexander the Great, were frequently depicted as wearing them. They were ubiquitous on helmets. Jerome may have been mistaken in his translation but the thought of Moses wearing horns on his head, if anyone thought of it all, was not particularly striking. As far as the Old Testament is concerned, they didn't come any more powerful than Moses.

Six hundred years elapsed between Jerome and Aelfric. Many paintings and mosaics of Moses have been discovered which date from within that interval. None of them depict Moses with horns. But shortly after Aelfric's Old English version described Moses' face as *gehyrned*, or horned, an illuminated copy of his manuscript appeared. It included various images of Moses with horns. Ruth Mellinkoff suggests that the creativity of eleventh-century, Anglo-Saxon art was such that it offered 'favourable conditions for the introduction of a novelty such as the horned Moses'.[6]

Aelfric had done nothing more than render Jerome's *cornuta* into its Anglo-Saxon equivalent. But the illustrations which accompanied his Old Testament paraphrase helped to launch the motif in Western art of Moses having horns. Over the coming centuries the horned Moses cropped up in church art and Bible illustrations across Europe, very often even in biblical scenes that precede the one in which his face became '*gehyrned*'. The most famous of all depictions is Michelangelo's 1513 statue of Moses.[7]

The real damage attributed to Aelfric's horns had very little to do with the character of Moses, and much to do with medieval superstitions about the Jews. If Moses was *gehyrned*, it followed, to the medieval mind, that all Jews had horns. In 1267 an ecclesiastical synod in Vienna ordered Jews to wear a horned hat. In the same period, Jews in France were required to wear a yellow wheel with a horn in the middle. The idea of the horned Jew became rooted in the popular imagination, it even survives in our time; Amy-Jill Levine, one of the foremost scholars of the Jewish origins of Christianity recounts that she has 'twice been asked where she had her horns removed'.[8]

From an ancient symbol of power and majesty, the horn became one of the most virulent symbols of anti-Semitism. And it all started because a twelfth-century Bible illustrator took Aelfric's translation too literally.

The Cathar Bible

There are very few periods in the history of religion more shameful and disastrous than that of the Crusades. The wars that Christian Europe launched against the Muslim East, the consequences of which are still felt today, and the slaughter of Jews that accompanied the Crusaders' knightly rampages, had little to do with the fact that the Bible could now be read in many languages. But the vernacular did become caught up in one crusading campaign, indeed it was made to share part of the blame. It was perhaps the most bizarre of all Crusades, the only 'holy war' which the Church waged against its own people. A Crusade which took place, not in the Holy Land, but in the Languedoc region of southern France.

The unfortunate victims of the twenty-year Crusade instigated in 1209 by Pope Innocent III were the sect known as Cathars. According to the Church, the Cathars were guilty of the Albigensian heresy, so named because of its origins in the town of Albi, near Toulouse. The Cathars were Christians, but; far from orthodox in their doctrines, they subscribed to a dualist theology in which two deities, one good and one evil, competed for control. Evil dominated the world as we know it but Good stood invisible behind it, waiting to redeem those whose deeds and virtues allowed them to complete a successful cycle of reincarnations. The Cathars believed that Jesus's teachings were those of the benevolent deity, but that the Church, with its predilection for material wealth and splendour, had fallen into the clutches of the malevolent spirit, the creator of this evil world. As a result the rituals of the Church were to be eschewed and there was certainly no reason to pay its tithes and taxes. Small wonder that the Cathars incensed Rome.

The popularity of the Cathar movement, which may have attracted up to four million followers in its heyday, owed much to the yawning chasm between the impoverished lives that ordinary people lived and the pampered privileges of the clergy. The peasants, who endured hardship and poverty, saw priests and bishops living lavish lifestyles, wearing fine clothes and living in splendid dwellings, some even inhabiting castles. Much of their wealth came from taxes and tithes levied upon the poor. The peasants resented this, and considered Catharism to be a noble and virtuous alternative. It became a social movement fuelled by the exploitation of the disadvantaged, just as much as it was a belief system. Cathars called the Catholic Church a harlot and the Pope the antichrist. The Church called the Cathars vermin, serpents and demons.[9]

At first the Church and Cathars tried to resolve their differences in public disputations, held in the courtyards and banqueting halls of great castles and noble homes. These were big, dramatic gatherings; peasants and landowners flocked from miles around to hear the Catholic priests take on the Cathar Perfects, as their spiritual leaders were called.

The main point at issue in the disputations was Jesus's message. The Cathars quoted exclusively from the New Testament, basing their arguments on the literal meaning of the text. They drew their quotations both from the Vulgate and its translation into their own Occitan language (a copy of the Cathar Bible survives in the Municipal Library of Lyon).[10] The Church cited both Old and New Testaments, but, in a tacit admission that they had little confidence in their own position, they refused to admit extracts from the Occitan translation into the debate. Stephen O'Shea, in his highly readable and entertaining history of the Cathars, notes that they prohibited quotes from the vernacular Bible to avoid 'twisted interpretations of revealed truth'.[11] The old canard, that a Bible which people understood would cause nothing but trouble, was alive and well.

It was inevitable of course that the public disputations would fail to produce a reconciliation. Tiring of futile debate, Rome resolved to adopt a more assertive policy. The Pope declared that Toulouse, the main city in Languedoc, was a centre of heretical corruption. He accused the senior baron in the *langue d'oc*, Count Raymond VI, of failing to defend the Church against the heresies taking root in his land. His legate, Peter of Castelnau, was sent to raise an army against Raymond. Peter excommunicated Raymond and tried to confiscate his land. When Peter was assassinated, the enraged Pope called for a Crusade.

The Crusade raged for twenty years. Eventually, following hundreds of thousands of deaths[12] and no prospect of an end in sight, a peace treaty was agreed. The once prosperous Languedoc region was destitute, its population annihilated. In 1229 a Council in Toulouse proclaimed that henceforth people were forbidden from reading the Old or New Testaments, even in their original languages, other than the Book of Psalms. They were expressly prohibited from having translations of the Bible. Even before the decree was issued, translations had been burned in Metz and Challis.[13] As Malcolm Lambert puts it, 'repression of translations as well as of heretical preachers was the simple disciplinary solution, especially when local prelates had narrow horizons'.[14] It was the first act in what was to become an endemic, medieval persecution of the translated Bible.

Banning the translated Bible was not enough for the Church. Pope Gregory IX determined to make absolutely sure that any future heresies were nipped in the bud; the hegemony of Rome must never again come under threat. In 1233 the Dominican Order was instructed to root out and destroy heresy. Its techniques were to be enquiry, investigation and interrogation. The institution became known as the Inquisition. It was to develop a fearsome reputation over the coming centuries.

Although the Crusade formally came to an end with the agreement of a peace treaty, the slaughter continued for a further fifteen years. In 1243 Royal forces laid siege to the hill-top fortress of Montségur where two hundred of the leading Cathars were holed up. Unable to survive the winter, the fortress's inhabitants surrendered. They were herded together into the snow and burned alive.[15]

Beguines and Beghards

Throughout the medieval period the translated Bible was buffeted by the politics of religion. Marguerite Porete's story is just one such case. Marguerite was not a Bible translator, but she was able to understand enough Latin to recite passages from the Bible in her own language. She wasn't unusual in her ability to do this. By the time she lived, in the thirteenth century, not all translations of the Bible were formal or scholarly. Informal translations were becoming quite common, as Marguerite's example shows.

Marguerite was a *beguine*. The *beguines*, and their male counterparts, *beghards*, were pious, wandering mendicants who preached religion to the masses and lived on alms. They were similar to nuns and monks, except they were not members of any of the religious orders licensed by the Church. Operating beyond the purview of the Church, they occasionally espoused beliefs that conflicted with orthodox Christian theology. The Church's attitude towards them fluctuated; at times they were tolerated, equally they could find themselves condemned as heretics.

Marguerite Porete had written a mystical treatise, *The Mirror of Simple Souls*. In her book she discussed, among other things, the annihilation of the soul, a process through which, so she believed, the human spirit could potentially be elevated to such a high level that it fused with the divine. Marguerite seemed to suggest that souls in this state were not bound by the ordinary laws of morality and could suffer no pangs of conscience. The book was condemned as heretical and Marguerite was instructed not to disseminate it. When she refused, she was condemned to a lingering and painful death, burned at the stake in Paris on 1 June 1310.[16]

Marguerite's alleged heresy was by no means clear-cut. Long before it was condemned her treatise had been read and approved by three well-known, orthodox theologians, and even after her death it remained popular and continued to circulate. In 1530 it passed an inspection by the archbishop of Tours. There seemed to be nothing fundamentally wrong with *The Mirror of Simple Souls*, and it has influenced Christian mystics and mysticism for centuries.

Marguerite was allegedly burned for the esoteric views that she expressed in her book, particularly for her understanding of the autonomy of the mystically annihilated soul. But her prosecutors took her statements out of context[17] and it seems likely that she was condemned primarily for political reasons, rather than for any theological offence. It appears she was executed to prove the orthodox credentials of the French king, Philip the Fair. He was in the middle of a campaign to ostracize the Knights Templar, a powerful monastic order to whom he was deeply in debt. His campaign, against such a wealthy and mighty faction, caused great concern among the highest echelons of the

Church. Executing the alleged heretic Marguerite was one of the strategies Philip adopted to demonstrate his orthodoxy, his unswerving loyalty to the tenets of the Church, his passion for rooting out all taints of heresy, acting solely to preserve correct belief with no ulterior motive.[18]

But if that was so, why choose Marguerite? There were many other ways Philip could have demonstrated his theological conformity. The answer is that the alleged heresy in Marguerite's mystical tract was only an excuse for her execution. The real reason was her 'crime' of translating the Bible. A quarter-century earlier, in 1274, the Council of Lyons had placed the *beguines* and *beghards* under a ban. Prominent among the charges against them was one of 'cultivating novelties in their vernacular exegeses of Scripture'.[19] As everyone knew, this offence of the 'vernacular exegesis of Scripture' contravened the prohibition enacted against the Cathars by the Council of Toulouse in 1229, forbidding the translation of the Bible. The *beguines* and *beghards* had offended against the pronouncements of Toulouse and Lyons by daring to read from the Bible using the Gallic language in 'conventicles, street corners, and public squares'.[20]

The *beguines* and *beghards* were placed under a ban due to their informal translation of the Bible into old French. Marguerite's execution was politically motivated – both in demonstrating Philip the Fair's loyalty to Rome and, just as importantly, as a warning to those who dared commit the offence of translating the Bible. After 1229, the popular Bible was under threat as never before. But it was in England that it would face its severest challenge.

The Morning Star of the Reformation

The fourteenth century was not a happy time in England. The plague of Black Death was rampant, killing nearly half the people in the country. The nation was perpetually at war, first with the Welsh, then the Scots and finally the French. The conflict with France, which ran for well over a century, was dubbed the Hundred Years War.

There were tensions too within English society. The old nobility were contending with the rise of a new merchant class. The poor had to suffer them both. Trumping all three factions were the friars and clerics, whose power transcended even that of the king. His authority was only in this world; even royal decrees meant nothing thereafter. The churchmen, however, could grant either salvation or damnation for all eternity. They could even countermand the severest heavenly judgement. Everything depended on the willingness of the sinner to open his purse.

As the century wore on the nobles and merchants increasingly grew to resent the power, wealth and corruption of the Church. As for the peasants, blighted by poor harvests, land shortages and an ever-growing burden of taxes, they railed and eventually rebelled against both the ruling classes and the clerics.

Religion of course was the sole bastion of relief in those days and it was to contemplative matters that traumatized peasants naturally turned in order to find solace. But the priests and friars had lost touch with their calling. Tormented souls and seekers after truth rarely turned to them for comfort or enlightenment; the churchmen had shown themselves to be self-absorbed, dry and uninspiring. Instead, new and unorthodox devotional approaches to religion became the fashion, inspired by activists like the Lollard evangelists and the Yorkshireman Richard Rolle, an Oxford-educated hermit, whose theological treatises were hugely popular.

The Lollards, also known as the Mumblers, were a loosely defined and poorly organized movement of itinerant preachers who shunned the formal structures of the Roman Church. They followed the teachings of John Wycliffe, a leading theologian and by far the most interesting churchman of his age. It was John Wycliffe, two centuries ahead of his time, who set out to produce the first full translation of the Bible into English.

Wycliffe was born during the 1320s, somewhere near the town in Yorkshire whose name he bore. His early career was very conventional. He studied theology, mathematics and natural science and developed a reputation as a thinker and writer. In 1360 Wycliffe became Master of Balliol College in Oxford. He was acknowledged as a preacher of note, a rising, if somewhat dissident, star within the Church. When he left Balliol, he was granted various clerical positions around the country.

But Wycliffe was too independent a mind for his chosen career. He began to depart from the well-trodden, conventional path expected of fourteenth-century churchmen. His defection began when the English Parliament refused to pay the Pope a tribute to which they had been committed long ago, by the late King John. The current instalment was already thirty-three years overdue and the Pope was pressing hard, but Parliament was resolute that they would not pay. The legislators were adamant that King John never had the power to commit the nation to send money overseas, not even to the Roman Church.

It was a seminal moment in England's relation with the papacy. It was also Wycliffe's first serious foray into politics. He was called in, as a theologian, to advise Parliament on the matter.

As he drew closer to the seats of power, Wycliffe was disturbed by what he saw. He was a fervent advocate of justice and humility, yet wherever he looked he saw corruption and self-interest. Nor was he alone in feeling that the Church was blind to, even complicit in, the nation's malaise; his concerns were shared by some in the Royal Household. Eight years after he was first summoned to advise Parliament, King Edward sent him across the English Channel, to Bruges, to negotiate a peace with France. While he was there he met the king's son, John of Gaunt, who had recently been ennobled as the Duke of Lancaster. The two men became close friends and Wycliffe, conscious that he could now rely on the protection of a powerful ally, felt more able to speak his mind. He came back to England a resolute man.

Wycliffe was determined to face down the corruption which pervaded the Church. He dreamed of a religious establishment that shunned wealth and power, one which had the interests of the poor at heart. He began to agitate in books and sermons against the authority of the Pope in England, arguing that the supreme ruler of any land should be its king, not a far-distant church leader. In one of his tracts he borrowed from the Cathar phrase book, describing the Pope as 'the anti-Christ, the proud, worldly priest of Rome, and the most cursed of clippers and cut-purses'.[21]

Wycliffe's attitude did not go down well in ecclesiastical circles. In 1377, when he was fifty-three years old, Wycliffe received a summons from the bishop of London to attend his court and explain the 'wonderful things which had streamed forth from his mouth'.[22] The bishop had finally lost patience; he had been coming under pressure from Rome for some time to do something about Wycliffe, and he could put off the day no longer.

John Wycliffe appeared before the bishop, accompanied by his friend the Duke of Lancaster, the son of the king. The hearing began with a violent row over whether or not Wycliffe should sit down. The Lord Marshal of England and the Duke of Lancaster insisted that Wycliffe's status allowed him to remain seated, the bishop demanded that he stand; to sit before his court would be an indignity. The Duke threatened to bring down the pride of the bishop and all the prelates in England. 'Do your best, Sir,'[23] responded the bishop, himself the son of a duke.

The hearing was a farce. The bishop was unable to tame Wycliffe and his circle of powerful allies. When the news reached Rome the Pope himself felt obliged to take to the fight. He issued a bull in which he accused Wycliffe of 'vomiting out of the filthy dungeon of his heart most wicked and damnable heresies'.[24] He demanded Wycliffe's arrest and eventually managed to have him declared a heretic and dismissed from Oxford University.

But the Pope's victory was short lived. He died the following year and the Catholic Church was rocked by a revolution at its very heart. The Papal Schism, as it has become known, led to the creation of a rival papacy. A second Pope, known to his enemies as the 'anti-pope', established his court in Avignon. The Church was in crisis, its reputation and authority had never been so low. John Wycliffe and his social conscience were no longer its most pressing topics.

Even so, the schism in the Church did not make things that much easier for Wycliffe in England. The country had its own problems. In 1381 the Peasant's Revolt broke out. Sparked by the king's attempt to impose a poll tax on the people, it rapidly turned into a popular uprising against the two forces that made the lives of the poor a misery: the institution of serfdom and the power of the Church. Among the key movers of the revolt were the Lollard preachers, Wycliffe's followers. And even though the nobility shared the rebels' dislike of the Church, and despite John of Gaunt still being Wycliffe's most powerful supporter, nevertheless the hapless Duke of Lancaster, son of the hated king, found himself one of the chief targets for the revolutionaries' ire.

The rebels' dislike of John of Gaunt put Wycliffe in an invidious position. His anti-papal rhetoric reflected the religious mood of the nation. By rights he should have supported the uprising. But he felt duty-bound to support his patron and ally and to come out against the revolt. Torn, and unable to commit to either party, Wycliffe was left with only one choice. He retreated to his books and his writings. He turned his attention to the Bible.

A cornerstone of Wycliffe's theology, enthusiastically supported by the Lollards, was that Scripture should be accessible to everyone. The Bible was the foundation of Christian belief and should not be the esoteric property of the clerics. But although parts of the Bible had previously been rendered into English there was still no complete translation. Ordinary people, who neither spoke Latin nor were able to read, only knew what they knew from the mouths of the clergy. Much of what they thought they knew, powerful convictions such as the fires of hell and the travails of purgatory, were not even part of Scripture. The Bible had become the property of the priests and monks; the decree issued by the Council of Toulouse in 1229 had played no small part in removing it from public scrutiny.

Wycliffe believed that the Bible was the path to salvation. He regarded the policy of withholding it from the masses to be an unpardonable sin. He was convinced that by reading an English Bible, or at least having it read to them, the laity would find grace. If nobody else would make an English version available to them, then he would. No earthly power would prevent him from carrying out what he considered to be his religious duty. A full translation of the Bible became an imperative for Wycliffe. It was to the accomplishment of this that he turned, following the Peasant's Revolt, when he knew that his remaining days on this earth were numbered.

But for all his determination, Wycliffe was no Jerome. Despite his theological erudition, he did not know Hebrew and he is unlikely to have known Greek. Like everyone else, the Bible he knew was the Latin Vulgate, and it was this that he and his assistants made use of for the first English translation. As with so many who had gone before him, Wycliffe's translation of the Bible was actually a translation of a translation.

Wycliffe lived long before the introduction of printing into Europe. His Bible could only be composed and reproduced in manuscript. Producing a hand-written copy of a work as lengthy as the Bible may be an endeavour of love but it is time consuming and laborious. Anyone wishing to buy one of

Wycliffe's manuscripts would have had to shell out a lot of money. This didn't seem to dent their popularity though. Today, more than six hundred years after the translation was made, it is believed that up to two hundred copies still exist.[25] Once, there would have been many more.

It goes without saying that Wycliffe's translated Bible provoked the wrath of the Church. Henry Knighton, a canon of St Mary's Abbey in Leicester, wrote that Wycliffe 'translated from Latin into the language not of angels but of Englishmen, so that he made...common and open to the laity, and to women who were able to read, [that] which used to be for literate and perceptive clerks, and spread the Evangelists' pearls to be trampled by swine'.[26]

Although Knighton appears not to have held a very high opinion of his congregants, his comments about the English language need to be seen in context. During the fourteenth century, English was only just beginning to recover from centuries of neglect. The Norman invasion, led by William the Conqueror in 1066, had installed French as the lingua franca of the nobility and educated classes. Latin was the language of religion and French the language spoken in the upper echelons of society. English was the old language, which only peasants spoke. It wasn't really until the fifteenth century, with the emergence of English nationalism, that the language came to be accepted by all classes. By that time some of the phrases that Wycliffe had coined from the New Testament, such as 'the wages of sin are death', had entered the vernacular as proverbs.[27]

Chaucer and Wycliffe dug the foundations for English as a literary language; two hundred years later Shakespeare and Tyndale would gild its spires. Knighton, who wrote in Latin, doesn't mention Chaucer; perhaps he had never heard of him. When he disparaged those who read English as swine it wasn't only class prejudice. It was just as much a case of disdain for a language he never came to appreciate.

The assumption that English was the speech of illiterates, below the refined talents of the nobility, reinforced the opposition to Wycliffe's translation. One only had to look, so the argument went, at the Lollards to see what could happen when the peasants got ideas of their own. Giving them access to the Bible, which they were obviously incapable of fully understanding, could only result in disaster. Knighton was in no doubt about this. Citing the conservative

French theologian William of Saint Amour; he wrote, 'We are probably close to the end, and therefore we are closer to the perils of the latest times, which are to come before the coming of Antichrist.'[28]

Opposition to Wycliffe's Bible became institutionalized within the ruling classes. Seven years after his death, in 1391, a bill was laid before Parliament to outlaw English Bible versions and to imprison anyone in possession of a copy. It was obvious that Wycliffe's work, which was now circulating freely, was the principal target. The bill was thrown out due to the intervention of Wycliffe's old friend, the Duke of Lancaster.

The Church then tried a different tack. In 1408 a synod in Oxford declared that no person, under pain of excommunication, was to translate the Bible into English. Thomas Arundel, Archbishop of Canterbury, wrote to the Pope denouncing Wycliffe as 'that pestilent wretch, of damnable memory, yea, the forerunner and disciple of antichrist who, as the complement of his wickedness, invented a new translation of the scriptures into his mother-tongue.'[29] No matter that Wycliffe was long dead by now; when it came to the medieval art of abuse, the memory of Wycliffe was as good a stone as any on which to whet the arrows of contumely.

But words alone are never enough. In 1427 Pope Martin issued an order for Wycliffe's remains, now forty years into their decomposition, to be exhumed and burned. The ashes were to be cast into a river, hoping no doubt that this act might arrest the currents of change that Wycliffe had anticipated, currents which were already undermining the nature of clerical authority.

John Wycliffe sowed the seeds, but it took a full two hundred years for his spiritual heirs to reap the fruits. It wasn't until the dawn of the sixteenth century, when the Renaissance was changing the way that people understood the world, when the Protestant Reformation was gathering pace, that his legacy began to crystallize.

Wycliffe predated the Reformation by two centuries. But he is often considered to have been its herald. He is sometimes referred to as the Morning Star of the Reformation. It has been suggested that it was he whom Chaucer had in mind when he created the character of the exemplary, virtuous parson in the *Canterbury Tales*.[30] Chaucer was a friend, and eventually the brother-in-law, of John of Gaunt, so this suggestion is not unrealistic. Wycliffe's ideas and the impact he had on society were enough to subject him to vitriol and condemnation while he was alive. But it was his translation of the Bible that ensured that the abuse would endure long after his death.

A Czech Heretic

To his persecutors in England, Wycliffe was more than merely a troublemaker whose obsession with church reform threatened their easy lives. The Peasants' Revolt had driven home to them the fragility of English society; as the luminary of the Lollard movement Wycliffe represented an ongoing threat to the nation's stability. But there was another side to Wycliffe. His English opponents probably never knew, and they almost certainly didn't care, that his name and influence was having an impact in places so alien they couldn't even begin to know where they were. The Bohemian city of Prague was far beyond their ken; even as recently as 1938 a British Prime Minister described it as a 'faraway place' populated by 'people of whom we know nothing'.[31] But one man in Prague had heard of John Wycliffe, and he was destined to pay with his life for what he knew.

Jan Michalóv of Husinec was burned at the stake in 1415 in the German city of Constance. Before he died he was stripped of his priesthood and his soul formally handed over to the devil. One of his disciples claimed that, as the flames licked his charred and blistered body, he died singing. A local chronicler, much more realistically, claimed that he died screaming.[32] How could he not?

Jan Michalóv is better known as Jan Hus. Fifty years younger than Wycliffe, Hus was born into a society that was teetering on the edge of social upheaval. As in so much of Europe, there was a growing sense of resentment about the wealth and power concentrated in the hands of a priesthood who were widely seen as corrupt. And, as elsewhere, matters were exacerbated by the presence of a small, over-privileged, secular class. In the case of Bohemia this privilege lay in the hands of a prosperous, socially dominant, German-speaking minority. By the time Hus came on the scene, stirrings of Czech nationalism were already in the air. All that was lacking was an inspirational figurehead.

Hus started out as a philosophy lecturer in Prague's university. There was little remarkable about his early academic career; he lived the life of a good and observant Catholic, he is even on record at one point as buying an indulgence for the remission of his sins. But it was around this time that he began to read Wycliffe's books, and to recognize the similarities between the English theologian's world and his own.

Hus's growing awareness of the problems in Czech society, and his desire to do something about them, led him to seek ordination. In 1402 he was appointed to a pulpit in one of Prague's private chapels. His sermons, which grew more radical as he became more confident, began to attract attention. And although he was an independent thinker, whose thoughts were shaped by the social conditions surrounding him, the extent of Wycliffe's influence can be gauged by the archbishop's reaction once Hus's anti-corruption message began to hit home. Appointed just a few months after Hus took up his pulpit, Archbishop Zbyněk, who had paid 2,800 gulden to get the job, initially supported Hus and his early calls for change. But once Hus's calls for clerical reform grew too vigorous, the archbishop ordered the confiscation and burning of Wycliffe's books. In the archbishop's mind at least, it was Wycliffe who was responsible for Hus's sedition. The destruction of Wycliffe's books was the first step in a process which would ultimately lead to Hus's death.

Central to Hus's reform agenda was to cement a sense of national identity through the development of the Czech language. Just as had happened in England, the peasant classes were emerging from centuries of ignorance and repression. They were identified as much by their language as by their poverty. Elevating the language was the obvious way to ameliorate their status. But old Czech was hardly a literary language; its orthography was complex and uncertain. In his treatise, *de orthographia bohemica*, Jan Hus set out a simplified system of pronunciation for the Czech alphabet. Although it has been modified somewhat since Hus first devised it, the system of signs and symbols above and below the letters which he introduced eventually became the basis for all Slavic languages that use the Latin alphabet.

Top of Hus's agenda was to provide the Czechs with a Bible they could read in their own language. It is not clear whether Hus himself takes the credit for translating the Bible into Czech, or whether he appointed a team of scholars working under his direction. But the Czech Bible that emerged in 1406, with a revision in 1414, is generally regarded as Hus's accomplishment; one of several theological innovations that led to his eventual arrest for heresy. To appreciate Hus's passion, and the Church's violent reaction to his translation, we need look no further than his assertion that the 'disciples of antichrist'[33] were keeping people away from the Bible.

Before he was finally murdered for his alleged heresy, Jan Hus was subjected to one of the most spectacular trials in history. Thomas Fudge describes how nearly every VIP in Europe travelled to the German city of Constance to watch the proceedings. One archbishop arrived with 600 horses; 700 prostitutes paraded through the streets, 500 people tragically drowned in the lake, two committed suicide and one was murdered. The Pope fell off his carriage into a snowdrift.[34] The carnival was so exhilarating that Hus's eventual conviction and barbaric execution must have seemed an anti-climax. But the violence didn't end there.

Hus's supporters of course foresaw the outcome of the trial. But that didn't imply they were resigned to it, or that they would take his execution lightly. When news of his death reached Bohemia, country-wide riots broke out. Churches and priests were attacked. The authorities retaliated in kind. Within a few short years the country was embroiled in a civil war. After King Wenceslas died in 1419 his successor Sigismund, egged on by the Pope, raised a foreign army and launched an attack against the Hussites, as they were now known. The fighting raged until 1436 and spread from Bohemia into neighbouring provinces. It wasn't until the Hussite camp became riven with its own internal arguments and disagreements that a path was cleared for a peace agreement. In the interim, thousands had died.

The Hussite wars marked one of the first great revolutions which would ultimately culminate in the Protestant Reformation and Europe's unhappy age of religious wars. But the Czech Bible lived on.

A Question of Language

Wycliffe's complaints against the Church were sparked by the corruption and venality in which the ecclesiastical hierarchy was steeped. As Henry VIII's archbishop, Thomas Cranmer, put it: 'the ungraciousness of damnable ambition, never-satisfied avarice, and the horrible enormity of vices had corrupted and taken the see of Rome'.[35] The Roman Church had grown lax and complacent; it had lost touch with its roots. Spirituality had been replaced by temporality; the nurturing of souls by the accumulation of wealth.

But greedy, over-stuffed friars and privilege-toting bishops were merely the visible manifestation of a deeper malaise, one which failed to appreciate, indeed tried its hardest to resist, the immense cultural upheaval taking place in Europe. The Renaissance was gathering pace. Nearly every field in which the human imagination could be exercised had its own giant, reshaping it, bringing it into the new, nearly modern world. A world that Christopher Columbus was busy making quite a lot bigger.

In Italy, Leonardo da Vinci was exercising his phenomenal intellect, fusing mathematics, art, anatomy and science to conjure up technically flawless, artistically immaculate blueprints of hitherto unimaginable contraptions, including a flying machine, a helicopter and an armoured vehicle.[36] In the same city, in Florence, his younger contemporary, Michelangelo, was demonstrating an artistic creativity and versatility that arguably has never been surpassed. In the same city Pico della Mirandola fused all the great philosophies of antiquity into one single, quasi-heretical theological system. To the north-east, in Poland, Nicolaus Copernicus was receiving his education. His astronomical proofs that the world did not stand at the centre of the universe would lay to rest the ancient, Greek understanding of nature and launch what became known as the scientific revolution.

It was matters of the intellect that would most challenge the Church. The long-established traditions of scholasticism; a method of religious enquiry beloved of the monks, with its roots in Aristotle and Augustine, had become distorted by theological nit-picking and specious casuistry. Fourteenth-century Italy saw the emergence of a new approach to thought and education: an intellectual torrent, unleashed principally by Francesco Petrarch's innovations in the study of classical literature, a new way of thinking rapidly spread throughout Europe. Known as Humanism, it laid the intellectual groundwork for the period we now call the Renaissance. Humanism extolled the virtues of mortal endeavour, attaching particular importance to the study of the classics. Humanist thinkers investigated language, history and culture, finding new ways of understanding people and society. In Jonathan Arnold's words, humanism was a movement to achieve 'eloquent expression of wisdom'.[37] Translation figured prominently in its armoury.

Even though Renaissance writers like Boccaccio, Machiavelli and Erasmus satirized and ridiculed the monks, the Church itself was not inimical to humanism as a discipline. Indeed some of the popes were among its most enthusiastic supporters. Nicholas V, who became pope in 1447, scoured Europe for rare copies of the great classics, employing teams of scholars to translate and transcribe them. A generation later Pope Sixtus IV summed up the humanist project when he wrote that 'nothing more excellent or more useful had been given by the Creator to mankind than classical studies which not only lead to the ornament and guidance of human life, but are applicable and useful to every particular situation'.[38]

It was Sixtus who set in motion the greatest achievement of Renaissance art; restoring the Sistine Chapel and engaging the first team of painters to create its frescoes. Michelangelo placed the gem in the project's crown when he began work on the chapel's ceiling in 1508.

But despite papal adulation of humanist ideals, the movement's emphasis on classical study would shortly contribute to the greatest schism the Church had encountered in its fifteen-hundred-year history. Humanism's affection for the language and culture of the ancient world brought fresh eyes to the study of the Bible. This in turn led to new ways of contemplating Scripture and, indirectly, to the Protestant Reformation.

Of all who contributed to the spread of the translated Bible, one figure more than any other deserves the greatest share of credit. Yet Desiderius Erasmus, the Dutch 'Prince of the Humanists', was far more than just a translator. The illegitimate son of a priest and a doctor's daughter, Erasmus was orphaned at an early age and spent most of his life travelling as an itinerant, albeit highly respected, scholar. His profound intellect and international reputation made it relatively easy for him to find patrons to support his studies and fund his travels. But his intellect demanded he tread his own path. He was an ordained priest but did not sit easily within the Catholic Church; a man with humanist leanings, but not infected with a reformer's zeal. Intellectually, Erasmus sat somewhere between Catholicism and Protestantism. He was his own man.

Erasmus believed that the Bible was the most profound of all texts and that the way to fully understand it was by making use of the tools and techniques first used by classical authors. Their exploitation and manipulation of language was the key to human understanding. The classical languages, Latin and Greek, were the tongues which underpinned all of Christian Europe's culture. To attain clarity of thought and expression one required a thorough understanding of the literature, culture and linguistic techniques of the classical, Greek and Roman world.[39]

Erasmus published his own edition of the Latin New Testament. Believing that the Vulgate had become corrupted by scribal error, he scoured as many reliable Greek manuscripts as he could find, reconstructed what he believed to be the authentic original text, and published it alongside both the Vulgate and his own Latin translation, complete with notes. His Greek reconstruction came in for criticism, largely because the manuscripts he used were nowhere near as reliable as he had imagined, but that wasn't really the point. Erasmus enabled readers of the Bible not only to access a revised and improved Latin text, but to compare it with the Greek and the Vulgate. Erasmus's version made it possible for those who so wished to draw their own conclusions about the Bible's meaning and interpretation.

But to fully engage with the Bible demanded more than a knowledge of Latin and Greek or an understanding of the classical world. A true appreciation of Scripture demanded familiarity with the tongue in which the earliest books of the Bible had been composed. And so it was that, centuries after Jerome and Origen, Hebrew began to re-emerge as an object of study. As is the way with these things, the charge was led at first by just a handful of enthusiasts, but the popularity of Hebrew study rapidly gathered pace. Eventually, Hebrew became an accepted part of the curriculum in universities across Europe.

Among the first Christian Hebraists, as these new enthusiasts were called, was a young Italian count, Giovanni Pico della Mirandola. Pico lived a short, but action-packed life. An Italian count, he was one of Italy's wealthiest men. He lived in Florence, where he kept up a correspondence and friendship with the ruler of Florence, Lorenzo de' Medici. His *Oration on the Dignity of Man* is considered one of the most important philosophical texts of the Renaissance.[40]

Pico developed a profound interest in Kabbalah, the Jewish mystical system which at the time was gaining currency in Italy.[41] He became convinced that beneath all the world's different esoteric and philosophical systems lay a common, unified undercurrent of knowledge, the core wisdom of humanity. Drawing together threads from these different systems, Pico composed his *Conclusiones*, a treatise containing 900 assertions that he claimed would harmonize all known religious, mystical and theological schools into one single doctrine. He intended to present his work to the Pope and the College of Cardinals, who, he imagined, would gather round to debate his ideas. But the Pope was not as compliant as Pico had hoped. He investigated the work and demanded that Pico retract thirteen of his assertions. Pico assented but concomitantly made things worse for himself by publishing an apology defending the retracted statements. The Pope responded by declaring the entire work heretical and ordered Pico's arrest.

Pico fled to France, where he was thrown into jail. It fell to Lorenzo de' Medici to negotiate his release. Pico's credit must have been running high in the Florentine court; it was only a year since he had caused a scandal in the city by running off with Margherita de' Medici, the wife of Lorenzo's cousin.

Pico laid the foundations of Christian Kabbalah by commissioning Latin translations of Hebrew Kabbalistic documents. He allied himself to the tyrannical preacher Savonarola who, it is reported, preached a sermon in 1494 of such apocalyptic proportions that it made Pico's hair stand on edge and Michelangelo flee the city in panic.[42] Encouraged by Savonarola to renounce all his earthly possessions, Pico gave away the entire fortune he had inherited, partly to his nephew but mostly to the Church.[43] Pico died, possibly poisoned, on the day that the republic of Florence finally fell to the armies of the French king, Charles VIII. Savonarola preached at his funeral. Pico was only thirty years old.

Pico learned Hebrew and Aramaic under the tutelage of Elijah del Medigo, a Jewish scholar who taught Kabbalah and the Aristotelian philosophy of Averroes to wealthy students in Padua and Venice. He also spent time with another Jew, Flavius Mithridates, with whom he studied Hebrew and who translated Kabbalistic tracts for him into Latin. But his indirect contribution to the history of Bible translations came not through his Jewish connections but through his influence on Johann Reuchlin, a judge in the Supreme Court of the German city of Speyer.

Reuchlin, rather unfairly, is best known for his lengthy dispute with Johannes Pfefferkorn. Pfefferkorn, a convert from Judaism, had instigated a campaign to have all Jewish books destroyed. A commission of enquiry was set up to investigate Pfefferkorn's proposal, to which Reuchlin was appointed. When the enquiry reported it transpired that all the commissioners had agreed that the Jewish Talmud and other works should be banned. The only commissioner who disagreed was Reuchlin, who insisted that, although they were products of a false religion, the Jewish books contained valuable legal information and theological arguments that deserved to be preserved. The proposed ban was also wrong, he argued, from a humanitarian point of view. The Jews had as much right to their books as anyone else.

Pfefferkorn took exception to Reuchlin's stance and a virulent war of words broke out between the two men. Pfefferkorn had Reuchlin arraigned on a charge of supporting the Jews. The case bounced from one appeal to another around the inquisitorial and papal courts until finally Reuchlin lost and was left bankrupted.[44] The Pfefferkorn affair had taken over his life. But Reuchlin's stature far surpassed the grubby accusations he was forced to defend.

Reuchlin met Pico in 1490 when he travelled on a diplomatic mission to Florence.[45] Reuchlin had already begun to learn Hebrew but Pico's infectious enthusiasm both for the language and for Kabbalah inspired him. On his return to Germany he engaged a Jewish tutor to help him improve his Hebrew. He later returned to Italy to study under the great Jewish biblical commentator, Ovadiah Sforno.

Reuchlin's significance to the history of the translated Bible is in the foundations that he laid for future translations from Hebrew. He didn't translate the Bible himself, other than the seven penitential psalms.[46] But he made Bible translations from Hebrew possible, both by promoting it as a scholarly language, and by providing the tools necessary to learn it. Conscious that there was a paucity of study aids for those who wanted to delve into the language, he published a Hebrew grammar, a lexicon and a Hebrew-Latin dictionary. His enthusiasm for the language was such that, even in the middle of his dispute with Pfefferkorn, he proposed that every university in Germany should engage two professors dedicated to promoting the study of Hebrew.[47]

Reuchlin's most important work was *De Arte Cabalistica*; a fictional account of a meeting between a Muslim, a Pythagorean and a Jewish Kabbalist. They converse successively on Messianism, numerology and the practical value of Kabbalah to Christianity. Of course the work was an anathema to Pfefferkorn and the Dominicans but was roundly approved by Humanists across Europe. One man in particular appreciated the value of Reuchlin's promotion of Hebrew, and the reasons for it. Commenting on 'the innocent and learned' Reuchlin's struggle against Pfefferkorn, Martin Luther wrote, 'You know that I greatly esteem and like the man, and perhaps my judgment will therefore be suspected, but my opinion is that in all his writings there is absolutely nothing dangerous.'[48] Luther's appreciation of Reuchlin, the Hebrew skills that Reuchlin made accessible, and his own study of the language would prove immensely significant for the future of the translated Bible.

Martin Luther's German Translation

Humanism itself was no threat to the Church, although the attitudes of some humanist thinkers towards theology and Scripture most certainly were. For the first time there was an interest in the sources and original language of Scripture, the genesis and veracity of belief. Some were even challenging accepted dogmas and time-honoured certainties.[49] And while this activity could have comfortably remained within academic and scholarly circles, it was thrust into the world of action by a ramping up of popular, anti-clerical sentiment, resentment at the power and wealth of the Church, which Wycliffe and his supporters had identified two centuries earlier. To cap it all, the new technology of printing was making it so much easier to disseminate ideas and influence thinking.

One week after Christopher Columbus set sail for America, Rodrigo Borgia bribed his way to the papal throne in Rome, where he took the name Alexander VI. Good looking, charming, witty and manipulative, Rodrigo is considered to have been the most corrupt Pope in history, keeping a string of mistresses and bestowing wealth, favours and titles on his illegitimate children. He granted Pico della Mirandola a pardon from the charges of heresy hanging over him and provoked a dispute with the pious but tyrannical friar Savonarola,[50] who was imposing his own uncompromising brand of religious asceticism upon the city of Florence. Savonarola's days were numbered – he would shortly be defrocked, hanged and his body cast to the flames. The philandering Pope was just the most important of his many enemies. But the preacher's call for a renewal of Christianity, and his success in turning the faithful of Florence against the religious establishment in Rome, was a portent; a sign of things to come.

Venality was hardly less rife in the monasteries and abbeys, where trade in the sale of indulgences for the forgiveness of sin was brisk. Indulgences, which for a fee would ease the conscience of the wayward, had been introduced during the Crusades. By the beginning of the sixteenth century they had become an indispensable way of raising money, both for those who sold them and for the Church at large. In 1507 their proceeds were earmarked to finance the building of the new St Peter's Church in Rome. Six years later they funded a dodgy deal between Pope Leo X and the twenty-four-year-old Prince Albert of Brandenburg, whereby the young Prince could add a third archbishopric to his string of titles.[51]

Just as ethically dubious as indulgences were dispensations. A priest under a vow of celibacy could, upon the payment of a sufficiently large sum of money, obtain a dispensation to take himself a mistress; or, for a further sum, to divest himself of one paramour and settle down with another. Dispensations could also be purchased for a son born from such a union to enter holy orders.

The papal establishment badly underestimated the scope and severity of the dissent that was taking hold. Few in Germany would have disagreed when Martin Luther declared: 'Roman avarice is the greatest of robbers that ever walked the earth. All goes into the Roman sack, which has no bottom, and all in the name of God.'[52]

Luther has gone down in the popular imagination as the man who nailed his ninety-five theses, protesting against the sale of indulgences, to the door of All Saints Church in Wittenberg. Behind the drama lay a disagreement that extended across the whole of the Christian belief spectrum; Luther quarrelled both theologically and politically with Rome. At the heart of his struggle was the interpretation of the Bible. One of Luther's most important and enduring acts was to translate the scriptures into German.

The long-held view of the Catholic Church was that the Bible could only be understood through interpretation. Only the Pope, who had been divinely ordained as the sole, unerring interpreter, could explain Scripture's meaning correctly. Luther strongly disagreed. He argued that there would be no point to having a Bible if it could only be understood through the medium of the Popes. 'Why not burn it all and content ourselves with these unlearned lords at Rome, who have the Holy Ghost within them…?'[53] he asked. On the contrary, argued Luther, human beings, even popes, cardinals and councils, can err. The only authority which could be relied upon was the unmediated word of God. And this was to be found in one place alone: in the Bible. This principle, of inexorable faith in the word of the Bible, became known as *sola scriptura,* 'only by scripture'. It was a key foundation of the Reformation.

Sola scriptura implies that the Bible needs to be taught based on an understanding of its original languages, whether Hebrew, Aramaic or Greek. Relying on a translation requires a trust in the translator's skill and choice of words; as such, translations cannot be considered to be *sola scriptura.* Luther appreciated the importance to *sola scriptura* of understanding the Hebrew language. But there was an implicit danger in promoting Hebrew education. The Jews had been analysing and interpreting the Old Testament for centuries, based on a thorough comprehension of Hebrew grammar. If Luther encouraged people to do what the Jews did, there was a very real risk that they would end up believing what the Jews believed. He couldn't have that; it would be worse in his eyes even than assenting to Catholic doctrine. Luther needed to find a different methodology that would help people to understand the sense of the Hebrew text.

Luther created an artificial distinction between grammatical and spiritual Hebrew. Grammatical Hebrew was what the Jews and their rabbis made use of; but in relying on it they missed the spiritual connotations of the language. *Sola scriptura* notwithstanding, in Luther's eyes Hebrew could only be a tool for understanding the original sense of the Bible if one transcended the simple grammatical meaning of the language and understood the spiritual context.

The rabbis had failed to do this, as Luther explained, in as abusive a manner as he could. He declared 'that is a great benefit that we have received the language from them but we must be aware of the dung of the rabbis, who have made of Holy Scripture a sort of privy into which they have deposited their foulness and their exceeding foolish opinions'.[54]

Four years after he circulated his ninety-five theses Luther was put on trial for heresy at the Diet of Worms, Emperor Charles V's court. It was clear from the outset that he would not be acquitted unless he recanted, which he was not prepared to do. Rather than wait for the verdict to be pronounced, he took flight. As he fled through the forest he was ambushed; kidnapped by his friends as part of an elaborate plot to stage his disappearance. By the time the court delivered its edict proclaiming him a heretic, he was long gone. He went into hiding under a false identity in Wartburg Castle. It was there that he began to undertake his translation of the Bible into German.

Luther's wasn't the first German Bible; sections of the Book of Psalms had been translated as early as the eighth century, and by 1518 eighteen German translations had been published.[55] Luther even made use of some, particularly an Anabaptist translation of the books of the Prophets which had appeared in 1527.[56] But Luther's Bible was different; not only because it became far more popular than any other, but because it was the first translation to have been made with an ideological agenda.

Luther established a *collegium biblicum*, or biblical college, with his colleagues Matthew Aurogallus and Philip Melanchthon (an enthusiast for Greek who, born as Philip Schwarzerd, had even translated his own name). They began with the New Testament, using the new critical Greek text that the Dutch scholar Desiderius Erasmus had compiled. They completed the entire work within eleven weeks; it went on sale on 25 September 1522.[57]

Luther harnessed his translation of the Bible to reinforce his theological outlook. He changed the order of the books in the New Testament, broadly following the sequence which Erasmus had established but relegating to the end those which he believed were not written by apostles and did not follow the views of Paul.[58] Crucially, he added just one word[59] to lay down a direct challenge to the doctrines of Rome. The Catholic Church held the view professed in the Epistle of James that salvation could be achieved equally through faith or through correct deeds. Luther maintained that it could be attained through faith *alone*. This single, one-word addition went to the heart of his theological dispute with Rome.

The additional word also emphasized the distinction between Protestantism and the faith of the Jews. The Jews had always stressed the indispensability of actions as a testimony to faith. Luther would have none of it. He was insistent that faith alone was all that was needed. Deeds, whether they were the observance of the Old Testament's laws or the purchase of indulgences, could never in his view be a route to salvation. As for the text in James which formed the basis of the Catholic position, Luther scathingly dismissed the book as an 'epistle of straw'.[60]

Although the New Testament only took a few weeks to translate, the Old Testament proved not to be so easy. It took Luther another ten years until his translation of it was complete. In part this was due to ill health. But the delay was also the result of Luther's need to reconcile the translation he was producing to his negative attitude towards the Jews and their interpretation of the Bible. The Old Testament, he believed, was a Christian text which anticipated the Trinity. The Jews however, whom he vigorously denounced with 'a scatological rhetoric mirroring the worst of medieval anti-Semitism',[61] had, in his view, refused to believe in the fulfilment of its promise.[62] Translating the Jewish Bible to accord with his reforming outlook was a complex task.

Luther's Old Testament was condemned by the Catholic Church for its structure as well as its theology. The principle of *sola scriptura*, of remaining faithful to the original words of the Bible, demanded that he include in his Old Testament only those books which had appeared in the Hebrew canon. For centuries there had been a debate about the validity of a collection of writings that had been included in the Greek Septuagint, but which were absent from the Hebrew text. Known as the Apocrypha, from a Greek root meaning 'concealed', and including works like books 1 and 2 of the Maccabees, Ecclesiasticus, Judith and Tobit, the biblical status of these texts had divided opinion among the early Church Fathers. Jerome had argued that they should not be included in the Old Testament, but they did find their way into a later recension of the Vulgate, and had generally been considered as a full and authentic part of the Bible ever since. Luther however, following *sola scriptura*, extracted them from the Old Testament, inserting them instead into a separate section. The consequence was that, in Rome's eyes, Luther had not just translated the Bible illegitimately and interpreted it wrongly, he had actually constructed a deficient Old Testament. In 1546 the Council of Trent, established in the wake of the Reformation to support and clarify Catholic doctrine, affirmed that the Apocrypha was part of the Old Testament canon. That remained the Catholic position ever since. Protestants disagree. Today the Apocrypha, which is now more commonly known as the Deuterocanon, or 'second canon', is included in Catholic Bibles but omitted altogether from most modern Protestant versions.

Predictably, the publication of Luther's translation created a backlash. However this time it was not the vernacular Bible that caused the most offence, but rather the translator himself. The Duke of Saxony, a long-standing opponent of Luther, ordered all copies of the translation in his lands to be confiscated and destroyed. His order backfired, and by drawing public attention to the translation's existence the Duke created additional demand for the work. Luther's sales increased. The Duke then turned to Jerome Emser, a loyal theologian, instructing him to produce a critique of Luther's Bible and to issue a competing translation. Emser did as he was bid, publishing both a lengthy polemic against Luther's work and his own translation. But his translation was based so closely on Luther's that the two works could scarcely be told apart. Emser even used the same illustrations! Even though thirty-eight editions of Emser's translation were eventually published it never came anywhere near attaining the same stature as Luther's work.[63]

Luther was anxious that his Bible be seen as a literary work grounded in exemplary use of the German language. He struggled at times to find the best form of words; one reason why the translation of the Old Testament took so long was that he and his team spent four days agonizing over the best way to render just three lines from the notoriously difficult book of Job. Excellence of language was more important to him than literal meaning; he was not afraid to deviate from the direct translation of a phrase in order to convey the sense better in German. Perhaps the best known example is his translation of the Vulgate's 'fat mountain' in Psalm 68.16. Not wanting to conjure up images of a mountain smeared with lard, he decided upon 'a fruitful mountain'.[64] The sense is the same but the Vulgate had already departed from the obscure Hebrew word which the Jewish grammarians, with whom Luther wanted no affinity, associate with the mountain's shape, rather than its fertility. Luther had merely ameliorated the Vulgate's terminology, instead of addressing the lexical issue.[65]

But even if the meaning of some words in his Bible deviated from the principles of *sola scriptura*, Luther's insistence on literary excellence was transformative. By producing a readable, literary, vernacular Bible, he made a substantial contribution to the structure and standardization of the German language. Wholly aside from its theological position, Luther's Bible remains a classic work of German literature today.

By the time of Luther's death in 1546 half a million of his Bibles had been sold. A consortium of businessmen grew rich on the sales. They didn't share the profits with Luther.

William Tyndale, an Englishman, was a younger contemporary of Luther. He too went down in history as a translator of the Bible. But his story, and his fate, were far more tragic than Luther's. Luther was a shrewd operator; the translation of the Bible was just one of many achievements that helped him create a vigorous and successful alternative to the hegemony of Rome. Tyndale, who translated the Bible into English, was far less confrontational and he paid for it with his life. The murderous age of Bible translations was heating up.

6

The Murder of Tyndale

No Place in All England

If credit can be given to any individual for the majestic language that suffuses
the English Bible, at least until its more recent revisions, that person has to be
William Tyndale. Some of the phrases he coined are used so frequently they've
even become clichés – 'fall flat on his face', 'go the extra mile', 'the powers
that be' and many more. Tyndale did for English what Luther had done for
German; his precision and artistry in translation standardized the vernacular.
David Daniell rightly says that 'he made a language for England';[1] so much of
later literature depends upon him.

Tyndale was born in 1494 to a relatively prosperous Gloucestershire family.
Educated at Magdalen College in Oxford, and then later in Cambridge, he
studied the works of Erasmus and of Luther. They were to define his life.

Tyndale was painfully aware that England was the only European country
not to possess a printed translation of the New Testament. Luther's German
translation was the immediate catalyst for him, but he almost certainly knew
that an Italian translation had been made as early as 1471 with Czech, Dutch and
Catalan versions following in quick succession and a Danish recension in 1524.

Tyndale was deeply conscious of the disadvantage that England was
under. He felt that his own early religious education had suffered due to
unlearned priests, and if an intelligent, educated man such as he had been left
in partial ignorance, what chance that less talented people could gain a true
understanding of Scripture?

Manuscript copies of Wycliffe's translation, although illegal, were still in circulation. The Lollards had made sure of that. As was an English paraphrase of the Gospels, made by William Caxton, the first English printer. With the Church's blessing and in the tradition of the *Diatessaron*, Caxton had produced an abridged version of Jesus's life. But it was all a far cry from an accessible, readable English Bible which educated lay people could read, and the illiterate have read to them.

Tyndale purposed to put the matter right. Following in the footsteps of Erasmus, he resolved to print an immaculately composed, English translation directly from the Greek. It would, he believed, place the Bible into the hands of the laity, circumvent the censorious influence of the clerics and revitalize the religious spirit of the nation.

Of course he couldn't just sit down and write a translation; the age was not yet ready for such autarchy. It wasn't just a question of money; naturally he would need to find finance for the printing costs but important as this was, even more essential was ecclesiastical sanction. A project of this nature could not possibly proceed without permission of the religious authorities. Fortunately, or so he thought, the bishop of London, Cuthbert Tunstall, would warm to the project. The bishop was a friend and fan of Erasmus, and he'd even worked with him on the second edition of his Greek New Testament. Tunstall would be just the man to become Tyndale's patron, to find him backers and steer him through the complex waters of church politics and ecclesiastical regulation.

Tyndale turned up at Tunstall's London residence, armed with a translation of a speech of the Greek orator, Isocrates, as proof of his scholarship. But Tunstall wouldn't see him. He certainly wouldn't help. Tyndale had miscalculated; he'd been too naive. He'd failed to realize that, however learned and honourable Tunstall may have been, he was an Establishment man with a position to uphold. Tyndale had already acquired a reputation as a Lutheran and potential trouble maker. Tunstall may have quietly sympathized with his intellectual aspirations but there was no chance that he would compromise his own standing within the Church, let alone his positions as bishop of London and Lord Privy Seal, to assist a little-known radical, an avowed admirer of the troublesome German reformer Luther; particularly when Tyndale's project had the potential to cause as much damage in England as Luther's translation was beginning to cause in Europe. Lutheran books had already been burned in England, and Cardinal Wolsey was busy rooting out anyone suspected of importing or distributing 'heretical' literature. The Church was a powerful landowner, the largest in London, and the greatest employer. It also owned many prisons. The fact that Tunstall didn't have Tyndale arrested when he brought the idea for a printed Bible to him suggests that privately he may have sympathized. But with his career, reputation and even his life at stake, Tunstall was never likely to put his head above the parapet.

But Tyndale did not give up. He turned to Humphrey Monmouth, a free-thinking alderman of London (who would eventually be cast into the Tower for reading heretical books and associating with Lutherans). Humphrey Monmouth belonged to a group known as the Christian Brethren, an informal ring of merchants who imported Lutheran books from Europe and supported scholars and translators. The books they imported were distributed through Lollard networks.[2]

Monmouth, who had heard Tyndale preach on a couple of occasions, offered him lodging within his house. Tyndale stayed for six months, studying 'most part of the day and of the night...he would eat but sodden meat...nor drink but small beer'.[3]

But for all the time he spent in Monmouth's home, Tyndale's plans for a translation of the Bible were making no progress. He took a position as a preacher at St Dunstan's in Fleet Street, but this did not satisfy his ambition; the opportunity to compose his translation was all that he craved. He grew increasingly frustrated by those who were in a position to sanction and support his endeavours but were not prepared to do so.

Tyndale came to the conclusion that London was just not the right place for him to work. Years later, in his prologue to the book of Genesis, he allowed himself to express the frustration he had felt. In a masterpiece of scorn and mockery he sounded off against ignorant and unlearned priests, boastful praters, pompous prelates and the Lord Chancellor, Cardinal Wolsey, who reviled and berated him 'as if he had been a dog'. He explains in the Prologue that, as a result of his experiences, he came to the realization 'not only that there was no room in my Lord of London's palace to translate the New Testament but also that there was no place to do it in all England, as experience doth now openly declare'.[4]

Tyndale's next move was to make contact with a group of German merchants and traders living in an area close to London Bridge, known as the Steelyard. The merchants were well connected with printers and bankers in Germany, and most importantly, were sympathetic to the Lutheran cause. Many of the so-called heretical books distributed in England had been imported by these men. With their help, and a little money donated to him by Humphrey Monmouth, Tyndale set off in April 1524 for Germany. He was next heard of in 1525 in Cologne.

Danger in Germany

If William Tyndale thought that relocating to Germany would solve his problems, he was sorely mistaken.

Not much is known about the first few months of Tyndale's sojourn in Germany. He is thought to have spent time in Hamburg and Wittenberg before travelling to Cologne. Somewhere along the way he was joined by William Roye, an apostate Franciscan friar who had also fled England after being accused of displaying heretical tendencies. Whether or not Roye had travelled to Germany with the intention of assisting Tyndale is not clear, but by 1525 the two men were working together in Peter Quentell's Cologne print shop, turning out their first copies of the New Testament.

Tyndale and Roye did not start as good friends and their relationship deteriorated the longer they worked together. In one of his tracts, *The Parable of the Wicked Mammon*, Tyndale describes Roye as 'somewhat crafty…whose tongue is able not only to make fools stark mad but also to deceive the wisest'. He depicts Roye as something of a parasite, attaching himself to new acquaintances only for as long as he needed their support and then, when things turned difficult, finding someone else to sponge off. Even though, as Tyndale acknowledges, Roye had been helpful to him in preparing the texts for printing, when their work came to an end he 'bade him farewell for our two lives and, as men say, for a day longer'. Tyndale also tells us that after the two men separated, Roye found himself new friends, and, when he had stored up enough money, headed for Strasbourg 'where he professeth wonderful faculties and maketh boast of no small things'.[5]

Roye apart, the city of Cologne should have been an ideal location for Tyndale. It was blessed with a thriving printing industry; Peter Quentell had printed a Dutch Bible there in 1478. But it wasn't a safe place for Tyndale to realize his printing ambitions. The city was under the authority of the Catholic archbishop, Hermann von Wied. In due course Wied would fall out with the papacy and drift towards Lutheranism, but at the time that Tyndale was in the city he was still fiercely opposed to the Reformers. He had even agitated at the Diet of Worms for Luther to be declared an outlaw. Cologne may have been a centre of printing but Tyndale was nervous, and cautious. He'd made too many enemies on the other side of the Channel; English spies were already hunting for him. The last thing he wanted was for von Wied to find out what he was up to.

Tyndale's caution was well founded. Just as he and Roye were on the point of completing their printing of the book of Matthew in Peter Quentell's print shop, they received news that the authorities were on to them. They'd been betrayed by Johann Cochlaeus, a local scholar and fierce opponent of Luther, who was having his own works printed in the same press. One drunken evening a printer let slip that the Bible was also being printed on the premises. Cochlaeus guessed immediately whose Bible it was. He swiftly reported the matter and spent the rest of his life dining out on the tale of how, when they were warned that their works were about to be seized, the two Englishmen snatched up the quarto sheets that had been printed and fled up the Rhine by boat to Worms.

Worms was a Lutheran city where, on the face of it, Tyndale should have been safe. But by now Tyndale was battle scarred and wary. He engaged a local printer, Peter Schoeffer, urging him to print as rapidly as he could. His overriding concern was to finish the New Testament and get as many copies as he could to England before anything else went wrong. He didn't bother to write a prologue or to add marginal notes. David Daniell suggests that the style of the epilogue and the list of errata suggests a man working under stress.[6]

Tyndale accomplished his objective. By the beginning of 1526 the New Testament was complete. The first copies arrived in England during March, probably smuggled across with the aid of the large expatriate English community in Antwerp. What began as a trickle turned into a deluge. Tyndale's Bible began arriving in its hundreds, concealed among consignments of other books from the continent. A network of distributors disbursed them across the country. None of the printed Bibles carried Tyndale's name, nor did they display the details of where they were printed. But nobody was in any doubt regarding who was behind them.

In the summer of that year Cardinal Wolsey convened a meeting of English bishops. They agreed that the recently arrived Bibles should be seized and burned, and that anyone found in possession of them should be dealt with severely. Archbishop Tunstall, upon whom Tyndale had placed such high hopes, preached a sermon in St Paul's in which he claimed to have identified two thousand errors in the new Bible. He summoned the booksellers in London, confiscated their stock and adjured them against having anything to do with the work of Tyndale and Roye. Having rounded up as many copies as he could of Tyndale's Bible, Tunstall had them publicly burned, on 28 October 1526.

Tyndale was horrified when he discovered that Bishop Tunstall had described his New Testament as *doctrinam perigranam*: strange learning.[7] He was even more horrified to discover that Tunstall had ordered his Bible to be publicly burned. This was the friend and colleague of Erasmus, the man whom Tyndale had once considered a potential ally. One can only guess at the extent of his disillusionment.

Still, if the story is to be believed, Tyndale did have one success at Tunstall's expense. A 1548 chronicle by Edward Hall tells of a visit to Antwerp by Tunstall.[8] While he was there, the bishop told a local merchant that he was keen to burn as many of Tyndale's Bibles as he could. The merchant told him that he could obtain a large quantity. A price was agreed. The merchant purchased the Bibles from Tyndale and handed them over to Tunstall to be burned. Tunstall was delighted. So was Tyndale. He used the proceeds to finance his next round of printing.

Neither Tunstall's efforts nor the wrath of the Church could stem the flow of Tyndale's printed Bibles into England. Even pirated copies began to appear, printed in Antwerp by Christopher von Endhoven. They were not of the same high quality as Tyndale's own imprint, but the market easily absorbed them. Little wonder that Wolsey, as anxious as ever to destroy Tyndale's work and covetous for greater recognition from Rome, was incensed.

Still, Wolsey had all the power of the state behind him. Nobody with a connection to Tyndale was safe. Thomas Bilney, a meek, scholarly lawyer, and by no means a rabid radical, was arrested and imprisoned in the Tower of London for a year. Unsure of his crime he recanted and repeated his genuine rejection of Luther. He was eventually released, a broken man and probably suicidal; his friends made sure he was never left alone. Other supporters and followers of Tyndale, including Humphrey Monmouth who had helped him when he first came to London, and the monk Richard Bayfield, were rounded up. Subjected to the full range of medieval torture they were grateful for those days in which they were only whipped, gagged and stocked. A group of young scholars in Oxford, members of Wolsey's own Cardinal College, were thrown into a dungeon where salt fish were stored. The stench killed them. All for the sake of a printed Bible, and a church hierarchy that had completely lost its sense of perspective.

A year later Thomas Hitton, a priest who had met Tyndale in Europe, was seized in Kent. His crime was said to be the preaching of heresy. He confessed to smuggling two printed Tyndale New Testaments into the country. They burned him alive, the first supporter of Tyndale to suffer such a fate. But only the first. A year later, the new bishop of London, John Stokesley, re-arrested Thomas Bilney and Richard Bayfield. They too were consumed alive in the flames. The murderous age of Bible translations had reached its peak.

Meanwhile, in Europe, the hunt for Tyndale was on. His pursuers didn't yet know it but he was hiding out with Miles Coverdale, a forty-two-year old priest from Yorkshire who had fled the country after preaching against the worship of images. There are conflicting reports about whether they were together in Hamburg or at the English House in Antwerp, which was Tyndale's base from 1528,[9] but what is certain is that they were collaborating on a further translation of the Bible. With Coverdale's help Tyndale was now printing English copies of the Pentateuch, which he was, quite unexpectedly, translating directly from the Hebrew.

Tyndale seems to have been the sort of man who always needs to push himself further. Once one project was over he needed another. So, when the New Testament translation was finished his natural next step was to make a start on translating the Old. Little matter that it required a knowledge of Hebrew; what he didn't know he could soon learn. That is exactly what he did. And even though he was master of eight different languages, Tyndale's grasp of biblical Hebrew is mind boggling.

Tyndale's achievements are so many that his astonishing competency in Hebrew is invariably overlooked. But when we consider that Hebrew bears no direct relation to any other European tongue, that its character set and method of transcription are wholly different, and that Tyndale came from a country where scholarship in the language was virtually unknown, the scope of his achievement comes into focus. Add to that the likelihood that he had no Hebrew teachers (although, as a result of Reuchlin's advocacy of Hebrew study, there were now primers, dictionaries and grammars to assist him) and we can see that his accurate, fluent, readable and stylistic translation of the difficult text of the Pentateuch is an accomplishment rarely equalled in the history of literary scholarship.

By 1530 Tyndale's new Pentateuch was making its way to England. Despite the controversies still raging around his New Testament he now was sufficiently confident to introduce the prologue to Genesis with the words 'W.T. to the reader'.

Tyndale's English Pentateuch eclipsed John Wycliffe's earlier translation. Not just because it was printed and portable. Nor because the English language had evolved in the century and a half since Wycliffe wrote. Tyndale did more than simply translate the Bible. He did so with a stylistic elegance that laid the foundations for English literature as we still know it today. If any moment can be pinpointed as that in which, following centuries of gestation, English finally became one the world's great languages, it must be the arrival of Tyndale's New Testament in 1526.

The Tyndale translation is as much a literary work as a religious text. Its prose exudes confidence, yet is imbued with simplicity. The stilted sentence construction of Wycliffe's fourteenth-century, Latin-based translation was brought to life in a free-flowing composition, which reflected the original Greek and Hebrew more closely. Wycliffe's '*Light be made and light was made*' became Tyndale's '*Let there be light and there was light.*'[10] '*Therefore yield ye to the Emperor those things that be the Emperor's*' was transmuted to '*Give therefore to Caesar that which is Caesar's.*'[11] Tyndale's phrases pepper the English language. 'Under the sun', 'my brother's keeper', 'apple of his eye', 'land of the living' are all his, and many more besides. He even made up new words; *scapegoat, long-suffering* and *busybody* are among the best known.[12] Even the Jewish festival of Passover owes its English name to Tyndale. Why? Because when he smote the Egyptian first-born the Angel of Death 'passed over' the houses of the Israelites.[13]

Betrayal

Things were changing in England. The row between Henry VIII and Rome over the question of his intended divorce was hotting up. Wolsey was dead, but not before he had been stripped of political office by a king impatient with his failure to obtain an annulment of his marriage to Catherine of Aragon. Thomas Cromwell was Henry VIII's right-hand man and, as anyone who has read Hilary Mantel's magnificent historical novels knows, his skill at political manipulation puts anything practised in the twenty-first century to shame. In an attempt to bring the dispute with Rome to a resolution, Cromwell drew Henry's attention to Tyndale's *The Obedience of a Christian Man and How Christian Rulers Ought to Govern*. Written in 1530, Tyndale's intention was to show how the practices of the Roman Church were driving people away from their faith. The faith itself was not to blame; in Tyndale's eyes it was the papacy which was culpable: it had usurped its authority and taken on powers which were reserved for lay people and kings. This was exactly the sort of thing that Henry wanted to hear; his quarrel was with the authority of the Pope, rather than with Catholic articles of faith. Cromwell suggested that Tyndale be rehabilitated, and Henry told him to see to the matter.

Cromwell contacted Stephen Vaughan, a London-based merchant whom he trusted to run sensitive errands. He asked Vaughan to go to the Continent, find Tyndale and persuade him to come home. But finding Tyndale, let alone convincing him, was not so easy.

Vaughan speculatively addressed letters to Tyndale in Frankfurt, Hamburg and Marburg. Unsurprisingly, none of them reached him. Eventually he received information that Tyndale was most probably in Antwerp, but as soon as he started rooting around there he came up against a wall of silence. None of Tyndale's friends were prepared to divulge the translator's presence to an envoy of the king's fixer, not after all the trouble Tyndale had already been through. Vaughan, undaunted, left messages at the English House in Antwerp, and generally made a nuisance of himself. Eventually Tyndale, worn down by people telling him that an English agent was looking for him, decided to meet the man. But he'd been hunted for so long that caution was almost instinctive. Not knowing anything about the mission on which Cromwell had sent Vaughan, he feared that the English envoy would arrive with armed men, ready to arrest him. He decided the best course of action would be for Vaughan to be invited to a secret meeting, in an undisclosed location, without being told whom he would meet.

Vaughan was led to a field outside Antwerp. There he met a man who claimed he was authorized to negotiate on Tyndale's behalf. It wasn't until Vaughan had reassured him that his intentions were honourable that his interlocutor told him that he was in fact talking to none other than Tyndale himself. But no deal was done. Tyndale offered to come back to England only if the king agreed to authorize the printing of an English Bible. Vaughan had no authority to agree to that and when the matter was eventually reported to Henry, he turned the idea down flat, despite Cromwell trying to convince him otherwise. Vaughan returned home empty-handed, Henry flew into one of his rages and Tyndale continued his life in exile.

Tyndale's decision not to accede to Henry's advances was not the wisest of his life. The next envoy sent from London had instructions not to negotiate with Tyndale but to arrest him. And even though the envoy, Thomas Elyot, despite spending a fortune on bribes, couldn't find Tyndale, as far as the translator's future was concerned, the writing was on the wall. (That's not one of Tyndale's phrases; he didn't translate the Book of Daniel.)

Meanwhile, a fourth edition of Christopher von Endhoven's pirated version was being prepared. The printer had engaged an English priest, George Joye, to oversee the work. Joye, like so many others, had been accused of heresy and fled England. Although he was no outstanding intellect, Joye had pretensions to greater knowledge than he actually had. He knew hardly any Greek yet took it upon himself to 'correct' Tyndale's translation by comparing it with the Latin Vulgate, which was itself of course a translation from Greek. Even more controversially, he even tinkered with Tyndale's theology, removing over twenty references to resurrection. To make matters worse, he did not sign his name on the title page of the pirated copy, implying that all the amendments were Tyndale's. Tyndale, who had just completed a revision of his New Testament translation, making use of new linguistic insights garnered from his ongoing Hebrew studies, had never previously commented on the pirated version. He'd believed it was beneath his dignity to do so. But when he heard how Joye had both plagiarized and bowdlerized his work he was thunderous. He took advantage of the publication of his revised version to write a new prologue sharply criticizing Joye.

But when compared to what was to come next, Joye was merely an inconvenient distraction. In 1535 a young, spoilt patrician, Henry Phillips, found himself in financial trouble. He had stolen money that his father had entrusted to him, and gambled away his fortune. Unable to return home he fled to the Continent, turning up in Antwerp where he presented himself as an extremely prosperous man of the world. Brian Moynahan[14] suggests he had been bribed by friends of Thomas More, the former Lord Chancellor of England and lifelong opponent of Tyndale, who was now languishing in the Tower of London.

Phillips was dissolute and disreputable, yet charming. He insinuated his way into the social life of the English merchants in Antwerp, among whom Tyndale moved freely. Tyndale seems to have found Phillips entertaining for, despite uncertainty voiced by Thomas Pointz, Tyndale's host in the English House, the two became companions. Tyndale invited Phillips one evening to go out to dine with him. As the two were leaving the English House, Phillips gesticulated to two thugs whom he had instructed to lie in wait at the doorway. They were officers of the Procurator General. Tyndale was seized and imprisoned in Vilvoorde castle, eighteen miles from Antwerp. It was the end. Tyndale never left.

Tyndale's arrest sent shock waves through the English expatriate community. They were furious, not just because they believed he had been guaranteed safety in Antwerp, but also because the English House was searched, the Procurator General's men trampling over their presumed diplomatic privileges. Thomas Pointz led a campaign to have Tyndale released, writing letters, riding to Maastricht and Brussels to present petitions, and travelling to England to enlist the help of Thomas Cromwell. Cromwell was only too aware that the Procurator General had provided the Holy Roman Emperor with a prize catch and was fuming at his inability to deprive him of it. But in this matter at least Cromwell was impotent and Pointz's campaign came to an abrupt end when Phillips turned on him, accusing him of heresy by helping Tyndale. Pointz was arrested. He escaped after three months but lost his business, his wealth and even his family; his Flemish wife would not bring the children to join him in England. He died impoverished, having destroyed his life for his friend.

In August 1536 Tyndale was found guilty by the Procurator General's investigating commission of heresy. He was stripped of his priesthood in a humiliating ceremony and handed over to the secular authorities for execution.

On 6 October 1536 William Tyndale was tied up at the stake. As a former churchman, the executioner was instructed to strangle him before burning his body, to save him pain. The strangulation failed. He died in the flames. Medieval accounts of burnings tell us that an immolation victim could take up to three days to expire. His contemporary biographer John Foxe wrote that Tyndale's final words were 'Lord, open the King of England's eyes.'

Aftermath and Backlash

As it happens, the king's eyes were already opening. The first glimmer of light had been his agreement that Stephen Vaughan should meet Tyndale. His final awakening came when his mistress, Anne Boleyn, became pregnant, forcing his hand over the annulment of his marriage to Catherine of Aragon. In 1534 the Act of Supremacy declared the English Church an independent entity, with Henry at its head. In the same year the bishops of the Canterbury Convocation petitioned for an English Bible. Pressurized by his bishops, and badgered by Thomas Cromwell's not-so-gentle urging, the king assented. When Miles

Coverdale, the fugitive English priest who had collaborated with Tyndale in Hamburg, dedicated a translation of the Bible to the king, there was no objection.

Although Coverdale's Bible has gone down in history as the first, full English Bible, most of the credit for it goes to others. Coverdale's skills as a linguist were not particularly sophisticated. He relied on other translations, including the Vulgate and Luther. But the text he made the most use of was Tyndale's. Coverdale's Bible was really Tyndale's, with Coverdale making use of his other sources to fill in those parts of the Old Testament which Tyndale had not managed to complete.

In 1537, a year after Tyndale's death, a second printed Bible appeared in England. It purported to be the work of a 'Thomas Matthew', a pseudonym designed to conceal the true identity of the translator. Matthew's Bible, as it came to be known, had been compiled by John Rogers, a friend of Tyndale. He had come across some unpublished translations of the Old Testament among Tyndale's papers. Rogers made a few editorial changes to Tyndale's translations, often losing the poetic sense of the original,[15] but compensated by including more of Tyndale's notes and annotations than had previously been published. Two-thirds of Matthew's Bible was the work of Tyndale.[16]

The printed English Bible was finally granted complete legitimacy in 1539 when Henry VIII decreed that every parish should obtain a copy of the Bible, of the largest possible size, placed in a public location where people could see it. Cromwell engaged Miles Coverdale to produce a standardized text. He had it printed in Paris, where it was nearly destroyed by the French Inquisitor General. Coverdale transferred the printing to England and the Great Bible, known as such due to its large size, became the first authorized, mandated Scripture in England. Cromwell took advantage of the first edition of the Bible for a spot of self-publicity. The title page carries a woodcut by Hans Holbein, dominated by an image of Henry on his throne handing the Bible to Cromwell. But Cromwell did not keep his place in the Bible for long. By the time the fourth edition appeared just over a year later, the king's great manipulator had been arrested, tried and executed; brought down by the many enemies he had made. On the frontispiece of the Great Bible's second edition, the king sits alone in regal majesty. Tyndale did not live to see the day.

The Great Bible was sanctified through kingly approval but it didn't mark the end of the translated Bible's woes. The beliefs and loyalties of ordinary people are far more complex than the politics of state and religion. Even though the English Church was now independent of Rome, many of its bishops were still uncomfortable with the popularization of the Bible. In 1540, not long after Cromwell had been booted out of power, into the Tower of London and finally onto the scaffold, a backlash against the Great Bible began. No more copies were printed and in 1543 an Act was passed forbidding unlicensed people from publicly reading the Bible, and the 'lower' classes from reading it altogether.

Things got worse in 1546 when the king proclaimed that nobody was to possess a copy of Tyndale's Bible, nor of Coverdale's. The Great Bible remained in the churches but the bishop of London ordered all other versions to be burned at St Paul's.[17] And despite a brief restoration of the translated Bible's fortunes during Edward VI's short reign, with a flurry of new translation activity, the respite was brief. Catholic Queen Mary I came to the throne, the Protestant Reformation faltered and, for a short while, the translated Bible in England was done for.

But not quite. The champions of the translated Bible translation could not be brushed aside so easily. Bible translation went underground. The most assiduous scholars relocated abroad, out of Mary's reach. An English translation, the work of fiercely anti-royalist Calvinists, was produced in Geneva in 1560. Based on a 1540 translation by Robert Olivetan, a cousin of Calvin, it received its final version at the hands of a committee in 1588. French and Italian versions were produced in Geneva during the same period, the translators in each of the three tongues drawing simultaneously upon the scholarship and erudition which suffused that Calvinist city in the mid- to late sixteenth century.

Smaller, cheaper, well printed and published with comprehensive notes, maps, summaries and tables, the Geneva Bible was immediately popular. It was also controversial. It made no attempt to conceal its translators' antipathy to monarchic rule. The English aristocracy hated it, but their distaste for its political agenda did not dent its popularity. New editions were published every year for the next half-century.[18]

The success of the Geneva Bible threw up a new kind of challenge. In England, the only land in Europe where the monarch was supreme head of the Church, a fiercely anti-royalist Bible had won the hearts of the masses and cornered the market. It felt, to the monarchy and the English Church, like a mockery and a provocation.

It would take the English Establishment half a century until they came up with an effective, enduring alternative to the Geneva Bible. Meanwhile, in Catholic Europe, the advocates of Bible translation were beginning to sense the early flushes of success.

7

Confound Their Strife

The Catholic Vernacular

Tyndale's translation was bold, and Luther's a significant contribution to the success of the Reformation. But they were only the best known among the translations of the sixteenth century. A trickle of undercurrents gradually swelled into a frenzy of activity; all at once it seemed as if translations of the Bible, which had been supressed so rigorously and for so long, were being produced in every corner of Europe, and in every tongue.

Printing, education and the stirrings of religious reform were the main contributors to this change. The translated Bible had long been regarded by Rome as dangerous; it was susceptible to theologically incorrect interpretations and potentially led people to misapprehend their faith.[1] But when weighed against the polemics of the reformers, against the argument that orthodox doctrine wilfully misrepresented the Bible, then the carefully managed publication of select translations for the use of Catholic worshippers began to appear to the Church as a sensible policy.

Although printing allowed texts to be made available more quickly, in greater quantity and with much greater accuracy than manuscript versions, not everyone was endeared of it. Printing was expensive, its cost fell upon the translator; many would-be authors of translated versions could not afford to have their work printed. Even when printed there was a danger of plagiarism; as Tyndale had discovered, the printing presses of Europe were infested by unscrupulous operators churning out and distributing the works of others, in inferior quality and far more cheaply.

There could also be a stigma attached to printing. Not everybody wanted their works to reach the masses. Some authors intended their literature for a restricted or elite audience. Even as late as the seventeenth century in Venice, the early home of printing, the Jewish polemicist Leon Modena, fearful of a backlash, chose to restrict his fierce, controversial assault on the Kabbalah to a manuscript edition.[2]

But printing was the new technology, and it walked hand in hand with advances in literacy. In 1504, a canon in Padua justified his writing of a commentary of the Song of Songs in the local dialect on the grounds that printing had brought knowledge of the Bible to uneducated people.[3] The masses were ready to receive the Bible in their own language; the translation of Scripture could no longer be dismissed as a Protestant heresy.

Emser's 1527 Catholic response to Luther's German translation had been followed by translations in France, Holland, Bohemia and Poland. English Catholics too were about to get their own version. But it wouldn't be printed in England; Mary was dead and her Protestant half-sister, Elizabeth I, was on the throne.

The Catholic Queen Mary had reigned little more than five years, before 'flu carried her off at the age of forty-two. The crown was on Elizabeth's head and it was once again the turn of the Catholics to be persecuted. Many fled, the leading scholars seeking refuge at a seminary in Douay, northern France. There, for the first time, they began work on an English-language, Catholic Bible, translated from the Vulgate.

The first copies of the Douay Bible rolled off the presses in 1582. A magistrates' decree had recently expelled all English residents from Douay and the seminary had temporarily decamped to Rheims. This upheaval, and associated financial problems, had meant that despite the whole Bible being translated, the college could only afford to print the New Testament. It took nearly thirty years for the Old Testament to appear, by which time the college was back at Douay. Conceived and printed in the two centres of Douay and Rheims, the entire work is unsurprisingly known as the Rheims–Douay Bible.

The Rheims–Douay Bible did not flourish. Its language was heavy and technical, its margin notes and commentaries overlong, its tone unabashedly polemical. It made few friends among Protestants, whom it castigated as heretics or equated with Canaanite idolaters. The first recension of the Rheims–Douay Bible survived for little more than a century before being comprehensively revised.

Changing Perceptions

Despite the appearance of Catholic, vernacular Bibles the controversies over translation did not abate. Both Catholics and Protestants used translation as a device for articulating their beliefs; rather than creating common ground between the two denominations, the act of translation drove them further apart. It all came down to the choice of words. The Protestants distanced themselves from the highly structured Roman hierarchy by preferring, for example, to speak of 'congregation' rather than 'church', 'senior' instead of 'priest'. But words alone did not account for the extent of the antipathy between the sects. Nor did disagreements over the order of the biblical canon, nor even the question of whether ultimate authority lay in the Church or the Bible, an issue which had sharply divided More from Tyndale.[4] Instead the controversy, as always, lay in the exercise of power, and the Protestant Reformation's assault on the long-founded hegemony of the Roman establishment.

It was this struggle over power and authority which led even Catholic translations, or more accurately translations made by Catholics, to be examined for traces of Protestant sympathies. Antonio Brucioli's Italian translation was one such case. Published in 1530, Brucioli was not the first Italian to try his hand at translation; a rendition from the Vulgate had been published in 1471, in Germany, by Nicolo Malermi. But Brucioli was already a controversial figure, his reputation tarnished long before he took up the art of Bible translation.

A member of the same circle as the political theorist Machiavelli, Brucioli had been banished from Florence in 1522, in the wake of a failed plot against the future Pope, Giulio de' Medici. Brucioli spent five years in exile in Lyon where he wrote his *Dialogues*, a discourse on moral philosophy.[5] In 1527, following the Medicis' fall from power, he returned to Florence where he once again found himself in trouble, this time accused of promoting Lutheranism. On the run for a second time, he now headed for Venice.

Brucioli in Venice underwent a transition from political philosopher and religious activist to the slightly more sedate profession of Bible translator. Even so, he was no priest and probably not much of a scholar. He had a reasonable command of Greek, from which he translated the New Testament. But although he claimed to have translated the Old Testament directly from the Hebrew, his knowledge of that language is suspect. It looks as if he drew heavily on an earlier Italian translation from the Vulgate, though he did not give the translator, Santi Pagnini, any credit for this.[6]

Political agitation is one of those traits that people find it difficult to abandon fully. Despite his reinvention as Bible translator Brucioli discovered that he couldn't quite shake off his penchant for making his opinions known. He wrote seven volumes of a commentary to accompany his Bible, in which he allowed his Protestant sympathies to become all too evident. Once again, trouble loomed. The Inquisition summoned him, and sentenced him to the third exile of his life, this time in Ferrara. His troubles didn't even end there. In 1548 he was arrested again and put on trial for heresy. When, instead of recanting, he stuck to his principles, he was imprisoned. He died, an impoverished and broken man.

Over the coming years Brucioli's translation of the Bible began to attract attention. It became increasingly popular, his creation ending up as far more of a success than his own life had turned out to be. Instead of being regarded as a fundamentally Catholic work, albeit heretical, it became accepted as a genuine Reformation text. It was reprinted frequently and ended up as the Bible of choice for Italian Protestants for many years. The Catholic Church responded in their traditional manner. In 1559 they placed it on the first ever Index of Prohibited Books.

One of the spin-offs from the invention of printing had been the requirement for printers to obtain a licence, known as a privilege, to print their book. Initially this was for their own benefit, to give them copyright over their works and prevent plagiarism. But it didn't take long for the licensing system to develop into a programme of theological scrutiny; in 1508 the governing body of Venice appointed a censor to examine a book for possible heresy, before agreeing to grant a privilege for its printing.[7] The sixteenth century saw the Holy See ban or censor a burgeoning number of books and authors, in an attempt to keep belief within tried and tested boundaries as the Protestant Reformation took hold. Eventually, in an attempt to control and regulate the ever-increasing number of books that even the censors were unable to expurgate, Pope Paul IV introduced the *Index Librorum Prohibitorum*. Although earlier lists of locally banned books had been published, the Index of Prohibited Books was the first comprehensive catalogue of works to be prohibited throughout the world. First published in 1559 the Index was regularly updated, until it was finally abolished in 1966.

The French philosopher Michel de Montaigne, whose own works had been scrutinized by the Church's censors, sympathized with the Vatican's antipathy to translation. He too doubted the skills of the masses to understand a vernacular Bible properly. In his essay *On Prayers* he wrote:

> And I do further believe that the liberty every one has taken to disperse the sacred writ into so many idioms carries with it a great deal more of danger than utility. The Jews, Mohammedans, and almost all other peoples, have reverentially espoused the language wherein their mysteries were first conceived, and have expressly, and not without colour of reason, forbidden the alteration of them into any other. Are we assured that in Biscay and in Brittany there are enough competent judges of this affair to establish this translation into their own language?[8]

Montaigne's defence of the old, traditional opposition to Bible translations was indicative of yet another shift in the post-Reformation, intellectual climate. Although the Vatican was now reconciled to the publication of approved, translated Bibles, opposition to the principle of Bible translation had not gone away. As Montaigne illustrates, it had now become a matter of personal opinion rather than an institutional quarrel. Sometimes these personal opinions flared up into out-and-out conflict.

The Protestant Reformation, in all its various incarnations, had forced theologians of every conviction and persuasion to clarify, articulate and frequently defend their own views. For many orthodox and conservative thinkers, their opposition to the translated Bible had little to do with support for the authority of the Pope. They saw the language of the translated

Bible, or the opinions cited in accompanying commentaries, as a challenge to their own personal beliefs. They responded just as personally. Thus, Sebastien Châteillon found himself castigated, not for the erratic quality of his translation, which vacillated between literary amplification and turgid archaism,[9] but because he dared to be outspoken. He had nit-picked over discrepancies in biblical readings, such as the number of Jacob's descendants who went to Egypt, a figure given as seventy in Genesis and seventy-five in Acts.[10] Even more daringly, he had called the erotic Song of Songs 'lascivious and obscene'.[11] Châteillon's opponents didn't mince their words. They called him an 'instrument of Satan'.

An equally personal disagreement had broken out in France, half a century before Montaigne, between the philosopher Jacques Lefèvre d'Étaples and the conservative scholars of the Paris Theology Faculty. At its root lay a virulent, doctrinal dispute over the identity of Mary Magdalene.

Lefèvre had written a treatise in which he argued that Mary Magdalene, as portrayed in the New Testament, was actually a composite of three different women who had been amalgamated into one by Christian tradition.[12] The treatise had aroused the ire of the Paris Theology Faculty and led to a three-year-long controversy which drew in a cast of theologians and humanists from across Europe, including Desiderius Erasmus and John Fisher, the bishop of Rochester, who would eventually be executed by Henry VIII for refusing to accept the king as the supreme head of the English Church.

While this controversy was simmering, the French king Francis I, a patron of artists, humanist scholars and reforming churchmen, endorsed a proposal from Lefèvre to create a French translation of the New Testament from the Latin Vulgate. As long as he basked in the king's favour Lefèvre was safe from the assault of his opponents. But the king fell victim to his own military adventuring and was captured in battle by forces of Charles V, the Holy Roman Emperor. Lefèvre found himself shorn of his royal protection, and at the mercy of his enemies in the Theology Faculty.

Under attack from the Paris theologians, Lefèvre saw no alternative but to flee to Strasbourg. With their enemy gone, his opponents, preferring the correctness of their own opinions in the Mary controversy to any qualms they may have had about scriptural sanctity, publicly burned his Bible.[13] It would take the ransoming of the king, and his own return to royal favour, before Lefèvre could complete his work; in 1530 his French translation of the complete Bible was published in Antwerp.

In theory, Lefèvre's Bible should have had an easy ride in France. Despite his theory about the three Marys, Lefèvre was not a reformer. True, he felt that the time was ripe for an internal reform of the Church and he shared the view that Scripture should be made available to the masses, because that was where truth was to be found. But he was a loyal Catholic, he'd had no truck with the Reformation. It was his position on the three Marys which was exploited by way of his translation of the Bible to attack him personally; in 1546 it too was banned.[14]

Brucioli and Lefèvre were not the only translators to confront orthodox belief and suffer persecution in return. In Antwerp, the printer Jacob van Liesveldt produced a Dutch Bible, based on Luther's translation. It was banned and in 1535 van Liesveldt's entire stock was burned. Unafraid, van Liesveldt continued to reprint his Bible. With each edition he added further notes displaying his Protestant leanings. The final straw came in 1542 with the publication of the sixth edition. By now van Liesveldt's Bible was carrying woodcut illustrations. One showed Satan, in the guise of a bearded monk, with goats' feet and a rosary. Van Liesveldt, who must have known that he wouldn't get away with it, was charged with heresy. Like so many others struggling for openness and intellectual integrity in Europe's great age of religious intolerance, van Liesveldt was put to death.

The story was similar throughout most of Europe. Translators and printers, emboldened by the Protestant Reformation, their own passion for the vernacular Bible, and the possibility of making a quick profit, were risking their lives to produce ever-new editions.

Brucioli, Lefèvre and van Liesveldt were just some of those who tested the Vatican's tolerance of the translated Bible. By 1559 the Roman leadership could take no more. Pope Paul IV issued a ban on vernacular versions. No Catholic translations appeared in Italy after that date. Existing translations continued to circulate and eventually the Catholic vernacular Bible did return. But many theological battles would be fought before then and the already sharp instruments of religious repression would be whetted ever more keenly.

The Spanish Inquisition

Jews had lived in Spain for the best part of a thousand years. It was a far larger, and better integrated Jewish community than anywhere else in Europe. The Jews knew Hebrew and Spanish. Until their expulsion in 1492, anyone who wanted a Spanish translation of the Old Testament could easily find an interpreter who would work directly from the original Hebrew. They did not need the Vulgate as a crib or intermediary. Unlike the rest of Europe, many of the early Spanish translations were made directly from Hebrew.

But Spain also conducted a more systematic and thorough Inquisition than the rest of Europe. A particular target of the Spanish Inquisition was the community of *conversos*, Jews who had been forcibly persuaded to convert to Christianity. During the century leading up to their eviction, more than half the Jews in Spain converted, nearly always at the point of a sword. For many *conversos* adoption of Christianity was a matter of expediency; they chose to preserve their lives at the expense of their religion. They were Christians in name but Jews at heart.

Many *conversos* secretly preserved their old Jewish customs, lighting the Sabbath candles in the recesses of their homes, not eating milk dishes with their meat, acknowledging, even if not fully observing, the Jewish festivals, and in some cases even gathering for clandestine prayer services.

As they looked into the activities of the *conversos*, the Inquisitors began to suspect that they were using Spanish copies of the Old Testament to practise their religion. An obvious repressive tactic therefore was to round up and destroy every copy of the Spanish Old Testament that could be found. The enthusiasm with which the Inquisitors went about their task explains why far fewer vernacular Old Testaments have survived in Spain, when compared to Germany, France and England.[15] Only one leaf remains of a 1417 translation made by Bonatius Ferrer. It was first printed in 1478, but by 1500 it had been all but fully destroyed. Ferrer was a monk, and his translation was almost certainly made from the Vulgate and intended for Christian use. It may never even have passed through Jewish or *converso* hands, but the Inquisition would not have bothered about details like that. The sole remaining leaf is preserved at the Hispanic Society in New York.

One Bible translated from the Hebrew did survive. It was commissioned, together with a commentary, by Don Luis de Guzmán, the Grand Master of the Military Order of Calatrava.[16] The putative translator, Moses Arragel, a Castilian rabbi, who probably felt that the request made of him was more of a command than a commission, was highly reluctant to carry out the work. He worried that both Christians and Jews would be offended; a Jewish commentary might scandalize Christian sensibilities while Jewish principles would be breached by Don Luis's plans for illustrating the edition. He was also concerned that differences between the Hebrew text that he would use and the well-known Latin Vulgate might expose unwanted divisions between the two traditions. But his reluctance to take on the work was to no avail. He came under extreme pressure to change his mind; ultimately, as with so many choices imposed by the medieval ruling classes, he had no alternative but to relent.

It took Moses Arragel eight years to complete the translation. The illustrations were overseen by two cousins of Don Luis and carried out by a team of monks. The whole work was completed in 1433. It contains 334 illustrations, alongside Arragel's extensive and erudite commentaries drawn from a variety of sources, and twenty-five pages of his correspondence with Don Luis. It was a remarkable work; all the more so because, shortly after it was completed, it vanished.

The Bible remained hidden for two centuries, either to protect it from the Inquisition or because one of the Inquisitors, conscious of its value, kept it somewhere safe. The Bible didn't resurface until 1622, when it turned up in the library of Madrid's Liria Palace, home of the Grand Duke of Alba. It remains there today; it is now known as the Alba Bible. A facsimile edition went on sale in 1992.[17]

The Alba Bible survived. Most other Spanish translations didn't. In Toledo in 1551 the Spanish Inquisition published their first Expurgatory Index, a list of banned and prohibited books. A second, fuller list followed in 1559.

The lists included all translated Bibles, including individual sections or other works that contained scriptural extracts.

But the banning of translated Bibles was only the beginning. Spain had already developed a penchant for book burning; a frenzy which began at the end of the fifteenth century with the immolation of Hebrew and Arabic works. Next came books on medicine, a class of work which was generally considered superstitious. Eventually, the Inquisition even burned Bibles, a matter which they seem to have considered utterly insignificant. Perhaps it was. Given the medieval fondness for torturing people and putting them to death by burning, possibly the most horrific and distressing ordeal ever devised, the immolation of books, even Bibles, seems quite mild. In 1559 a Jesuit reported that they had burned 'mountains of books' in their college. Two years later, when an officer of the Inquisition asked what he should do with the numerous Bibles he had confiscated, the answer came back, 'Burn them.'[18]

People were burned too. Many of them. Cardinal Francisco Ximenes de Cisneros, former confessor to Queen Isabella, archbishop of Toledo and Grand Inquisitor, is reputed to have presided over the burning of 2,500 *conversos* during his period in office. Ximenes, who had spent six years in prison as a young man, in protest at not being awarded a benefice promised to him by the Pope, was, on two occasions, appointed regent of Castile. He expelled 400 monks who had broken their celibacy vows from Andalusia, imposed forced conversions on the Muslims of Granada, led Spanish military activity in North Africa and conquered the Algerian port of Oran. He also found time to put his domineering personality to good use. In 1500 he founded a university at Alcalá de Henares, a city known as Complutum in Latin, where he sponsored a polyglot translation of the Bible. The six-volume work, known as the Complutensian Bible, contained parallel Hebrew, Greek, Latin and Aramaic columns. Ironically, while translated Bibles were being burned across Spain, Ximenes, agent *par excellence* of the Inquisition, took it upon himself to initiate one of the most ambitious Bible translation projects of the age.

While Spain was burning people and translated Bibles, its freshly expelled Jews were trying to put down roots elsewhere. As were many *conversos*, who felt unable any longer to tolerate the Inquisition's continual scrutiny of their lives for hints of relapse or heresy. The Jews, with co-religionists across Europe and the Mediterranean lands, found it easier to relocate than the *conversos*, who carried their stigma with them; neither accepted by Christians who considered them to be Jews, nor by Jews who regarded them as Christians. A few brave or influential souls did try to ease their plight. One such woman was the aristocratic Doña Gracia Nasi.

Doña Gracia had been born as Beatrice de Luna, a descendant of Portuguese *conversos*. The widow of a wealthy gem dealer and well integrated into aristocratic Christian society, Beatrice de Luna devoted her life and fabulous wealth to combating the activities of the Inquisition and helping *conversos* to flee the Iberian peninsula. She didn't have an easy time of it. A rift with her sister led her to being unjustly denounced in both Venice and France. In Venice, her sister alleged that she was a secret Jewess who planned to escape to Turkey with all her wealth. In France, a co-conspirator told a similar story to the government. Her wealth was confiscated in both lands and she was cast into jail. It was a stupendous fall from her earlier exalted status. Had it not been for her nephew's deft use of the family's extensive diplomatic connections, her time in jail may have marked the end of her.

On her release, Beatrice de Luna saw no further reason to continue to conceal her Jewish origins. She began to use her Jewish name of Doña Gracia and moved to Ferrara in Italy, where she once again threw herself in to helping *conversos* flee the Inquisition. When, in 1556, 36 *conversos* were burned to death in the Italian seafaring town of Ancona, she used her considerable economic and political muscle to agitate, unsuccessfully as it turned out, for a boycott of the city's port.[19]

It's the Ladino language which connects Doña Gracia's story to that of the translated Bible. Ladino is considered today to be a Jewish language, but it didn't begin life as such; it was one of the dialects spoken in Spain at the end of the fifteenth century, when the Jews were expelled. It was written, like all Spanish languages, in the Latin alphabet.

The refugees took the dialect into exile with them as their spoken tongue. It evolved organically, as languages do, influenced in part by the speech the Jews heard around them in their new locations. Back in Spain it evolved along a separate trajectory, eventually merging into Castilian Spanish. The result was that the Jewish exiles, who no longer knew Spain, continued to speak a dialect of Spanish long forgotten in their former homeland. Now identified as a Jewish language, Ladino continued to evolve until it reached a point at which it was barely recognizable as a Spanish dialect. And it was written not in the Latin alphabet but in Hebrew script.

In 1553, Doña Gracia undertook her final journey, to Constantinople, where she lived out the remainder of her life. The same year an edition of the Bible in Ladino was printed in Ferrara. Doña Gracia underwrote the costs of its printing. It was dedicated to Ercole I, Duke of Este, ruler of a fiefdom which had long been hospitable to the Jews. A second edition of the Ladino Bible appeared shortly thereafter, this time consecrated to Doña Gracia. The publishers declared that they were offering it to 'one so noble and magnanimous, that it would adorn her nobility'.[20]

These pioneering, printed Ladino translations still made use of the Latin rather than Hebrew script. They represented one of very few medieval translations undertaken by Jews, for the use of Jews. A far cry from those translations written in the other Jewish vernacular; the Yiddish versions that were composed around the same time in Northern Europe. They too were made for Jews, but not by Jews. They were made by Christian missionaries.

The Yiddish New Testament

Johann Reuchlin, the German scholar who inspired Luther to translate the Old Testament from Hebrew, knew something of Yiddish. The vernacular of Northern Europe's Jews was relatively easy for him; it is a mixture of his native German tongue and Hebrew, the language to which he devoted his scholarship. He had in his library two Hebrew Bibles containing Yiddish translations of the hardest words, and he had come across Yiddish footnotes in other works that he consulted.[21]

Reuchlin's Hebrew grammar and lexicon had made it possible for Christian scholars to study Hebrew without recourse to Jewish teachers and, provided they spoke German, to understand a great deal of Yiddish. Because of Reuchlin, Christians could converse with Jews in their own language. This gave evangelical Christians an opportunity to take the translated Bible back to an arena it hadn't entered since the days of Mesrop Mashtots and Little Wolf. Once again the Bible was to be translated for missionary purposes.

The first Yiddish translation of the New Testament was printed in 1540 in Cracow. It came about through a collaboration between two Jewish converts to Christianity: Johann Harzuge who translated the Bible and Samuel Helicz who, with his brothers, Asher and Elyakim, had opened Cracow's first Jewish printing press in 1534. They only kept it open for one year, then closed it for three. When it reopened, the brothers had new names; they were Paul, Andreas and Johannes, and they were no longer Jews. They had converted to Catholicism.

In the dedication to his Yiddish New Testament, Paul Helicz wrote that he hoped his work would give Jews the opportunity to learn the truth about Christianity and eventually lead them to conversion. In reality he knew that, far from reading it, they were not likely to even pick it up. After converting to Christianity the brothers had carried on printing Hebrew books. The Jews, who considered the brothers renegades, had taken their business elsewhere. The brothers had appealed to the courts for financial support, claiming that their status as converts had prejudiced their market against them. The king issued a decree obliging the Jews to buy up all the brothers' unsold Hebrew stock; 3,850 books valued at 1,600 florins. The royal decree simply made the Helicz brothers even more unpopular. There was no way now that the Jews were likely to buy Paul's Yiddish New Testament, and he knew it.

A year after he published his Yiddish New Testament, Paul Helicz sold up and left town. It has been suggested that the real reason he'd published the New Testament in Yiddish was to ingratiate himself with his patron, Piotr Gamrat, Bishop of Cracow. It assuredly was never likely to be a commercial success.[22]

In 1592, Elias Schadeus, former professor of Hebrew at Strasbourg University and a preacher at the city's cathedral, published a Yiddish edition of five New Testament books. Unlike Helicz, Schadeus was a dedicated missionary. He believed that by publishing in Yiddish he was offering a service which Jewish readers would find useful. He didn't get it quite right; Yiddish is an informal language, containing many words that can be expressed either in German or Hebrew. Its chief distinguishing characteristic, on paper, is that it is written in Hebrew characters rather than in Latin script. Whenever he had an opportunity to choose between a German or Hebrew equivalent for a word, Schadeus chose the German. His translation ended up little different from Luther's German Bible, but written in Hebrew characters.

In a preface to one of his other books, Schadeus records his reluctance to translate the entire New Testament into Yiddish. He doesn't explain why, but Paulus Fagius, a contemporary who had translated many Hebrew books into Latin, is more forthcoming. In his German introduction to the Yiddish Bible published in 1544, he tells his Christian readers that, ideally, he would have preferred the Jews to read the Bible in a different language, rather than 'having to drink the Jewish drivel with which they besmirched the worthy, holy book'.[23]

Schadeus and Fagius both lived and worked in Strasbourg. The ferocity of Fagius's language reveals that relations between Jews and Christians in the city were not genial. Officially, the Jews shouldn't even have been there. They were expelled from Strasbourg in 1390 and not formally let back in until 1791. When Martin Bucer, a Hebraist who arrived in Strasbourg in 1523, was asked by the local count whether a Christian authority should tolerate Jews living among them, he recommended that the Jews be expelled. If that were not possible, harsh measures should be introduced to punish them for their inability to see the truth, and a policy of instruction in Christianity should be applied. Their synagogues were to be burned and they were to be obliged to attend Christian sermons. The only way they could avoid all this would be to convert. The attitude of Hebraists like Bucer explains the context in which the Yiddish Bible was published.

Earlier Christian Hebraists, people like Pico della Mirandola and Johannes Reuchlin, had studied the language with Jewish teachers. But by the middle of the sixteenth century, through the courtesy of Reuchlin and others, the Hebraists had enough tools at their disposal to no longer need instruction from Jews. It wasn't just that Jewish grammarians and linguists no longer had anything to offer them. Hebrew, they insisted, was no longer a Jewish language. It had been replaced, so they said, by Yiddish. Sebastian Münster, a cartographer and professor of Hebrew in Basel, explained that, just as the

Jews had adopted Aramaic as their vernacular when exiled to Babylon, so too in his time they had adopted Yiddish. Were they to return to their homeland, he claimed, they would institute Yiddish as their national language, because they had all but forgotten Hebrew.[24] As far as sixteenth-century Hebraists were concerned, Hebrew was an ancient, classical language, like Latin and Greek; an academic discipline to bring them closer to the origins of Christianity. Yiddish however was, for them, a tool for converting the Jews.

The battle to get the Jews to forsake their faith for Christianity was an ongoing, eschatological activity; an enterprise for missionaries, scholars and polemicists. It didn't make much difference to the lives of ordinary people whether or not the Jews converted. Out there in the harsh world, far removed from the concerns of professors and theologians, more menacing struggles were taking place. Europe's old elites were being challenged as never before. The Hussite revolt in the Czech lands had only been the curtain raiser. Between 1524 and 1648 thousands would die in uprisings and revolutions across Northern and Central Europe. And although the various revolts and insurrections are collectively classed as Europe's Religious Wars, their immediate causes had far more to do with poverty and social injustice than with the competing theological claims of Rome and Reformers.

Even so, religion was never far from the battle; the popular revolt against privilege could scarcely avoid threatening the power and wealth of the Church. To some minds, the changes they were witnessing were wholly numinous, animated by divine forces far beyond their comprehension. Such people believed the world was approaching the end of days. It was, they were certain, to be an extraordinary time. It demanded extraordinary deeds. Nowhere was more extraordinary than the German city of Münster during the years 1534 and 1535. The translated Bible, quite unwittingly, sat at the heart of events.

John of Leiden and the Münster Revolt

In 1937 a German journalist, Friedrich Reck-Malleczewen, wrote *Bockelson: A Tale of Mass Insanity*.[25] Ostensibly a history of events in Münster, Reck-Malleczewen's book was a thinly disguised attack on the Nazi regime. His refusal to be drafted into the army, his hatred of Hitler, 'the stereotype of the head waiter'[26] whose face 'waggled with unhealthy cushions of fat...slaggy, gelatinous, sick'[27] and his revulsion at the deeds of the Third Reich, would inevitably lead to his murder in the Dachau extermination camp. But his recounting of events in sixteenth-century Münster as a forewarning of the evils of Nazi Germany is both prescient and terrifying. The Münster revolutionaries and the Third Reich shared many characteristics; not the least of which, as John Gray points out, was the millenarian belief that through their eradication of the evils of the old they would usher in the dawn of a new age.[28]

Luther's translation of the Bible, and the centrality of Scripture to the Reformers' theology, opened up new avenues of religious thought. But for religious conservatives the Reformation set in train a series of events which seemed to vindicate their age-old fears. Once people could read the Bible for themselves, they did indeed start to have their own ideas; exactly as the opponents of the vernacular Bible had predicted. One faction in particular – they were too diffuse in their beliefs to be classified as a sect – found neither the Catholic Church nor Luther's reforms satisfactory. Known as Anabaptists, they held themselves aloof from wider society, living in tightly knit communities where worldly possessions were, at least in theory, shared. Each community had its own prophetic leader who was followed uncritically. But what they had in common was a distaste for theological speculation and complex religious ritual. Instead they followed the Bible, and only the Bible, which they read, or had read to them, in their own language. The fence which they erected around their communities was one of re-baptism; it is what the name Anabaptist means. To be a member of the community one had to be re-baptized, as an adult. Without undergoing re-baptism, one could not join.

Anabaptists are a reputable Christian sect. But many religious movements are forced at some point in their history to respond to a deviant tendency, which, through extreme cynicism or misplaced fundamentalism, behaves tyrannically, or worse. In Münster, as Reck-Malleczewen's analogy intimates, it was worse.

In 1532 the German city of Münster became a Lutheran town. The transition from Catholicism was the result of popular pressure, the power of the town guilds and, most importantly, the influence and preaching of Bernt Rothmann, a young, charismatic orator who drew large crowds to hear his sermons. Lutheran preachers were installed in the town's churches and the Lutheran translation of the Bible adopted. And that is where matters could have rested, had it not been for the arrival in Münster, just a year later, of followers of Melchior Hoffman, a mesmeric and inspirational Anabaptist visionary. His followers preached Hoffman's message of imminent redemption. It struck a chord among the working people of Münster. Rothmann was also seduced. He abandoned his Lutheranism, declared himself an Anabaptist, placed himself at the head of the local movement and called upon the townspeople to follow the example of early Christianity by renouncing all personal possessions and holding all property in common.

Had everyone within Münster's walls bought into the communal model equally, and if the town had managed to erect a bulwark against the outside world, the experiment may have had some chance of success. But by all accounts the appeal of a relatively prosperous, egalitarian city where everything was shared attracted a large number of opportunists, chancers and ne'er-do-wells. Knowing what we do today about how outsiders and immigrants are blamed for society's ills, we may take such reports with a pinch of salt. But what is beyond doubt is that within a very short time the more prosperous citizens and Town Council were trying, ineffectually, to expel Rothmann and his Anabaptist supporters. The stand-off between the Town Council and Rothmann's followers was ongoing in Münster when, at the beginning of 1534, the radical Anabaptist movement underwent a change of leadership. That was when the trouble really started.

Melchior Hoffman, the prophetic visionary who was responsible for the blossoming and growth of Anabaptism, had been arrested in Strasbourg. His opponents imprisoned him in a cage, inside a tower. He would never leave. For all his idealistic eschatology, Hoffman had been a man of peace. His successor, Jan Matthys, was not. Matthys was an unyielding revolutionary, a man who believed that the End of Time could only be brought about by putting unbelievers to the sword. In early 1534, just as Rothmann was facing expulsion from Münster, the first of Matthys's apostles reached the city. They were greeted with fanatical excitement, the balance of power in the city swung in favour of the Anabaptists and Rothmann was saved.

John Bockelson, otherwise known as John of Leiden, was twenty-five years old when he arrived in Münster as one of Jan Matthys's apostles. He had only converted to Anabaptism a couple of months earlier. But he was ambitious, beguiling and thoroughly unscrupulous. Bockelson knew only too well how to make his mark. He set about seeking powerful allies, quickly falling in with the leader of the Guilds, a cloth merchant named Knipperdolling. The two men clicked; Bockelson would in due course marry Knipperdolling's daughter.

On 8 February 1534 Bockelson and Knipperdolling ran frenetically through the town, calling upon all to repent of their sins. It had all the makings of a stunt but the effect was electric. The entire population, if the reports are to be believed, was convulsed with an outbreak of hysteria. People swooned in the streets, screaming and foaming at the mouth. As the frenzy reached a climax, a band of armed Anabaptists seized control of the Town Hall.

Bockelson had manipulated himself into a position of power. He arranged for a call to go out from Münster to other Anabaptist communities. The world was to be destroyed before Easter. Only Münster would be saved. Everyone was to join them. Immigrants were to bring food, clothing, money, but most importantly, weapons. Sure enough, they came. So too did Jan Matthys. Bockelson yielded to his authority.

With Matthys and Bockelson now a team, Münster was wholly under the control of the Anabaptists. Most able-bodied Lutherans fled. Matthys wanted to execute any who remained, but Knipperdolling restrained him. It wouldn't look good to the outside world, he said. Instead, in the first of many foreshadowings of Nazi Germany, the weak, infirm and elderly were driven from town, accompanied by the hurling of stones and the hysterical cackles of possessed, demented townspeople.

Münster was not wholly abandoned to its fate. In those days, Northern German states were governed by prince-bishops; secular authorities who had achieved, or bought, ecclesiastical ordination. As insanity tightened its grip on the town the local bishop began raising an army of mercenaries. On 28 February he laid siege to Münster.

Even now, an occasional voice of protest could be heard within Münster's city walls. Not everyone had succumbed to the madness. A blacksmith tried to rustle up support to depose Matthys from his self-appointed status as town leader. Matthys had him brought to the town centre. He was executed while the crowd sang a hymn.

Matthys declared that the spirit of communal ownership was to be rigidly enforced. All money was to be confiscated. Anyone who refused would be executed. He sacked the cathedral and ordered all its books burned. In mid-March, Matthys declared that the only book permitted in Münster would be the Bible, by which he meant the Bible that people could read and understand: the translated Bible.

His megalomania spiralling out of control, Matthys determined that this was the time to break the siege. He set off with a contingent of men towards the bishop's lines. As the sortie drew near fighting broke out and Matthys was killed. Briefly, the hopes of the townspeople were raised. But Matthys's death turned out to be no salvation. Power passed to Bockelson. Like the hydra, the terror divided and multiplied.

Münster had already seen its fair share of powerful, compelling mystagogues. Rothmann, Hoffman and Matthys had each made full advantage of their charismatic, hypnotic powers. But Bockelson outclassed them all. It was on his canvas that Reck-Malleczewen painted Hitler. Bockelson, or John of Leiden as he was known, may only have had a small empire. But given the chance, he too could have ranked among the world's greatest ever villains.

Bockelson's first act of communal leadership was to act the showman. He ran naked through the town, finally falling into a three-day swoon. Even when catatonic he could mesmerize. When he finally spoke he had the whole population firmly in his grasp. Bockelson's reign of terror was about to begin.

His first act was to institute a system of forced labour. Men were either conscripted into the army or worked for the community. In either case they were not paid. Greed, lying and slander were made capital offences. Any youth who disobeyed their parents, any wife who rebelled against her husband, was to be put to death. Adopting the biblical commandment to 'Be Fruitful and Multiply', he demanded polygamy. Briefly, this proved to be a step too far.

Outrage at the insistence that they were to take extra wives precipitated the men of the town into a brief rebellion. Bockelson and Knipperdolling were thrown into jail. But the two men had recruited a small, personal militia; foreigners who owed no allegiance to anyone in the town and had no qualms about allying themselves to the despotic cause. The prison holding Bockelson and Knipperdolling was soon breached, the two madmen liberated and their enemies killed.

Bockelson guessed that to promote polygamy he would need to lead by example. He established a harem of fifteen wives; whether they were seized or seduced we will never know. He passed a law obliging all girls over a certain age to marry. He ordained that, if an existing wife quarrelled with one of her husband's new brides, she was to be put to death. But this too met with resistance; if Bockelson had anything remotely resembling an Achilles' heel it was his incompetence at sexual politics.

The women who were now forced to share their husbands finally asserted themselves. They demanded the right to divorce. Bockelson assented. He legalized divorce and transformed polygamy into free love. His acolytes set off to the town's perimeter, to the siege, to persuade the few mercenaries whom the bishop had managed to recruit to come and join the fun.

Bockelson's crowning megalomaniacal act was to proclaim himself Messiah. He arranged for one of his 'prophets' to anoint him and pronounce him King of Jerusalem. He declared himself to have power over all the nations and warned the assembled crowd, on pain of death, not to resist his orders. Over the course of the next three days his preachers went about the town, delivering a similar message.

A throne was erected in the marketplace for the new Messiah, who dressed himself in the finest robes, wreathed with gold and silver. He processed through the town, his queen by his side, attended by an elaborately uniformed retinue. When he sat on the throne, a page stood on either side. One held a sword, the other the Bible, driving home the message that this was the tyranny of the translated Bible.

There must have been some in Münster who recognized the madness for what it was. If so, they were wise to keep their counsel. For the brainwashing grew ever more intense. Bockelson's impelling of the people towards their alleged spiritual destiny never flagged. They were told, in October 1534, that when they heard a thrice-repeated blast of trumpets, they were all to make their way to the town square. There they would miraculously be endowed with supernatural strength. Quoting Leviticus, Bockelson told them that 'five of you will pursue a hundred; a hundred of you will drive away ten thousand, and your enemies will fall before you at the sword'.[29] On the heels of this illusory victory they would march triumphantly to the Promised Land, enduring neither hunger nor fatigue. It was to be the victorious redemption of the Israelites.

Sure enough, the trumpets sounded thrice and the people, too terrified or robotic to resist, assembled in the town square. Bockelson and his retinue arrived, girded in their armour. And then, to everyone's utter consternation, as if teasing a crowd of children, Bockelson cancelled the promised expedition. The whole thing had been, so he said, a test of their loyalty. Now that they had proved themselves they were invited to a banquet. Tables were brought, the people sat down to dine and, for amusement, Bockelson beheaded a captured mercenary in front of their eyes.

The murders intensified. Three women were executed, one for bigamy, one for disobeying her husband and the third for mocking a preacher. A group of mercenaries who had defected to Bockelson became too rowdy in a tavern and were shot. The Münster regime was enjoying absolute power, and becoming ever more confident. In August 1534 the bishop attacked, and was repulsed so efficiently that his forces abandoned him. John of Leiden was riding high.

Now was the time, Bockelson decided, to send envoys to spread his message beyond the town. It was a defensive measure. The bishop had busily been recruiting new forces to strengthen the siege. Notwithstanding his messianic agenda and desire to proclaim his delusions to the world, John of Leiden never lost sight of the military situation. He urgently needed armed reinforcements from neighbouring Anabaptist communities.

The situation beyond the walls of Münster was not as he imagined. The world was not watching his pantomime in raptures of admiration. Some of his envoys did manage to stir up support; a thousand Anabaptists gathered in Groningen, planning to march to Münster. But they were defeated by the local duke. An uprising in Amsterdam briefly captured the Town Hall, before it was put down. Three boats carrying Anabaptist pilgrims set off up the river to Münster. They were sunk, with all passengers drowned. Various other brief outbreaks of armed rebellion or messianic fervour were quickly put down by the authorities. It seems that plans hatched in Münster were not despatched to his supporters elsewhere as securely as Bockelson and his allies had assumed. Increasingly the authorities were on to him. Ammunition dumps were raided, collaborators in neighbouring towns arrested. All the while, the siege grew heavier.

The beginning of the end came in April 1535, when the Imperial states agreed to contribute to a further strengthening of the siege. The blockade finally started to have an impact; the townspeople began to starve. What little food they still had was confiscated by Bockelson to feed his own troops and supporters. The people, reduced to eating grass and the bodies of dead animals, began to turn upon him. Bockelson assured them that he'd had a vision that redemption would come by Easter. Then he told them that the cobblestones would turn to bread. He ordained a three-day festival of dancing, races and competitions for the starving people. Finally, when the famine was so intense that he had no option, he told the most desperate they could leave.

The bishop treated the refugees no more kindly than Bockelson had done. Unable to discriminate between famine victims and potential spies or insurrectionists, he judged them all equally unfavourably. He refused to let them through his lines. For five weeks they starved between the walls of the town and the ramparts of the siege.

Meanwhile, in the town, Bockleson's reign of terror continued. Anyone planning to leave, or speaking out against him, was executed; Bockelson carrying out most of the beheadings himself. If he had a plan at all, it was either that he really did believe redemption would come, or that he was willing for the whole of Münster to starve to death. In the end, neither happened. Two men escaped from the town and showed the besiegers how best to penetrate the defences. Münster was invaded and the Anabaptists, despite an assurance of safe conduct, were executed over the course of the next few days.

Bockleson didn't get off so lightly. The bishop ordered that a chain be placed around his neck and that he be led around, naked, like a performing bear. When the local towns and villages grew tired of seeing the tyrant in chains, he and Knipperdolling were tortured to death with red hot irons. With their passing Münster's torment finally came to an end.[30]

The bizarre horror of Münster was of course not caused by the translation of the Bible. But the fact that the translated Bible was the only book allowed in Münster, and that its eschatological outlook underpinned the madness, makes it difficult to imagine whether the same events could have taken place in its absence. Of course, horror depends upon neither Bible nor religion; the perversions of Nazi Germany prove that only too well. And in the whole history of the translated Bible, John of Leiden's messianic kingdom of Münster is the only event to which the opponents of the vernacular Scripture can point and say 'we were right'. But even to this day, radical fundamentalism hasn't gone away. And religious extremism relies upon a revealed, unmediated, literal reading of Scripture, one which rejects the prism of human interpretation.

8

King James's Bible

The New King

If any English-language translation of Scripture warrants the epithet 'The Bible' it is the version bearing the name of King James. The sixteenth century had seen William Tyndale's Bible lay the foundations for English literature. By the end of the century William Shakespeare's pen was elevating the language to unprecedented heights. The King James Bible, born out of this rich literary tradition, did not let its progenitors down. It remains an almost inconceivable rarity, a translation that competes with the original for beauty, clarity of expression and turn of phrase. Clearly the ancient Bible was not written in English. But reading the King James version, one might almost think it was.

The murderous climate that had seen Tyndale and his supporters cruelly executed, had assuaged. New initiatives in education, facilitated by social progress, the Protestant Reformation and, to a lesser degree, the English Renaissance,[1] had vastly improved literacy. It has been estimated that erudition increased so rapidly during the later decades of the sixteenth century that by 1600 one-third of the male population could read. And with literacy came exhortation after exhortation for people to read the Bible, whether in Latin or in English.[2]

The flowering of reading skills brought the Bible to the masses. This wasn't universally seen as a good thing. Although the 1543 law that forbade the reading of the Bible by women and the working classes was unjust and proving unworkable, the fear which had led to the Act, that the ability to read the Bible would lead to new ideas, was well founded. The translated Bible, and its accompanying commentaries, became powerful weapons in the struggle by political radicals against the established social order, and by Puritans against the authority and structure of the new, English Church.[3]

But the Bible which liberates can also be the Bible that controls. Radicals point to biblical teachings that bolster their arguments and give them moral legitimacy. Conversely, political and religious establishments, who through the weight of their authority assume ownership of the Bible, may present it in a manner which counters the radical view.

The most valuable weapon in the use of the Bible as propaganda is translation. In a variation of Humpty Dumpty's dictum, 'When I use a word, it means just what I choose it to mean',[4] the ability of a translator to select the most polemically appropriate meaning can radically alter the way a biblical passage is perceived. Tyndale had deliberately translated the Greek *ekklesia* as 'congregation' rather than 'church' to counter the primacy of the Pope. In a more nuanced way, the King James rendering of 1 Corinthians 10.11, 'Now all these things happened unto them for examples' contrasts with the Rheims–Douay version's 'Now all these things happened to them in figure'. Rheims–Douay had followed Augustine in suggesting that the punishments meted out to the Israelites in the wilderness were intrinsic to their status as Jews, King James implies they were simply illustrations of what can happen to people who complain.[5] With the creation of the King James Bible, the age of the Bible translator living in fear for his life had drawn to an end. Replacing it was a new era, of the Bible translator as sophisticated, theological polemicist.

James VI had been king of Scotland for thirty-five years when he was told that the English crown was now his. His reign over the Scots had commenced when he was still a wee mite. As monarch of anarchic, brawling Scotland he'd had little money and even fewer allies. But he had a brain, had learned to be cunning and had waited for the day when the English sceptre would be in his hand. He was a man on a mission, and his mission was not solely one of self-interest.

James was determined to unite the fractured realm over which he had been newly crowned. The country had been riven by doctrinal quarrels for far too long, and in those days religion and politics walked hand in hand. The Catholics were no longer a force to be reckoned with, Elizabeth had made sure of that. But the Protestants were sharply and politically divided. The vast majority of churchmen, those who carried the greatest influence, rejected Rome and much of what they perceived as Catholic dogma, but they still wished to retain many of the symbols and rituals of the Catholic Church. Theirs was a truly English compromise. On the opposing flank of Protestantism was a small, vociferous band of Puritans, who rejected all hint of pomp and ceremonial. Theirs was a faith of the heart, devoid of external ritual; a faith that did not need, in John Milton's words, 'the weak and fallible office of the senses'.[6]

The Puritans believed that England's Reformation was incomplete.[7] They looked longingly towards strict, Presbyterian Scotland and to Europe, with its austere Calvinism. They dreamed of a more rigorous Protestantism taking root in England and they saw James as the monarch who would usher in the change. James's accession was to be the moment they had waited for, the arrival of a new king who, although nominally Catholic, had been reared under the tutelage of Presbyterian governors, a king fully conversant with everything they held dear. They believed he was the ruler who would advance their cause.

James's journey from Edinburgh to his London coronation was deliberately protracted. It was a month-long procession, contrived by the young king to display himself to his new subjects; seducing them with grand gestures of largesse, endowing them with his beneficent protection, a glorious new monarch for a splendid nation. As he journeyed southwards, James's retinue was assailed by a delegation of Puritans carrying a petition signed by, it was said, one thousand of their clergymen. The Millenary Petition, as it became known, demanded a thorough overhaul of the Protestant Church to rid it of popish practices and bring it into line with the European Reformation.

The king agreed to consider the petition. In his heart of hearts he knew that he would never agree to the Puritan demands; the good life was too attractive to him to have it curtailed by gloomy, naysaying zealots. But he was determined to unite his country and perhaps he was still high from the enthusiastic reception his subjects had given him; from the lavish fare and hunting parties which the English nobility from Northumberland to Hertfordshire had laid on. The opportunity to be seen to be doing something to unite the disparate factions, no matter how little would actually be accomplished, was too great for James to overlook. He could afford to make a grand gesture to the Puritans, to show that he was willing to address their discontent. Nothing would come of it, he knew this, but nevertheless James responded to the Puritan petition by calling a conference, to be held at Hampton Court, at which representatives of the established English Church and the Puritans would put their heads together and resolve their differences.

Discarding the Geneva Bible

Had James allowed the Puritans a free rein in choosing their delegates, the conference may have progressed towards a reconciliation between the two factions. But as it was, only four Puritan delegates were invited, and each one of them was an old friend or schoolmate of several of the sea of bishops arrayed against them. The modestly attired, self-effacing Puritans appeared uncomfortable and incongruous in the opulent, regal court studded with satin-clad prelates; the conference gave the impression of an intimate gathering of the self-interested. The truly radical Puritans, those causing all the trouble, who wished to purge England of its bishops and ceremonials, were not present.

With the odds stacked against them, the Hampton Court conference of 1603 would never produce a satisfactory outcome for the Puritans. But it did present James with an opportunity. It helped him to rid the country of the Geneva Bible, favourite of the Puritans and popular with the masses, with its anti-monarchist overtones. James's disdain for the Geneva Bible was not just personal; it was a matter of principle. James was a firm believer in the doctrine of the Divine Right of Kings, that the king is not subject to any worldly authority or control. The Geneva Bible undermined this doctrine; many of the notes in its margins implied that all kings were tyrants, and it fumed against them.[8]

There had already been one attempt during Elizabeth's reign to supersede the partisan Geneva Bible with one more appropriate to a national Church.

The English ecclesia had never fully accepted the non-hierarchical ideals of the European Reformation; structurally the Church in England had done little more than replace the Pope with the monarch as its supreme head. But the 'official' Bible the English Church had commissioned during Elizabeth's reign had failed to catch on. The Bishops' Bible, so called because it was compiled by a team of fourteen bishops, had even won itself a derisory nickname. People called it the 'Treacle Bible', because of its rendition of Jeremiah's 'is there no balm in Gilead?' as 'is there no treacle?'[9] In contrast to the Bishops' Bible, treated as an object of mockery, the Geneva Bible, with its extensive notes and subversive anti-royalism, won the hearts of the masses. The English religious and royal establishments couldn't wait to see the back of it.

The Hampton Court conference had been bogged down for days in futile argumentation when the leader of the Puritan delegation, John Reynolds, President of Corpus Christi College in Oxford, made a proposal designed to break the impasse. Reynolds suggested that henceforth both factions should use the same translation of the Bible, as a way of demonstrating their common interest. Reynolds probably didn't mean that a new translation needed to be made; his intention was almost certainly to dispense with the Bishops' Bible in favour of the Geneva. But the king jumped at the idea; he saw it as a way of getting rid of the Geneva Bible altogether, by means of a new, universally acceptable, translation.[10]

James had made up his mind about the Geneva Bible, even before the Conference was called. He was very clear about what he wanted, and now that the proposal was in the air he didn't mince his words. 'I profess that I could never see a Bible well translated in English, but I think that of all, that of Geneva is the worst. I wish some special pains were taken for a uniform translation, which should be done by the best learned in both universities, then reviewed by the bishops, presented to the privy council, lastly ratified by royal authority to be read in the whole church, and no other.'[11]

The new Bible was to be constructed by an academic committee and overseen by the bishops, before being passed to the secular authorities for approval. In pointed contrast to the ethos of the Geneva Bible, it was to receive royal sanction before being released to the churches. Whether this last stipulation was ever met is uncertain but, as Alister McGrath points out, 'the fact that there is no known royal "authorisation" for the translation cannot necessarily be taken to imply that such "authorisation" was not forthcoming'.[12]

The Making of King James

Much has been written about the making of the King James Bible. Yet there is a dearth of hard evidence about both the build-up to the process, and the act of translation itself. The few original documents often contradict each other and the gaps in what we know can only be filled by hypothesis. According to David Norton's analysis of the translation's textual history: 'The evidence we do have tells a lot about the work but not enough to clear up all mysteries...: speculation and guesswork will be unavoidable as we try to establish just how the text was created.'[13]

Among the facts that are as certain as history can ever be is that the committee was to be headed by Richard Bancroft, the tough, pragmatic bishop of London. Bancroft had taken part in the Hampton Court conference. He had ridiculed the idea of a translation when Reynolds proposed it. But he soon came round. One of the factors that won him over was the realization that chairing the translation committee was an excellent way to win the king's favour. Bancroft was the front runner for the soon-to-become-vacant position of Archbishop of Canterbury; John Whitgift, the current incumbent, was on his deathbed, and the appointment of his successor was in James's gift. Bancroft's sudden enthusiasm for the Bible project paid off. He was put in charge of the committee and, as a reward for his selfless work on the translation, was appointed Archbishop of Canterbury in October 1604.

Bancroft was a fanatical opponent of the Puritans, considering their austere solemnity a threat to England's Protestant reformation. His disdain for the self-effacing Puritans exceeded even his dislike of the militant Catholic extremists who would, on 5 November 1605, try to blow up Parliament in the Gunpowder Plot. Bancroft had cut his political teeth rooting out Presbyterians during Queen Elizabeth's reign. Now, as head of the translation committee, he had his opportunity to emasculate the Puritan challenge, once and for all.

First, however, Bancroft had to get the committee into a workable shape. The king had not just ordered him to recruit the most appropriate translators. He'd also charged him with the tricky task of finding the money to pay for the project. Bancroft was not given a budget but his manipulative skills soon helped him devise a solution that was neat and to the point. The bishops at the Hampton Court conference had ingratiated themselves to the king by obsequiously endorsing his enthusiasm for the new translation. Now Bancroft would get them to pay for their flattery. He passed responsibility for funding the translation on to them, informing them that they were to provide livings for the translators. The bishops would pay the translators' salaries and the translators would carry out their work for Bancroft.

Bancroft managed to dispose of the funding situation to his own satisfaction. But his solution didn't work well for the translators. Not all were granted a living; not everyone got paid. In the end Robert Cecil, the King's Lord Treasurer, had to find the money by doing a deal with Robert Barker, the head of a firm of printers who'd had a monopoly on printing English Bibles since 1577. Cecil persuaded him to pay the sum of £3,500 for a licence to publish the finished translation.[14] But by the time the deal was done it no longer mattered to Bancroft; the translation was virtually complete, he was Archbishop of Canterbury and no longer interested in the details of the project's financing.

A more delicate task for Bancroft was to get a diplomatically acceptable balance of voices on the translation committee. Although the unspoken purpose of the translation was to assert the authority of the English Church, the Puritans could not simply be left out in the cold. They had been represented at the Hampton Court conference, the translation had even been the Puritan John Reynolds' idea. To exclude them from the process of translation would have been an invitation to all-out sectarian conflict.

It wasn't simply a question of Bancroft selecting those Puritans who were best versed in the Hebrew and Greek languages. There was the king to consider. In his eyes, the new Bible would unite his fractured kingdom. This meant that only moderate Puritans, those who wished to remain with the religious establishment, could be included. The monarch would not brook a committee that included Separatists, that troublesome brand of Puritan which saw no value in a united Church and agitated for each congregation to be an independent entity. Bancroft needed to manage the selection of Puritan delegates very carefully.

His solution was to divide the translation committee into six separate companies, each comprising nine people. Two of the companies were to be based in Westminster, two in Oxford and two in Cambridge. Moderate Puritans would be put in charge of two of the companies, John Reynolds, whose idea the translation had been, in Oxford and Laurence Chaderton in Cambridge. Bancroft hoped that the independence of each company, together with the authority of Reynolds and Chaderton, would satisfy any concerns the Puritans may have had of being outmanoeuvred.

Bancroft's next challenge was to ensure that, despite each translation company working independently, the style of the final product was consistent throughout, remaining free of sectarian bias and influence. We can't say if he consciously adopted the model laid out in the Septuagint legend, or whether it was just a coincidence, but he put in place a system of cross checking that resonated with echoes of Alexandria.

Each company was allocated particular books of the Bible to translate. Every scholar in the company was to work on the same passage. Just like the Alexandrian translators, they would translate independently. When finished, they would confer, compare and agree. Once the company was agreed, their work was passed to the other companies for consideration and assent. A general meeting would then approve everything. Finally, supervisors from the universities were to ensure consistency of translation between similar passages appearing in different places. The system of checks and balances that Bancroft put in place was just about as watertight as it could possibly be. All this, and more, was set out in sixteen rules that Bancroft drew up.

It is often thought that the King James Bible was a new work, composed from scratch by its translators. But that wasn't so, as the first of Bancroft's sixteen rules made clear. The translation was to be, and is, a revision of the Bishops' Bible, which in itself was based on previous versions, going all the way back to Tyndale. The translators themselves stress this in their Preface to the reader: 'we never thought from the beginning, that we should need to make a new Translation, nor yet to make of a bad one a good one ... but to make a good one better, or out of many good ones, one principal good one'.[15]

As much as 94 per cent of the New Testament translation in King James comes directly from Tyndale.[16]

The new Bible was intended to top the pinnacle of all English translations since Tyndale. Its culminating virtue is as much, if not more, in its style and exquisite use of language as it is in content. For, elegant as it is, Tyndale's version scarcely approaches the majesty and poetic style of the King James Bible, even though in many cases the later translators merely made cosmetic changes. We need only to compare one random example, this one taken from the story of Noah's Ark, to see the difference:

> Tyndale: And after the end of forty days Noah opened the window of the ark which he had made. And sent forth a raven which went out ever going and coming again until the waters were dried up upon the earth. Then sent he forth a dove from him to wit whether the waters were fallen from of the earth. And when the dove could find no resting place for her foot she returned to him again unto the ark for the waters were upon the face of all the earth. And he put out his hand and took her and pulled her to him in to the ark.
>
> KJB: And it came to pass at the end of forty days, that Noah opened the window of the ark which he had made. And he sent forth a raven, which went forth to and fro, until the waters were dried up from off the earth. Also he sent forth a dove from him, to see if the waters were abated from off the face of the ground. But the dove found no rest for the sole of her foot, and she returned unto him into the ark, for the waters were on the face of the whole earth: then he put forth his hand, and took her, and pulled her in unto him into the ark.[17]

Another of Bancroft's rules, the third in his hierarchy, was unashamedly polemical. It was designed to show the Puritans and Presbyterians that the English Church would brook no compromise when it came to questions of religious authority or ecclesiastical governance. The rule looks innocent enough: The old ecclesiastical words to be kept, viz.: 'as the word 'Church' not to be translated 'Congregation' etc'. But behind this apparent loyalty to the old terminology lay a fractious dispute, which goes to the heart of the Reformation. The early Reformers were forcefully opposed to the hierarchical edifice of the Roman Church. Strict Protestantism was to have no such structure; it was to be a flat composition with no intermediaries, privileged or otherwise, between people and the divine. The hierarchical Church was to be replaced by the egalitarian Congregation. Tyndale makes this point quite clearly. In his translation of Matthew 16.18, he has Jesus saying to Peter, 'On this rock I will build my congregation', deliberately changing the Greek word *ecclesia* from its historic designation as Church. Bancroft would have none of it. English Protestantism had a Church, James was its head and the Archbishop of Canterbury the 'Primate of All England'. To avoid all doubt, and keep the Puritans in their place, Rule 3 insisted that the Greek word *ecclesia* was to be translated as Church, not congregation. It seems like a minor point, but, sadly, so do most Bible translation controversies.

Other rules emphasized the need for continuity from the older versions. The translators were to retain the original chapter and verse numbers. When they were in doubt as to the best word to use they should stick to the old, familiar ones. But they were also not to include any notes or commentaries; the king did not want another variety of the highly annotated, dogmatically ideological, anti-monarchist Geneva Bible. The only material to appear in the margins was cross references to other biblical passages, or the occasional clarification of an ambiguous word in the translation. One additional rule, added a little later,[18] required 'three or four of the most ancient and grave divines'[19] from either Oxford or Cambridge to oversee the translation, to ensure consistency of translation. There is some doubt about whether this rule was followed, although we do know the name of one of the ancient divines appointed to the task, George Ryves, Warden of New College, Oxford.

The remainder of Bancroft's rules were procedural, setting out the ways the various translators and companies were to communicate with each other.

The first translators were recruited in 1604. A careful reading of their translations indicates that, despite the king's disapproval of the Geneva Bible, this was one of the sources they consulted. They also seem to have used the Latin translation from the Hebrew made by Solomon Münster in 1536, and the work of the thirteenth-century, Jewish grammarian David Kimchi.[20] Other than this, very little is known about their day-to-day activities or how they went about their work. Their story doesn't surface again until 1608, by which time they were ready to start planning the general meeting which would agree the final version. Each company was to nominate two people to attend the meeting, to be held at Stationers' Hall in London. It took a year to get them all together, at least one translator, Andrew Downes, professor of Greek at Cambridge, refusing to come on the grounds that he had not been paid. The king sent him £50 and he relented.[21]

Errors and Disappointment

History is silent about events between the general meeting and the eventual publication of the King James Bible in 1611. It's likely that the final printed version was prepared, not as we might have expected from a full manuscript of the translators' work, but from scribblings onto a particular copy of the Bishops' Bible. The transcript had been unbound and its individual pages separated. The translators' amendments and alterations were little more than notes in the page margins. The whole thing had been passed on to the printers to prepare the final version.[22]

This sounds like a clumsy way of going about things. Notes in the margins are unlikely to be very clear, the possibility of misprints finding their way into the printed text is very high. It would seem more reasonable to assume, even at the dawn of printing technology, that the printers would receive a clean copy of the translation, proofread and laid out the way the editors wanted it to appear. But there is an annotated Bishops' Bible in Oxford's Bodleian Library[23] which contains a clue suggesting that this was the copy that was sent to the printers. A direct translation of the original Hebrew in Hosea 6.5 reads 'Therefore I have hewn them, through the prophets' and from its second printing onwards the King James Bible reads 'I have hewed'. But the first printing reads 'I have shewed'. Presumably the printers of the second edition assumed this was a misprint; 'shewed' is not a correct translation of the Hebrew and it is quite reasonable to assume that a careless printer slipped in an extra 's' at the front of 'hewed' by mistake. But that is not so. The hand-written margin notes in the Bodleian Library's copy of the Bishops' Bible also read 'I have shewed'. This strange rendering may have been an attempt by the translators to make sense of a difficult Hebrew verse, but it raises the possibility that the first edition of the King James Bible was printed from the Bodleian's annotated version of the Bishops' Bible, and not as we might have expected, from a clean, well-laid-out draft.[24]

The details of how and when the King James Bible was published are equally cloudy. Because it was little more than an upgrade on previous versions of the Bible it was never registered as a new publication in the Stationers' Register, the official register of published books. Nor is there any record of its actual publication date. And even though it is known as the Authorized Version, no document has ever been found granting it this title, nor declaring that it is indeed Authorized. It is not even known whether James's stipulation that the Bible be ratified by royal authority was ever carried out.

Given the unlikely manner of its production, it is not surprising that the newly published Bible was full of errors. And not just because the Bible may have been typeset from hand-written notes in the margin. Early printing was still a laborious, complicated process. The printed King James Bible comprised 366 sheets, of four pages each. Each sheet needed to be typeset, printed and proofread individually. All this required considerable effort and the opportunity for slip-ups was substantial. Then there was the question of cost. Printing may have been cheaper than manuscript writing, but it was still expensive. Corners were cut wherever possible to try and save money. David Norton counts 351 printer errors in the first edition and another 28 'hidden' mistakes, where a typo would not be noticed because the reading continues to make sense, even though it is wrong. Like the misprint in Daniel 6.13 which reads 'the children of the captivity' instead of 'the captivity of the children'. But, as Norton points out, this number of less than 400 words represents about one mistake for every three and a half chapters, which is not bad, considering the scale of the task. Certainly none of the errors come close to the classic misprint in the 1631 'Wicked Bible' which forgot to include the word 'not' in 'Thou shalt not commit adultery'. The careless printers of that edition were fined £300; every copy they had sold was recalled, their entire stock destroyed and their licence to print the Bible revoked. But not every owner of the Wicked Bible returned their copy. It is still, according to some internet sites, possible to acquire one. It will cost you in the region of $100,000.

Despite the build-up, the effort and the expectation, when the King James Bible hit the market, it flopped. It didn't win many fans among the general public, and as every church already had their Great Bible, most were not willing to run to the cost of replacing it with the new version. A long time passed before it found favour. Oliver Cromwell's puritan-leaning Protectorate, which had come to power in 1653 in the aftermath of the Civil War, were implacably averse to the King James Bible. It represented everything they despised about the monarchy. In the guise of a unifying project the translation had proved to be little more than a tool to diminish the influence of the Puritans. It was not until 1660, when Cromwell was dead and the throne restored in the person of Charles II, that the time grew ripe for the King James Bible to capture the stage in all its majestic, Protestant, English glory.

Part Three

Enlightenment

9

A New Role

King James Vindicated

It had taken until the latter part of the seventeenth century for the King James Bible to take its place as the unique, indispensable version for English-speaking Protestants. Until then, despite all efforts to the contrary, the Geneva Bible had continued as the popular text of choice. Printing of the Geneva Bible had even been banned in England, but this didn't stop copies being imported from the Netherlands. Nor did England's political situation help. In the increasingly fractious quarrel between Royalists and Parliament the King James Bible was, quite naturally, associated with the monarchy and all that it stood for. In contrast, the Geneva Bible was the favoured text of the burgeoning Puritan camp which stood foursquare behind the Parliamentarians in their attempts to curtail the autocratic rule of James's son, Charles I.

Reliance on the Geneva translation became even greater in the years following the civil war. King Charles I had been executed and the monarchy abolished. Oliver Cromwell was Lord Protector and his Puritan regime was in control. There was no way now that a Bible translation brought into being by royal decree would eclipse a version that had made its ideological opposition to monarchies abundantly clear. In the battle of the Bibles, the conflict between Parliamentarians and Royalists was played out all over again. Just like the Puritan regime, the Geneva Bible briefly prevailed.

But England's republican experiment soon crumbled, and with it went the popularity of the Geneva translation. In 1660 the royal throne was restored and the scales tipped, never to be realigned. Now, in an England ostensibly at peace with its royal heritage the King James Bible stood proud, a sovereign text, a pillar of the monarchy, exquisite and demonstrable proof of the majesty and stability that only a hereditary king could guarantee. The Geneva Bible was finished; King James ruled supreme.

In North America too, the Geneva Bible was soon eclipsed. It had been carried there by the early Puritan settlers, desperate to escape the intolerance and persecution of England's Protestant establishment. But the lure of the New World soon overtook the parochial interests of the early settlers. Pioneers kept arriving, religious separatism gave way to nation building, and a disharmony of immigrant tongues coalesced around a common language. The King James Bible, with its measured tolerance, linguistic artistry and theological moderation proved a more than satisfactory primer for the American razing of the Tower of Babel. The King James Bible's pivotal role in shaping the American language, its influence on the way people spoke and wrote, was not lost on Noah Webster, the man who was acclaimed in the following century as the architect of the New World's diction, the philologist who would make a translation of the Bible one of the highlights of his career.

But Webster's lexicography, and his Bible, is still some way off as far as our story is concerned. Back in the Old World, the Renaissance had faded, the Protestant Reformation had put down roots across Northern Europe and now, as the turmoil of the seventeenth century dissolved into the history books, the Enlightenment was taking its place on the switchback of civilization. Translating the Bible was no longer controversial; nobody denied Bible translators the right to live or to perform their craft. That the Bible could be translated was taken for granted, and now its role was about to change. The early translators had used common language to bring Scripture to the masses. Now, in a spectacular reversal of that aim, one man was about to use Scripture to provide the masses with a more thorough grasp of common language. That man was Moses Mendelssohn. The masses he wanted to elevate linguistically were the Jews.

Teaching German to the Jews

Throughout most of their history Jewish communities had been far less interested than their Christian counterparts in Bible translations. The ancient practice of reading an Aramaic translation in the synagogue alongside the Hebrew Bible had died out, and had not been replicated in any other tongue. It wasn't necessary; traditional methods of Bible interpretation, which relied heavily on a close analysis of the Hebrew text, meant that Jews still retained an intimate connection with their ancestral language. For most Jewish children, learning Hebrew was a key part of the educational curriculum. Fluency in Hebrew, combined with the tendency for Jews to live separately, either corralled into ghettos or in self-selecting insular communities, led to them developing their own dialects. Many Jews were not even adept at speaking the languages of the lands in which they lived. This kept them distant from the great social, scientific and technical advances of the eighteenth century. As the world advanced, small, provincial Jewish communities found themselves falling behind.

Conservatives in the Jewish world saw this isolation as a good thing, strengthening Jewish identity and reducing the likelihood of assimilation. One man didn't see it that way. When Moses Mendelssohn decided that it was high time for insular Jews to enter the modern world, it was obvious to him that the first step had to be for them to learn German. He knew how to do this; he would make them a German Bible translation. Mendelssohn was clear about what he needed to do. The controversy he stirred up took him quite unawares.

Moses Mendelssohn was born to a poor but scholarly family in Dessau, 80 miles south-west of Berlin on 6 September 1729. Like most Jews, the Mendelssohn family lived in a small, inward-looking community, neither celebrated by the German people among whom they lived, nor particularly concerned about engaging with them. Their first language was Yiddish; they had a working grasp of German, which isn't that different from Yiddish anyway, but the German they knew was only really for the practical business of living reasonably peaceably among their neighbours.

Mendelssohn was a frail, serious boy with a physical frame that would prove weak in later life. But his mind made up for all that his body lacked.

He excelled at school and at the age of eleven was picked out as one of a very small number of Dessau's Jewish boys deemed worthy of further education. This was not as emancipating as it sounds. Secondary education in an eighteenth-century Jewish environment meant studying the Talmud and religious law, usually, as in Mendelssohn's case, in the cramped and fusty home of the local rabbi. Talmudic education is profoundly challenging, intellectually demanding and mind expanding. But, as the sole topic on the curriculum, it hardly equipped students to go out into a world in which the shoots of the Aufklärung, the German enlightenment, were beginning to emerge. Over the coming decades Kant, Bach, Haydn, Goethe and Schiller, to name just a few, would all make their mark on the world at large. It was not even thinkable that a poor, Talmudic student from a small, provincial, Jewish community could be numbered among them. But even if Moses Mendelssohn was not yet ready to articulate this as his ambition, time proved that it was what he wanted. Fortunately for him, it is exactly what he achieved.

Moses Mendelssohn's great fortune was that his childhood teacher was no ordinary, rural rabbi. David Fränkel, who seems to have been something of a father figure to the young Mendelssohn,[1] was one of the leading rabbinic scholars of his time, one of the very few people to have written a detailed commentary on the relatively obscure and inaccessible Jerusalem Talmud.[2] Fränkel, who probably found the majority of boys in Dessau less than invigorating in their intellectual abilities, recognized Mendelssohn's potential. Here was a young student who had the gifts to break out from the narrow future otherwise prescribed for him. Fränkel took the boy under his wing and Mendelssohn seized the opportunity. When his mentor was offered the post of Chief Rabbi of Berlin, the fourteen-year-old Mendelssohn followed him.

Decamping to Berlin was no easy matter. Residency was tightly controlled. Friedrich the Great, Prussia's ruler, maintained tight controls on immigration into his flagship capital. Jews were only allowed to live in the city if they were economically useful. An expulsion of Jews had taken place in 1737, but even that had not reduced the number in the city to the permitted level. The consequence was that only a small number of wealthy, mercantile Jewish families felt secure in Berlin, no more than 1,500 souls altogether. But even they were only secure if they fulfilled the royally imposed obligation of ensuring their community remained exclusive, a responsibility they were to discharge by stationing guards at the only two city gates through which Jews were permitted to enter. The guards were instructed to keep out Jewish hawkers, traders or opportunists who might fancy their chances at eking out a living in the great city. According to the story, which probably has a ring of truth to it, Mendelssohn was only allowed to enter Berlin after he had managed to convince the gatekeeper that he was coming solely for the purpose of studying under the chief rabbi. He would, he assured the guard, although he couldn't have been certain, be supported by charitable Jews in the city. He had no intention of becoming a drain on the capital's resources.

Yet it was his life as a fourteen-year-old, impoverished Talmud scholar in Berlin that propelled Mendelssohn towards a career that would, twenty years later, see him beating Immanuel Kant in an essay competition sponsored by the Berlin Royal Academy of Science. His steady climb to philosophy's stratosphere all came about because of a book.

Just before he arrived in Berlin a printing press near Dessau had published the *Guide for the Perplexed*, the pre-eminent work of Jewish philosophy written by the acclaimed, twelfth-century sage Moses Maimonides. Jewish philosophy had declined in popularity over the ensuing centuries and Maimonides's work had not been reprinted for two hundred years. Mendelssohn had come across the new edition of the *Guide* while still in Dessau but was perhaps too young to fully appreciate it. Now, a copy sat in the Berlin library where Mendelssohn pored over his Talmud studies. This time, when he set eyes on it, he was transfixed. Even though it was a complicated, medieval, Aristotelian tract, Mendelssohn imbibed its pages, and set his sights far beyond. Philosophy became all-consuming for him; he couldn't get enough. Years later he would say that the curvature of the spine from which he suffered so badly was brought on by the hours he spent bent over Maimonides's work.

It was Talmudic study that brought Mendelssohn into contact with philosophy, but it was philosophy that would lead him away from religious scholarship. The taste that Maimonides gave him encouraged him to learn more. He had been schooled within narrow confines, now he felt impelled towards a greater understanding of the world beyond. It wouldn't be an easy task for the Yiddish-speaking youth with an inexpert grasp of colloquial German. He would need to immerse himself in languages he had never even heard; French to read the publications of the *Academie Royal des Sciences et Belles-Lettres*, Latin and Greek for scholarly texts. And not just languages; there were philosophical and scientific concepts to get to grips with, technical vocabularies to understand and masses of literature to read if he was to bring himself up to a level of knowledge befitting his intellectual capability. It would also require him, and this was an even greater challenge, to step outside the social world in which he felt comfortable, and hurl himself, as best he could, into a self-important, exclusive, Berlin intellectual circle that didn't know him, had no reason to want to know him and would almost certainly look down upon the arriviste, the country Jew, uneducated and newly arrived in the city.

But none of this fazed him. Armed with a dictionary, and the benefit of a friend who taught him a smattering of grammar, he started his new intellectual journey by acquiring a Latin copy of John Locke's *Essay Concerning Human Understanding*. It took considerable effort to plough through the strange language and obscure concepts, but the more he read, the more he wanted to read. Philosophy, he was certain, was the discipline that he intended to study.

His breakthrough into Berlin's salon society came when a friend introduced him to the critic and dramatist Gotthold Ephraim Lessing, who was on the lookout for a challenging chess opponent. The two men became close friends. In 1755 Mendelssohn asked Lessing to read a manuscript he had written. Some months later, when he asked how he was getting on with it, the playwright handed him a bound and printed copy. Lessing had published *Philosophical Conversations*, the first of what would become Mendelssohn's many books, without even telling him. By the end of the next decade, when his magnum opus *Phaedon*, modelled on Plato's dialogue of the same name, had been reprinted fifteen times and translated into every European language, Mendelssohn's philosophical reputation was riding high. He became known as the Jewish Socrates.

But fame and respect turned out to be a double-edged sword. One of his correspondents, the Zurich pastor Johann Lavater, who had already tangled with Goethe and Rousseau, believed that converting Mendelssohn to Christianity would set in motion the messianic redemption.[3] Lavater had just translated a work by the French philosopher Charles Bonnet, which he believed provided a wholly logical proof of the truth of Christianity. He dedicated his translation to Mendelssohn and called upon him to either refute its arguments or to do what Lavater claimed Socrates would have done, and convert to Christianity.

Mendelssohn was stung by the attack. For the first time in his scholarly career he found that his Jewishness was in the spotlight. It made him profoundly uncomfortable; in common with most Jews at the time he felt that he owed a debt of gratitude to the Christian country which had granted settlement rights to his people, but he had no wish to involve himself in doctrinal polemics. Although he felt obliged to respond publicly to Lavater's challenge, which he did in a lengthy letter, he was unprepared both for the counter-rebuttal that the Swiss preacher issued and the ensuing, lengthy, public debate in which he found himself embroiled. The whole affair made him ill and distracted him for a number of years from his philosophical activities.

Mendelssohn was not the only one struggling to come to terms with the disparity between religious and national identity. Over the course of the next decade a vigorous debate emerged on the question of emancipation and civil rights. His friend Lessing had already scripted *die Juden*, a comedy which caused controversy with its favourable treatment of the Jews. He would follow this up in 1779 with *Nathan the Wise*, a drama set in Jerusalem during the Crusades, which presented a powerful case for religious tolerance. In the political arena, the historian Christian Dohm would, in 1781, publish *Concerning the Civic Improvement of the Jews*, an essay calling for their emancipation. A year later the Hapsburg emperor Joseph II would issue the Edict of Tolerance which added the Jewish religion to the list of non-Catholic faiths that he had emancipated the previous year. Religious toleration and the emancipation of minorities was a hot political topic.

Mendelssohn, the Jew who had made a personal transition from excluded minority to mainstream German society, the scholar whose intellectual credentials were undisputed yet who was still vulnerable to the religious hubris of people like Lavater, the philosopher whose election to the Berlin Academy was about to be vetoed by the emperor on the grounds of his religious affiliation, threw himself into this debate. The 1770s was to become the decade in which Mendelssohn added the twin titles of political theoretician and architect of an emancipated Judaism to his growing list of achievements.

Central to the demand for emancipation was the need to encourage village Jews, who were detached and alienated from German society, to recognize the opportunities ahead of them. The push towards tolerance would only be worthwhile if Germany's Jews were willing to seek a fuller role in mainstream German life. An essential ingredient in this was for them to learn the German language in preference to the Yiddish they commonly spoke. Adopting German as their common language would smooth the path to emancipation and provide the Jews with access to German and European literature. This in turn would open their minds to new ideas.

Mendelssohn decided that the best way for the Jews to learn German was to present them with a text with which they were familiar, but written in the national language. The obvious choice was the Bible. A German translation of the Bible would not only encourage Yiddish-speaking Jews to better understand the language of their host culture, it would also serve to launch a cultural renaissance, a programme of education that would reignite an attachment to the ideas and humanity of the Bible.

A year after the Lavater affair, in 1770, Mendelssohn began to translate the Book of Psalms from Hebrew into German. It wasn't published until 1783, by which time he had completed a translation for his children of the whole of the Pentateuch.

Up to this point all German Bibles had been translated by Christians, with annotations or even commentaries that displayed a Christian understanding of the text. Mendelssohn wanted his translation to reflect the Jewish way of understanding the Bible, and to draw out the full meaning and style of the Hebrew text. He decided that including a commentary, based on traditional Jewish sources, alongside the translation was the most effective way to achieve this. He gathered together a group of scholars, mainly friends, to collaborate with him. The commentary was printed on the lower half of the page, with the original Hebrew text and German translation in parallel columns at the top. The whole work became known, by the Hebrew title of the commentary, as the *Bi'ur*.

Excommunication

In the *Bi'ur*'s first edition the German translation was written in Hebrew characters, the alphabet with which his intended Jewish readership was familiar. But the work proved far more popular than Mendelssohn imagined it would be. It displayed a literary elegance and clarity of language which contrasted favourably with the now archaic Luther translation. Christian scholars and churchmen also wanted to read it; of the 800 subscribers to the first edition, many were not Jews.[4] A translation written in Hebrew lettering was clearly not appropriate. A second printing of Genesis in German characters quickly followed.

But this was the translated Bible and, predictably, despite its obvious popularity Mendelssohn's translation was not without its detractors. Some of the more traditional rabbis voiced objections. Their fear was different from the now obsolete concerns of the medieval Church; that making the Bible available to lay perusal might lead to unorthodox ideas. Jewish education had always been founded on Bible study; there could hardly be any objection to whichever language it was read in. Instead, Mendelssohn's detractors voiced more prosaic reasons. Encouraging students to use the Bible as a means of learning German, they argued, would reduce the time they had available for serious religious education. That at least was the fear they spoke out loud. Less publicly articulated was a deep-rooted opposition to the whole emancipation project; they feared that it would lead to assimilation and ultimately to loss of Jewish identity. The fact that four of Mendelssohn's six children converted to Christianity and that only one of his nine grandchildren remained a Jew is perhaps a vindication of their point of view.

Whether Mendelssohn's German Pentateuch really hastened the conversion of many German Jews to Christianity is a matter for debate. But one thing is certain. As future generations of emancipated German Jews successively fell further and further out of touch with the Hebrew language, they turned to Mendelssohn's *Bi'ur* to help them understand Scripture. Mendelssohn's translated Bible started out as a way of teaching Yiddish-speaking Jews German. It ended up as the one enduring link German-speaking Jews had with their Hebrew faith.

The opponents of Mendelssohn's Bible translation didn't try to kill him, those days had gone, but rumours did start to circulate of a plan for his excommunication. The most concerted opposition came from the rabbi of Altona. Altona is now a district of Hamburg in Germany, but in those days it was ruled by the Danish monarchy. Mendelssohn, however, had powerful allies in Denmark. He was able to outflank the rabbi by arranging for a subscription to the translation to be taken out on behalf of the Danish king, Christian VII. Christian, who was plagued by mental illness, was only the monarch in name; Denmark was ruled by his stepmother. But this didn't matter. Obtaining royal approval was all Mendelssohn needed to neutralize the threat from Altona's rabbi. The rumoured excommunication never took place and Mendelssohn's translation achieved its aim. It was adopted as the textbook in Berlin's first Jewish free school and provided a conduit for Germany's Jews into mainstream society. It had been the first Jewish translation since the days of Saadia Gaon to be made for ideological purposes. Arguably, it was the last.

10

The Early American Bible

The Bay Psalm Book

The first settlers on American soil brought with them the Bibles they had used in their now forsaken homelands. For the English settlers this meant either the Geneva Bible, beloved of the Puritans, or the King James version. A copy of the King James Bible, printed in 1620 and carried by John Alden, the ship's carpenter on the *Mayflower*, still survives at Plymouth's Pilgrim Hall Museum in Massachusetts.

But although existing European versions dominated in America during the seventeenth and eighteenth centuries, the continent's story of the translated Bible really begins in Massachusetts Bay in 1640 with the book of Psalms. And although it is only one volume and not the whole Bible, nor is it particularly controversial, the Bay Psalm Book, as it is known, is worth a mention.

The very fact that the book exists at all shows just how intense the rivalry between religious sects can be, particularly when, to an outside observer, there seems to be very little difference between them. When two similar factions compete for authenticity, they each need to find a unique way of expressing their identity. For the settlers in Massachusetts Bay, their unique identity was expressed through their own translation of the book of Psalms.

One of the great, popular innovations of the Reformation had been the public singing of hymns and psalms. Congregational singing allowed people to feel involved; they became participants in their religious services, rather than merely an audience. The singing of psalms in church was popular and many families also sang together at home.

The first Puritans to arrive in America were already singing from an English Book of Psalms, translated by Henry Ainsworth, an English pastor in Amsterdam. But the founders of the Bay Colony still clung to an older translation, one which Ainsworth had found so clumsy in its style and language that it impelled him to produce his version. The Bay Colony settlers did not like their older translation, but nor would they adopt Ainsworth's version, because *that* was the one used by the Pilgrims in the nearby Plymouth colony. And although there was little to distinguish the Bay Puritans from the Plymouth Pilgrims, in terms of their beliefs and the way they practised their religion, the Pilgrims were Separatists, having broken away from the Church of England, and the Bay settlers were Non-Separatists. Therefore the Bay Settlers would not use the translation of the book of Psalms the Pilgrims used. Instead they wrote their own.

The Bay Psalm Book is no more stylistically elegant than the Ainsworth version, possibly even less so, and it underwent a number of revisions over the ensuing years.[1] But, doctrinal differences and local rivalries aside, the real significance of the Bay Psalter is that it was the first book ever to be written and printed in America. It is also very rare, and therefore extremely valuable. Of the 1,700 copies which made up the first edition, only eleven are known to have survived. A copy which went on sale at Sotheby's in 2013 sold for $13m, making the Bay Psalter the most expensive printed book in the world today, a distinction it attained solely because two similar Puritan denominations could not bring themselves to use the same psalm book.

The Early American Bible

The King James Bible reigned supreme in America for the best part of three hundred years. Its success was not for lack of competition; the nineteenth century saw a flurry of American translations, some of them highly idiosyncratic. Still, nothing could dislodge the King James version. David Daniell compares the situation in the United States with that in England where, despite the King James's dominance, there was always healthy competition from the Geneva, the Douay and others. But in the United States, despite nearly every other area of culture demonstrating an energetic and inimitable American stamp, as far as religion was concerned the King James Bible, with all its English, monarchist associations, remained unchallenged.[2]

Other languages were not similarly inhibited. As early as the sixteenth and seventeenth centuries, even before the English arrived, Spanish Christian missionaries were translating parts of the Bible into Native American languages. In 1663 John Eliot, a Puritan minister who had been involved with the translation of the Bay Psalm Book, produced the first full Native American translation of the Bible, in the Natick dialect of the Algonquian language.

Eliot, who believed that the Native Americans were descended from the Ten Lost Tribes of Israel,[3] reportedly learned Algonquian with the aid of an 'unpaid servant'.[4] By all accounts Algonquian was a difficult language to inscribe; the Naticks had no written alphabet and like Little Wolf, Mesrop and Cyril before him, Eliot had to create one. But unlike his predecessors he did not go to the trouble of devising a new script, he simply transcribed the Native American phonemes into the Western alphabet, which he then taught to his prospective converts.

By 1655 Eliot had translated the Book of Psalms and with the aid of his Algonquian helper was working his way through Genesis and Matthew. He'd received funding from the New England Company, a society established by Oliver Cromwell's Parliament in 1649 for the express purpose of proselyting the Algonquin Americans. One condition of the Company's funding was that Eliot should seek help with the translation from those who knew the Algonquians and their language better than he. He doesn't seem to have done this and, once the translation was underway, doubts were raised about whether his work was actually intelligible to the Algonquians. Eliot responded forthrightly, asserting that he had read some of his translation to a group of Native Americans who 'manifested that they did understand what I read, perfectly, in respect of the language'.[5] But, although rarely voiced during the three years it took to typeset and print the Bible, the doubts persisted. Printing was finally complete in May 1663. One thousand copies came off the press and a second edition was prepared. But when a third edition was suggested, Cotton Mather, a Commissioner of the Company and Eliot's biographer, advised against it. In his submission he referred to reports he had heard from the Algonquians: 'There are many words of Mr. Eliot's forming which they never understood. This they say is a grief to them. Such a knowledge in their Bibles as our English ordinarily have in ours, they seldom any of them have; and there seems to be as much difficulty to bring them into a competent knowledge of the scriptures, as it would be to get a sensible acquaintance with the English tongue.'[6] Eliot's landmark translation of the Bible into the Algonquian language was not deemed a great success.

Like the Bay Psalm Book, the Algonquian Bible occupies a significant role in the history of American printing. The Bay Psalter was the first ever American printed book and the Algonquian the first printed Bible. And, like the Bay Psalm Book, the Algonquian Bible has become a collector's item, a first edition selling in 2013 for $400,000.

But not even the printing of a Bible in the Algonquian tongue was enough to stimulate the much more straightforward enterprise of composing an English-language translation in America. For decades the King James retained its monopoly among English speakers. It wasn't until the aftermath of the Revolution, when it was high time to dispense with the memory of the English monarchy, and the Bible that bore a royal name, that American versions began to appear.

The charge was led by Charles Thomson, a Revolutionary leader himself, who had arrived in America as a child from Ireland, together with the remnants of his family.

Thomson's childhood had not been happy. One of six children, he lost his mother when he was ten years old. Their father, certain that they would have a better future in America, packed the family onto a boat; within a few weeks he too had fallen sick and expired. The ship's captain helped himself to the father's money and, as soon as the vessel docked, dumped the kids in the New Castle port, where they were separated. Charles found himself taken in by a blacksmith but fled as soon as he discovered that his benefactor was making plans to have him indentured as an apprentice. Blacksmithing was not something Charles Thomson had ever planned to do. The boy had greater ambitions.

Escaping from the blacksmith's forge turned out to be the best thing he had ever done. As he trudged aimlessly towards wherever his next destination might be, he fell into conversation, if the story is to be believed, with a passing lady. As adults do, she asked him what he wanted to be when he grew up. When he told her he wanted to be a scholar, she whisked him up, took him home and sent him to school.[7] If this all sounds a bit like a fairy story, maybe it is. The only thing we really know is that Charles Thomson did get himself an education, and suffered a distinguished career.

After a brief career as a teacher and merchant, Thomson became drawn into revolutionary politics. He led Philadelphia's Liberty Party and served as secretary to the Continental Congress, the representative body of the thirteen colonies during the War of Independence. Hs role as Secretary made him the official charged with telling George Washington that he had been elected President of the United States. Given his distinguished service, Thomson hoped that he would be offered a post in Washington's government. Deeply disappointed not to be offered anything, and disillusioned with politics, he went into retirement. It was then that his relevance to the history of the translated Bible began.

Thomson was preparing to write a history of the American Revolution when he happened to walk past a store from which was extruding the hubbub of an auction. He heard the auctioneer proclaiming the sale of 'an unknown, outlandish book'.[8] Intrigued, Thomson walked in, bid for it, and watched the gavel fall. He found himself the owner of a section of the Greek Septuagint. Two years later he came across the remaining parts, in the same store. He snapped those up too.

Thomson spent twenty years translating the Septuagint, finally publishing it in 1808 together with an English translation of the Greek New Testament. At Thomas Jefferson's suggestion, Thomson printed his Bible in octavo format (meaning each sheet of paper was folded into eight leaves, with an approximate size of six by nine inches). Jefferson assured him this was the size that most readers preferred. But the sale of his Bible proved unprofitable. Ebenezer Hazard, Thomson's partner in the publishing enterprise, eventually bought up the unsold stock and stored it in his attic for years. When he died, the entire stock was sold for waste paper.[9]

Thomson's English Septuagint is a majestic and effusive piece of nineteenth-century literature. He had no qualms about sacrificing word-for-word equivalence on the twin altars of elegance and readability. His translation has attracted a certain amount of merriment, but this is largely because we no longer speak as they did in the nineteenth century, and because we are familiar with the Hebrew Bible, not the Septuagint. Thomson's rendering of the Garden of Eden as the 'garden of pleasure'[10] risks bringing images into our twenty-first-century minds that would probably horrify him. But the Septuagint author knew that the underlying sense of the Hebrew name Eden is 'pleasure', so Thomson, although innocently graphic, is correct. And in Psalm 23 where just two Hebrew words are typically translated as 'my cup runneth over', Thomson's elaborate 'and thine exhilarating cup is the very best' is just a more fulsome way of rendering the Septuagint's 'your cup was supremely intoxicating'.[11]

Charles Thomson's Bible was not a commercial success but it did break new ground. It was the first English version of the Old Testament from the Septuagint ever made. It was also the first English translation of the Bible in America. Many more would follow.

Noah Webster's Expurgated Translation

If any one individual is responsible for the distinctive vitality of American English, it is Noah Webster. Trained as a teacher, and with a keen interest in pedagogy, Webster was acutely aware that the American way of life was rapidly diverging from its origins in England. The challenges and rigours of living in an emergent society were so different from old England's staid and comfortable ways, and America's newly won political independence was propelling the nation towards cultural self-sufficiency. Even the very diction of the two English-speaking nations was bifurcating; the natural consequence of the evolution of language, a phenomenon we can easily spot if we compare audio recordings made half a century ago with the way we talk now.

Yet for all these differences, America's educational system was still dependent upon the Old World's teaching methods and textbooks. The United States desperately needed its own pedagogical tools, resources that would enable schoolchildren to develop a greater awareness of their own identity and to engage more fully with the language and literature that was coming to define the new nation's self-perception. Noah Webster spotted the challenge, and took it up.

In 1783 Webster published the *American Spelling Book,* more popularly known as the 'Blue Backed Speller'. Estimated to have sold more than 100 million copies, Webster's speller has never been out of print. He followed this success up with a grammar and a reader. And although these were all significant accomplishments, the achievement for which he is best remembered was first announced in June 1800, when he placed an advert in a Connecticut newspaper telling the world that he was about to start work on a 'Dictionary of the American Language'.[12] Twenty-eight years, 70,000 entries and several grandchildren later, Webster's *American Dictionary of the English Language* was published. He had written every entry himself. Incarnated today as Webster's *Third New International Dictionary*, it remains a standard work.

Webster's announcement of a new American dictionary was greeted with ridicule. The idea of an American language was laughable, his critics argued. Still, mockery was nothing new for Webster; for nearly fifty years he had been vilified for his 'vulgar perversions, horrible irregularity, subtle poison, and illiterate and pernicious ideas about language',[13] all of which testified to his critics' uncomfortable feelings about America's divergence from Europe. Thomas Jefferson, who profoundly disagreed with Webster's ultra-conservative political views, described him as 'a mere pedagogue, of very limited understanding'.[14]

But Webster was more interested in principles than popularity. Snatches of the King James version offended his sensitivities about the correct use of language. He found the vocabulary and grammar archaic, and some of the phrases the King James Bible used were, he believed, downright indelicate. In addition to inaccuracies in grammar, such as 'which' for 'who', 'his' for 'its', 'shall' for 'will' and 'should' for 'would', Webster noted that 'There are also some quaint and vulgar phrases which are not relished by those who love a pure style, and which are not in accordance with the general tenor of the language. To these may be added many words and phrases, very offensive to delicacy and even to decency.'[15] As America's pre-eminent lexicographer, Webster felt responsible for producing a revised version of the King James Bible with a language more in tune with the sensibilities of the time.

But for all his bluster, Webster actually made very few amendments to the King James version; he found no more than 150 words or phrases altogether that he decided needed to be revised. Even then he wasn't consistent, often amending some occurrences of a word or phrases, and leaving others unaltered. Among the most striking are his amendments to the gentlemen in Kings and Samuel[16] 'who pisseth against the wall'. They are transformed into nothing more than 'males'. He partially sanitizes the low-lifes of Isaiah 36.12 who, according to King James and the Hebrew, 'eat their own dung and drink their own piss'. In Webster's translation they merely 'devour their vilest excretions'. Over and again Webster's prudishness destroys both the startling, graphic impact of the verse and the direct sense of the original Hebrew.

Some of Webster's amendments may have been considered more tasteful in 1833 when his Bible appeared, but they now seem even more archaic than the phrases they were designed to replace. In Genesis 20.18 King James tells us that 'the Lord had fast closed up all the wombs of the house of Abimelech...'. Webster, finding the word 'womb' too indelicate, translates 'For the Lord had made barren all the females...'. Not that he was unduly worried about his personal sensitivities. More importantly, he worried that some of the graphic imagery of the King James Bible, the naming of body parts and the use of evocative words like 'stinketh',[17] would be 'so offensive, especially to females, as to create a reluctance in young persons to attend Bible classes and schools'.[18] David Daniell quite rightly ridicules this fear, pointing out that the language of the King James Bible is hardly likely to disturb schoolchildren who have always been 'streetwise enough to know where to find the dirty bits and giggle over them'.[19]

Noah Webster's Bible enjoyed limited success. It ran to a second edition in 1841 and was used for a while in Congregational churches. But its popularity didn't last long. Its price dropped from $3 when first published, to $2 and then to $1.50. It was reprinted once but then disappeared from view altogether. It has experienced something of a renaissance today, but more for its curiosity value than anything else. Not that it was the only curious, nineteenth-century Bible notable for the singularity of its composition rather than its religious utility. Julia Smith's was another.

The First Woman Translator

In a spectacular reversal of history, controversy and persecution – far from being the consequences of a Bible translation – were in one particular case, its cause. In a small town in nineteenth-century America, prejudice and victimization led to the publication of a Bible translation. One made even more notable by the fact that, as far as we know, for the first time in over two millennia the translation was the work of a woman. And not just any woman; Julia Smith, the first woman to translate the Bible, was by all accounts a quite extraordinary character.

In 1884, at the age of ninety-one, Julia Smith made her final public appearance, delivering an off-the-cuff address to a meeting of the Connecticut State Suffrage Association.[20] She had spent much of her life at the forefront of the struggle for women's votes, a consequence of the discrimination she'd faced as an unmarried woman. The publication of her Bible translation was engendered by a similar cause. Both facets of her character – her principled, assertive reaction to discrimination and her scholarly absorption in Bible translation – were the direct result of personal victimization, the unique education her parents had given her, and her own, profound, intellectual ability.

Julia Smith was born in May 1792, the youngest of four daughters. A fifth would soon arrive. Her mother Hannah was, according to Julia's account, a highly educated woman, unusual for those times, whose father had taught her Latin and French and who shared his taste for astronomy. Hannah, who devoted her life to the temperance and anti-slavery movements, raised her daughters in the spirit of her own commitment to social justice. Julia's father, Zephaniah, had trained as a Congregationalist minister but had fallen out with his congregation. At the time of Julia's birth, Zephaniah was studying for what would turn out to be a highly successful legal career.

Julia and her sisters were raised in an intensely intellectual environment. This was still a world in which boys were educated and girls were not. But with no sons to educate, and knowing of no reason why girls should not receive an equivalent level of attention, Hannah and Zephaniah gave their daughters the very best education that their considerable wealth could provide. A life of needlework and home-making was not what they had in mind for their daughters. The five girls studied French, Latin, Greek, history and mathematics, and were further encouraged each to develop her own unique talents. The oldest daughter built her own boat, and invented a device for shoeing cattle, which was adopted by local blacksmiths. The second was a talented horticulturist who developed her own varieties of fruit. The third daughter was an accomplished artist and teacher of French while Julia's youngest sister, Abby, was a political campaigner, an activist in the movement for women's votes.[21] But Julia's talents excelled them all.

Julia's diary, a thirty-year-long endeavour which she wrote in French, just for fun, shows that in addition to novels, newspapers and history she read Virgil's epic poetry, the works of the medieval theologian Erasmus, the sermons of John Knox, Shakespeare's plays and many other classics, textbooks on law, mathematics and chemistry. Over a ten-year period, from 1824, she read through the Old Testament three times annually and the New Testament eleven times. But however much of a bookworm she was, she was more than just a drudge; her diaries record dances, social excursions to neighbours, charity work and the frequent entertaining of visitors to the family home. All in all, Julia's was the sort of normal social life one would expect from a well-off, small-town young lady at the beginning of the nineteenth century. Indeed, her sociability surpassed that of her sisters; she was the only one of her siblings to marry, despite managing to put off the event until she was eighty-seven years old.

In the 1830s, William Miller, a Vermont farmer and preacher, experienced visions which he believed to be prophetic, about the imminent Second Coming. He found a text in the book of Daniel which convinced him he could place a precise date on the event; Jesus would return on 22 October 1844. Miller announced his prediction in churches, at public meetings, in tracts and in pamphlets. His utopian prophecies caused a commotion; people flocked to hear him. During the course of the decade the number of his followers burgeoned; as the eschatological moment approached reports began to circulate of believers selling their homes and possessions in preparation for their imminent ascension; of farmers refusing to harvest their crops for the coming year as to do so would show bad faith and tempt Providence to delay the redemption. When, in February 1843, a comet appeared in the sky it seemed a sure sign that Miller's prophecy was true. Even the Smith sisters were intrigued. They decide to examine the Bible for themselves, to see if they could find support for Miller's predictions.

Although they had read the Bible in English many times, Julia felt that to really examine it properly she should study it in its original languages.

Between 1845 and 1860 Julia Smith translated the Bible. She made five different translations, each time trying to get closer to the original meaning. Twice she translated from the Septuagint and once from the Vulgate, drawing on the Latin and Greek her parents had endowed her with. Then she translated it from the Hebrew, even though there was nobody in the area to teach her. She learned the language alone, working only from a lexicon and cross-referencing with the King James Bible. It was an astonishing feat of self-education.

Nobody knows for sure how Julia procured a copy of the Hebrew Old Testament. Such things were not readily available in nineteenth-century Connecticut. She did have a friend in a nearby town, an Episcopalian minister named Samuel Jarvis, whose extensive library included many Bibles, among them Tyndale's, the Bishops' and the Douay. The best guess is that she borrowed a Hebrew Old Testament from him, if indeed he had one.

Julia's self-taught Hebrew education resulted in a somewhat idiosyncratic translation. Not that she minded. Unlike the King James translators she was not seeking to create a readable, literary English Bible that the public would warm to and accept as their own. She was translating for her own purposes and trying, in English, to get as close to the original Hebrew as she possibly could, irrespective of style or nuance. In an interview that she gave many years later she confirmed this approach. 'I have consulted no commentators. It was not man's opinion that I wanted...but the literal meaning.'[22]

Julia was aware that the King James translators, like many before them, had inserted words into their translation to make better sense. Biblical Hebrew has no verb corresponding to 'is'; the word is simply taken for granted. Other pronouns are sometimes missing. The King James Bible had frequently inserted such words for greater clarity, using italics to signify an interpolation. Julia Smith chose not to add any clarifying words to her translation. Emily Sampson may be right in suggesting that Julia believed that the true meaning of the text only comes out in in the reader's struggle to comprehend; anything which eliminates this struggle by smoothing out the language is counter-productive. In Genesis 22.1, in the King James version, Abraham says 'Here I *am*.' Julia has him say 'Here, I.'[23] Similarly, the King James tells us that Noah's flood did not begin to subside 'until the tenth month, in the tenth *month*, on the first *day* of the month, were the tops of the mountains seen'. Julia Smith however follows the Hebrew literally: 'until the tenth month, in the tenth on the one of the month the heads of the mountains were seen'.[24]

After she had finished her first Hebrew draft, Julia Smith decided to make a second translation. She may have found the first version too stilted even for her tastes. In her second translation she paid closer attention to the subtleties of Hebrew grammar. This time she took account of a Hebrew grammatical device which changes the tense of a verb from future to past; a device she'd ignored the first time round. In her first version nearly every verb which indicated a past event had been translated as if it would take place in the future. Once she paid closer attention to the conversion of tenses from future to past, her Bible made better sense. But she didn't introduce the modification because she had an audience in mind; her second translation, like the first, was made for her own personal use. Originally, she'd had no intention of publishing either version. But she felt compelled to do so, when she and her sisters found themselves the victims of discriminatory, misogynistic prejudice on the part of the local tax authorities.

The problems began in June 1869, when the local tax collector visited the home in the town of Glastonbury, Connecticut, where Julia and her four sisters lived. He had come long before he was expected, to collect a tax that didn't fall due until the following autumn. He came early because the town was struggling to pay the wages of its labourers, and he'd picked on the Smith household because they were all women. Normally, the local tax burden fell only upon men, but the male taxpayers in the town had refused to pay before the levy fell due. The tax collector guessed that the wealthy Smith sisters would be a soft touch. He was right, they paid. But having got money out of them once, he tried again, sending the Smith sisters a second bill in October of that year for the same amount. He explained that the money was needed this time in order to employ someone to record the names of all the men who were eligible to vote.

This time the sisters were more resilient. They asked whether, as taxpayers, their names would also be recorded on the voting register. When told that paying tax did not qualify them to vote, that the franchise was reserved for men only, Julia was outraged. She was being asked to shell out for men to receive a right which was denied to her as a woman. Julia Smith and her sisters, who had been brought up to promote and fight for social justice for others, suddenly saw themselves as people to whom the same justice was denied. She and her sister Abby determined to do something about it. They joined the women's suffrage campaign.

Three years later the tax collector turned up again. This time he called to advise them that their taxes had been increased. It wasn't an increase which applied to the whole town: only the Smith sisters and two other widows were liable for the extra charge; none of the men had been asked to pay more. Once again the sisters dutifully paid the tax, but they swore they would pay nothing more until they had a say in how the money was spent.

The following year the authorities in Glastonbury, standing firm against what had become a national campaign for women's suffrage, reaffirmed their refusal to register the Smith sisters as voters. Soon afterwards, when the tax demand arrived at a level higher than for any other property in the town, the eighty-one-year-old Julia, and her seventy-six-year-old sister Abby refused to pay. The slogan 'No taxation without representation', a complaint first hurled at the British crown during the Revolutionary era, had once again become a rallying cry in a national campaign. The Smith sisters took it to heart. The more certain it became that the authorities in Glastonbury were unable to comprehend the changes taking place in the world beyond their town, the more the Smith sisters dug their heels in. They would not pay their taxes without being granted the right to vote.

The response of the town authorities to the sisters' tax strike was to seize seven of their eight Alderney cows. It was a heavy-handed gesture that proved to be a step too far. The evocative image of the elderly sisters' cows being sadly led away in a procession to be auctioned became national news. The *Boston Post* proclaimed that the Smiths' cows would 'take their place in history with Caligula's horse, the goose that by its cackling saved Rome, the wolf that suckled Romulus and Remus, and the ass that spoke for Balaam'.[25]

Still the sisters refused to pay, and still the town pressed for their money. The next step in the saga came when the authorities moved to seize the sisters' property. It took Julia and Abby some time to find an attorney who would agree to represent them; they encountered a similar level of prejudice from the legal profession as they had already received from the tax authorities. Eventually however they did find a lawyer and the case went to court. The sisters won the first round, the town immediately lodged an appeal, and the judge delayed proceedings for so long that it seemed obvious to Julia and Abby that his intention was to wear them down.

Julia Smith had one card she could play. It wasn't directly relevant to her case but it made a point. She was convinced that the only reason she and her sister had been picked out was because the town thought that women were easy prey; that they had neither the political muscle nor the intellectual capability to stand up to men. Julia resolved to do something 'more than any man has ever done'.[26] She decided to publish her translations of the Bible. Bible translation was, she acknowledged, 'the most difficult task that the most erudite scholars can set themselves'. It was time the town officials understood that 'the woman who knew not enough to manage what she rightfully and lawfully owned had actually done what no man ever had'.[27]

This was not arrogance on Julia Smith's part. She did not consider herself better than anyone else for having translated the Bible. But she did think she should be sufficiently respected that men would not take advantage of her.

Julia Smith translated the Bible for her personal satisfaction, as a means of affirming her own skill to herself. She never intended it for educational or congregational use. Even so, its publication received a mean-spirited reception in some small-minded quarters; one newspaper, which had not even seen her translation, declared that it simply proved that some women will deign to do things for which they are not suited.

Nor did it stop the town from pursuing her for her taxes. Towards the end of her life, after Abby had died, Julia married Amos Parker, a lawyer from New Hampshire. In a magnanimous gesture of male responsibility he took it upon himself to pay the tax bill for her. Julia was not at all pleased; reimbursing him was the mildest of her responses.[28]

Julia Smith's Bible does not stand out as one of the great translations, nor indeed as one of the most popular. It was never intended to be; only one thousand copies were printed, many of which were given away. But it is remarkable for at least two reasons. One, because of the role it played in the struggle for women's rights and representation. The other because, of all the Bible translations ever made, controversy was the stimulus for its publication, not the consequence.

11

The Quest for Meaning

The Push for Revision

Julia Smith and Noah Webster were just two of several lone, idiosyncratic translators, each trying to produce a Bible more relevant than the now archaic King James version. During the nineteenth century pressure for a new revision of the translation continued to grow, fuelled by a desire for greater readability, a scholarly wish to crystallize the definitive biblical text and new discoveries of ancient manuscripts.

It had become clear that, despite the work of Erasmus, and of Theodore Beza, a sixteenth-century Calvinist who followed in his footsteps with an even more definitive edition of the Greek New Testament, the classical base text used for the King James Bible was far from accurate. Indeed the King James version had only been in existence for sixteen years when a previously unknown manuscript, the *Codex Alexandrinus,* was sent to James by the patriarch of Constantinople. It only differed in minor details from the texts known up until that point, but far from advancing the quest for an original, authentic, definitive text of the Bible, it supported the growing awareness that such a thing probably never even existed. The Bible is composed of many books, all written by different people, in different times and at different places. The Old and New Testaments, as we know them today, were originally nothing more than compilations of these different books, and who is to say that every compiler had identical texts in front of them when they integrated them into a single codex?

When, in 1844, the German scholar and explorer Constantine von Tischendorf was winched in a basket over the impregnable walls of St Catherine's Convent in the Sinai desert, he little knew that he was about to become the latest antiquity hunter to rewrite Bible history. Inside the monastery's warm, dry library, perfect conditions for preserving ancient manuscripts, Tischendorf found a fourth-century codex, so heavy that one person could not lift it. The *Codex Sinaiticus* contained all the books of the Bible. It was the oldest and most complete Bible manuscript ever found. In an age captivated by archaeological exploration, Tischendorf's discovery seized the popular imagination. His account of his adventure, suitably embellished for public appeal, ran to eight editions. More recently, however, his report has been challenged. As has his 'borrowing' of the codex, to have it copied in St Petersburg before returning it undamaged. The codex has never been returned to the monastery from whence it came.[1]

Tischendorf's discovery lit the fuse for a flurry of research into the reconstruction of the elusive, original biblical text. It reached a crescendo in 1881 when the English scholars Westcott and Hort published the definitive *New Testament in the Original Greek*. It has been estimated that between Tischendorf's initial visit to St Catherine's in 1844 and Westcott and Hort's 1881 publication the number of known Greek manuscripts of the New Testament increased from 1,000 to 3,000. Rather than getting closer to the primordial prototype, any hope of recovering an original, definitive version of the Bible was slipping further and further away.

As awareness of the Bible's textual history increased, the emphasis shifted from reconstruction of the past to making the present intelligible. Pressure for a revised, modernized version grew. In 1832 the professor of Greek at Cambridge University, James Scholefield, published *Hints for an Improved Translation of the New Testament*. Dedicated to the Priests, Bishops, and Deacons, Scholefield acknowledged that to 'call the public attention to the consideration of any supposed improvements in the authorised versions of our Bibles is needlessly to unsettle men's minds', but if difficulties in understanding the Bible come from a defective translation, then it is 'an act of charity and duty to clear away that duty as much as possible'.[2] To achieve that aim, Scholefield worked his way, verse by verse, through the Greek text of the New Testament, suggesting amendments to the King James Version and inserting often lengthy notes to justify his choices.

In 1856 Canon William Selwyn published his *Notes on the Proposed Amendment of the Authorised Version*. He stressed that the spread of the English language throughout the world, and the role of the Authorized Version as the basis for missionary translations, had enhanced the importance of Scholefield's work one hundredfold. He urged the establishment of a committee of translators, working to the same principles as had guided the redactors of the King James version to amend and update the language of the seventeenth-century masterpiece.[3]

But it wasn't until 1870, in the Convocation of Canterbury, a venerable assembly of English churchmen, that a formal initiative was instigated to revise the King James version. A committee was appointed, mainly consisting of Anglicans but including Baptists, Congregationalists, Methodists, Presbyterians and a Polish-born, Jewish convert to Christianity. Two years later, the committee's work was extended to the USA, with the establishment of a parallel commission. The result was the publication, in England in 1885, of the Revised Version of the Old and New Testaments. It included an appendix listing the recommendations of the American committee. But voices in America were not satisfied with having their recommendations tucked away in an appendix. Illegal, pirated translations incorporating some of the proposed amendments began circulating in the United States. Even the staid, uncontroversial Oxford and Cambridge University presses got in on the act, publishing the American Revised Bible.[4] In response, the American committee, sensing that they were losing control of their own work, decided to issue their authenticated, proprietary translation. Choosing a title was a problem, the number of available options for the publication was shrinking, and every variation on 'revised' and 'revision' had already been appropriated. They named their volume the American Standard Version. It was published in 1901.

Religion and Politics in Russia

For the best part of a thousand years, the Slavonic Bible, originally translated in Moravia by Cyril and Methodius, had tenaciously clung to its status as the official Scripture of the Orthodox Russian Church. But as the nineteenth century dawned, its dominance seemed less assured. Old Slavonic was an archaic language that few could comprehend. A modern Russian translation, which ordinary people could use and understand, seemed to be a self-evident imperative. Every other country in Europe had one, and Russian society was increasingly opening up to cultural trends blowing in from the West.

In 1812, the recently formed British and Foreign Bible Society helped to establish a branch in St Petersburg. The British and Foreign Bible Society had been founded in 1804. Its founding impetus had come from a Welsh clergyman, Thomas Charles, who approached the Religious Tract Society complaining of a shortage of Welsh-language Bibles in the Principality. He asked the Religious Tract Society, who published Christian literature, to help cater for the need. As the Society set about considering his request it became clear that the Welsh issue was merely part of a much wider problem. If Wales, a part of Great Britain itself, was short of Bibles, then how much more likely were other countries in the British Empire to be in a similar position? Indeed, they mooted, it was more than possible that some of the more remote colonies and outposts had no Bible available in their native tongue at all. What was obviously needed was a means of translating the Bible into each and every patois which needed it, and then, once translated, the wherewithal to distribute copies widely, and cost-effectively.

And so it was decided to form 'A Society for Promoting a more extensive Circulation of the Holy Scriptures, both at Home and Abroad',[5] a name which soon became shortened to the more elegant British and Foreign Bible Society. Among its most prominent backers was William Wilberforce, the anti-slavery campaigner and member of parliament.

The new Society rapidly got to work. It despatched envoys across the world, to encourage and facilitate the establishment of local branches, formed in its own image. They sent a Scot named John Paterson to represent them in Russia and Scandinavia; it was he who initiated the foundation of the St Petersburg Bible Society.

Although the British played a seminal and evangelical role in its establishment, given the political complexities of nineteenth-century Russia, the new St Petersburg Bible Society is unlikely to have succeeded had it not been for the active patronage of the emperor, Alexander I.

The St Petersburg Bible Society's early vison was ambitious; it aimed to provide translations of the Bible for those people of the Russian Empire who did not speak the Imperial language, and to further the use of the Slavonic Bible within Russia itself. But it was Alexander I who harnessed its ambition, broadened its remit and turned it from a local society into a politically vulnerable, religiously controversial, state-backed institution.

Stephen Batalden, in his book *Russian Bible Wars*,[6] suggests that one reason for Alexander's support of the Society was his own personal, existential crisis in the wake of St Petersburg's fall to Napoleon's forces in 1812. In a state of despair, Alexander I turned to his adviser and friend, Prince Alexander Golitsyn. Golitsyn recommended that the emperor seek solace in Scripture. The emperor took the advice to heart, undergoing an intense religious awakening which eventually manifested itself in his promotion of the Holy Alliance, a coalition of European rulers set up after the defeat of Napoleon, ostensibly to encourage the use of Christian principles in international diplomacy.

Alexander's new piety also found an outlet at home when, in 1816, he issued a decree empowering the former St Petersburg, now the Russian, Bible Society, to translate and publish Scripture in modern Russian. The need for an Imperial decree to permit a translation of the Bible might sound like overkill, an echo of the patronage of King James. But it was an essential tactic; there was no other way to override the antagonism of the Orthodox Church. For, just as countless religious establishments had done before them, the Russian Church opposed any new translation of the Bible. The Old Slavonic text had served them perfectly well for a millennium; they saw no reason to change. The only power in the Empire which could override their objections was the throne; in Imperial Russia the emperor's fiat held sway even over the wishes of the Church. In his decree the emperor noted that the Greek Orthodox Church had recently approved the translation of the Bible into Modern Greek; this, he determined, was adequate precedent for a similar move in Russia.

The emperor issued his decree and a fresh controversy broke out. Even if momentum towards a Russian-language translation now appeared unstoppable, one fractious issue remained unresolved. The Old Slavonic Bible had been translated from the Greek Septuagint. But contemporary Russian Bible scholars argued that the new translation should be based on the accepted Hebrew text. As had happened so many times in history, the dispute pitted conservative churchmen against scholarly modernizers. Gerasim Pavskii, the best known of the translators and a man who would become the focus of a later controversy, thought he had disposed of the argument when he produced a compromise translation of the Old Testament's book of Psalms. He translated from the Hebrew but used the Septuagint's numbering, which differed from the Hebrew, and he included an additional psalm which only appears in the ancient Greek version. But Pavskii's ingenuous *fait accompli* only made things worse.

One of the stimuli behind John Paterson's creation of a Bible Society in St Petersburg had been the popularity of a spiritual system of freemasonry, which regarded the Bible as the key to understanding the supernatural world. While this system remained in vogue, conditions were ideal for a popular Bible, and for a Society to promote it. But Russian freemasonry was highly politicized; several of the Masonic lodges were suspected of revolutionary leanings. By the time that Pavskii's translation of the *Octateuch*, the first eight books of the Old Testament, was underway a counter-revolutionary mood was infiltrating Russia, one which saw freemasonry, fringe spiritual movements and reformist factions as threats to social stability. In 1822 Alexander I closed all Russia's Masonic lodges. The Bible Society, which had a number of mystically inclined masons among its members, began to come under scrutiny. It was certainly not the time for them to print or publish a translation of the *Octateuch*, particularly one made by Gerasim Pavskii, whose translation of Psalms had antagonized the conservatives.

Over the next couple of years the fortunes of the Bible Society deteriorated. The next crisis came when two charismatic Roman Catholic priests from Germany, Ignaz Lindl and Johannes Gossner, began preaching to large crowds and attracting substantial followings. The two preachers were not shy about their evangelical leanings and reformist sympathies, attributes guaranteed to attract the opprobrium of the Church. The Bible Society, for its part, appeared to be inextricably linked to the two German preachers. The secretary of the Society had assisted in revising the Russian translation of

Gossner's New Testament commentary, a friend of Paterson had circulated it and Prince Golitsyn, the President of the Society and the emperor's former adviser, had personally given it his patronage. Matters became even stickier when Lindl abandoned his priestly celibacy and secretly slipped away to get married. When the translator of Gossner's commentary mysteriously died, prompting suspicions of supernatural intervention, the writing was on the wall for the Society.

Pressure from the Orthodox Church continued. The Society was accused of being too closely involved with sectarians and reformist ideas. Its opponents argued that it had outlived its purpose. The Society was no longer needed; there was sufficient stock of translated Bibles to last for many years. Church leaders agitated for it to be closed.

The emperor tried to find a middle way. He removed Alexander Golitsyn, the friend who had advised him to seek comfort in the Bible, from his post as President of the Society. In his place he appointed Serafim, the Metropolitan, or senior archbishop, of St Petersburg. Serafim, who had sat on the governing body of the Society for ten years, was one of the two churchmen who had led the campaign of opposition to it. The last thing he wanted was the job of President. He suggested instead that the Society be closed. The emperor did not agree, an impasse was reached, and the Society fell into a state of decline. But Alexander was nearing the end of his life. A year after his death in 1825, the new emperor Nicholas I issued an order closing the Society and restoring the status quo prior to its establishment. Henceforth, Bibles were only to be published in Slavonic. The Russian *Octateuch*, which by now had been printed, was never bound or distributed. It remained in storage. Meanwhile Bible translation in Russia went underground.[7]

Gerasim Pavskii, who had translated the Book of Psalms and overseen the translation of the *Octateuch* for the Bible Society, was considered to be the most gifted Russian Hebraist of his era.[8] He was also seen as a high flyer in the church hierarchy. Since leaving his post as a director of the Bible Society he had taught at the St Petersburg Academy, been appointed as archpriest in the Kazan Cathedral and served as religious tutor to the Grand Prince and Princess. But in 1835 he fell out with his superior over his proposed educational programme for the Grand Prince. His exalted status began to unravel. It was merely a foreshadowing of what was to come.

The closure of the Bible Society had not curtailed Pavskii's translation work. By the time he took up his post as professor of Hebrew at the St Petersburg Academy, he had rendered most of the Hebrew Old Testament into Russian. He made his translations available to his students as part of his lecture notes. His students, knowing that no other Russian edition of the Old Testament existed, spotted an opportunity. In 1838, after Pavskii had left the Academy, his former students cashed in. Pavskii's lecture notes, which were in essence his translations of the Old Testament, were lithographed and secretly circulated.

The notes quickly became popular, and copies were soon to be found in theological colleges throughout the empire. Between 1838 and 1841, three separate editions of Pavskii's Russian Old Testament were clandestinely published. The Church was outraged. A double offence had been committed; not only had the Old Testament been rendered into modern Russian instead of Slavonic but the translation was based on the Hebrew text, rather than the Septuagint.

The underground availability of a modern, Russian Old Testament was made even more exciting by its ecclesiastical illegitimacy. It was sought after, even by those from whom the Church expected better things. A contemporary writer recalled that, when it was first published, not only did he order a copy of the illegal translation, but so too did the Archimandrite, or rector, of his seminary. Indeed, so he said, even the bishop of Tobol'sk had more than once borrowed his copy.[9]

Sadly, the church authorities were not so enthusiastic. An instructor at the Moscow Academy reported the distribution of the prohibited version of the Old Testament to the Academy inspector, who in turn informed the Metropolitans of Moscow, St Petersburg and Kiev, as well as the synodal chancery. The matter was placed before the Holy Synod. They swung into action.

A commission of investigation was established and a feverish hunt took place for copies of the lithographed translation. Instructions were sent to all diocesan bishops to recover all printed or hand-written copies of the translations, and to examine whether any seminary teachers caught in possession of a copy held unorthodox beliefs. Everyone who was found to be in possession of a copy was interrogated. Pavskii himself was summoned by the inquisitors in 1842 and again in 1844. He was cleared of participating in the distribution of the translation. But that didn't stop them from burning his Bible; in nineteenth-century Russia the thirteenth-century tradition of burning illegitimate Bibles underwent something of a revival.

The investigating commission determined that 490 lithographed copies of Pavskii's translation had been made, in addition to an unknown quantity of manuscripts. The inquisitors recovered 308 copies and burned them all, bar three. We know this because the Holy Synod archive contains 4,000 pages of once-secret documents pertaining to the investigation.[10]

For decades, the fallout from the Pavskii affair inhibited further progress towards a popularly available Russian-language Bible. One of the bishops, devastated by the clumsy and aggressive manner in which the investigation had been conducted, lamented that 'they only take things away from us – what do they ever give us in their stead?'[11]

Of course, as was always the case, the popular Bible eventually prevailed. In May 1858 the Holy Synod, no less, petitioned Emperor Alexander to approve the resumption of Old Testament translation. Even drawing up the petition had been troublesome; those who opposed it feared it would undermine the authority of the Slavonic version, and damage the Russian Church's relations with its Slavic and Near Eastern Orthodox neighbours. Even as Russia modernized, the issue of Bible translation remained as bound up as ever in questions of politics and authority.

Still, the translation went ahead. The Synodal Bible, the first to be approved in the Russian language, was finally published in 1876. It was a triumph for those who believed in making the Bible popularly accessible, but it didn't mark the end of the Russian state's influence on the politics of scriptural translations. During the Soviet era, as part of its policy of containment of religious practice, the state controlled the publication and distribution of the Russian Bible. No new translations were undertaken for more than a century. The next popular version didn't appear until 2011, following the collapse of the Soviet Union.

The Return of Bible Burning

Back in the English-speaking world, the Revised Version was enduring a rocky ride. It had been received enthusiastically when first published in 1881; two million copies were sold in London in the first four days, half of the orders coming from America. The *Chicago Tribune* printed the entire New Testament in its regular Sunday edition. The entrepreneurial bandwagon quickly got into gear, and within a few short weeks it was possible to buy cheap pirated copies. More critical readers could obtain an edition listing all the differences between the new translation and the King James version, while Bible specialists could buy a volume which set the Revised Version alongside Westcott and Hort's recently published *New Testament in the Original Greek*.[12]

But the excitement quickly dimmed. In the nineteenth-century age of exploration and progress, Bible translators were no longer murdered or persecuted. But living in a more tolerant world did not lessen the emotional attachment of ordinary people to the particular edition of the translated Bible with which they were most familiar. Religion is at least as much of the heart as of the mind, and for many people the words of the Bible they had grown up with were comforting and reassuring; changing its language to make it less archaic, or to conform more accurately to the original, may have been a rational thing to do, but it could prove very unsettling.

Not that the Revised Version's critics necessarily presented their unease as an emotional phenomenon; 'I don't like it' is not a persuasive argument. It was far more effective for an opponent of the new version to identify faults, general or specific, with the actual translation itself. And so Charles Haddon Spurgeon, perhaps the best known and most popular British preacher of his age, called the Revised Version 'Strong in Greek but weak in English'.[13] Even so, despite his dislike of its language, Spurgeon did appreciate the scholarship in the new version, particularly where it corrected some of the errors overlooked by the King James translators.[14]

The lukewarm reception given to the Revised Version naturally distressed those who had been involved in its production. In a series of addresses arguing for greater adoption of the Revised Version by churches, Charles Ellicott, bishop of Gloucester and Bristol and a founding member of the committee, lamented that the translators had collectively spent a total of twenty-four years on their efforts, only to find that 'partly from indifference, partly from a vague fear of disquieting a congregation... the old Version is still read'. He considered loyalty to the three-hundred-year-old King James Version inexplicable in the light of 'a current Version from which errors are removed, and in which obscurities are dissipated'.[15]

A slightly more optimistic reaction came from the western side of the Atlantic. Although Philip Schaff, a church historian and member of the American translation committee, was disappointed that of all the American denominations, only the Baptists had formally adopted the Revised Version, he remained confident that 'English readers will not be contented with King James' Version. They know that something better can be made... the Revised Version is not free from defects, I would have had some things different if I had been the only one to be consulted. But on the whole, the Revision is a vast improvement upon the Version of 1611'.[16]

Vast improvement it may have been, but the Revised Version hardly had time to become established in the USA before it was superseded in 1901 by its twin, the American Standard Version. The two editions barely differed; the Standard Version merely contained those amendments recommended by the American translation committee of the Revised Version, which their British counterparts had rejected. But even the Standard Version did not prevail for long. By the 1930s calls were going out for a further revision; one which was a little braver than the Standard and Revised Versions in rejecting archaisms, and which took account of even more early Greek manuscripts which had come to light since the Revised Version had been compiled.

And so it was that in 1937 a coalition of white, Protestant professors, drawn from across the denominations, assembled to begin work on the Revised Standard Version (the proliferation of similarly named Bible translations was becoming dizzying). There were no Catholics on the Committee; the fundamental theological difference as to whether authority was vested in the Bible or the Ecclesia meant that Catholics would not necessarily grant every newly discovered manuscript greater authenticity than the Vulgate, the sanctity of which was rooted in the earliest days of the Church. But there was a Jew; Harry Orlinsky of the Hebrew Union College was invited to join in 1941.

Some opponents of the translation castigated the committee for co-opting a non-Christian, and none rejoiced more in the opportunity to condemn the committee than Gerald Winrod, a Kansas preacher not long previously indicted for Nazi sympathies, who described their project as the 'bastard offspring of Talmudism'.

The Revised Standard Version was not solely attacked for having a Jew on its committee. The most dramatic opposition came shortly after its publication in 1952 from North Carolina. Luther Hux, a conservatively inclined Baptist pastor, was horrified to discover that in the new version Isaiah was no longer prophesying that a virgin would give birth; instead the mother of the child who would be named Immanuel was described merely as 'a young woman'.[17] This was the revival of an ancient controversy; its origins went back to the Septuagint's translation of the Hebrew word *almah* as virgin, although elsewhere rendering the same word as 'maiden'.[18] Hux, who no doubt knew what he was looking for when he turned to Isaiah, was well aware of the textual implications. Replacing the virgin with a young woman went to the heart of a major interpretative dispute between Christianity and Judaism: was Isaiah foretelling the birth of Jesus, or not?

Hux was not a man to stand idly by when what he believed to be the integrity of the Bible was challenged. In the spirit of the medieval inquisitors, he announced that he would burn the new Bible. On a Sunday evening at the end of 1952, Hux delivered a two-hour sermon before leading his congregation out into the cold November air. He gave each one an American flag, held aloft a copy of the Revised Standard Version, ripped out the page containing the offending translation and burned it. Sensing that act was somewhat less dramatic than the promise, he had only burned a single page, he yelled, 'I never said I would burn the Bible. I said I would burn a fraud.'[19] An anonymous Bible burner was more courageous. A few weeks after Hux's histrionics the chairman of the Standard Bible Committee received a box full of ashes. Its accompanying note proclaimed that it was the remains of a copy of the Revised Standard Version.

Controversy over the Revised Standard Version continued throughout the 1950s. It was not just its theology which came under attack. Senator Joseph McCarthy's House Committee on Un-American Activities investigated the translators for Communist sympathies. In 1960 the US Air Force Reserve published a training manual which warned recruits to avoid the RSV Bible which, so they claimed, had included among its translators thirty people 'affiliated with "Communist fronts"'.[20] When the matter became public, the manual was speedily withdrawn and the Defence Secretary apologized.

Arguments even raged over the non-appearance of italics. The Bible's predecessor, the American Standard Version, had followed the King James in italicizing all words which did not appear in the original Hebrew or Greek, but which had been interpolated into the text for clarity. This allowed readers to distinguish between the 'real' Bible and editorial adjustments. The Revised Standard Version, however, in the interests of readability, left the italics out. The Version's many opponents complained that it could not be trusted as a literal translation. And notwithstanding a few minor amendments, designed to soothe ruffled conservative feelings, appearing in subsequent editions, the controversy did not abate. Instead it led to yet another similarly named translation appearing a few years later; this one was the New American Standard Bible, distinguished by its literal translation, and use of italics. The New Testament appeared in 1963 and the complete Bible in 1971. The Bible bandwagon just kept on rolling.

A similar process had taken place in England, beginning in 1946. A coalition of scholars drawn from British universities and representing all the main Protestant denominations began working on a Bible 'to be made in the language of the present day'.[21] The New Testament was published in 1961 with the Old Testament and Apocrypha following nine years later.

The New English Bible's desire to reflect present-day language immediately placed it under fire. Among its many critics, the poet T. S. Eliot wrote 'We are…entitled to expect from a panel chosen from among the most distinguished scholars of our day at least a work of dignified mediocrity. When we find that we are offered something far below that modest level, something which astonishes in its combination of the vulgar, the trivial, and the pedantic, we ask in alarm: "What is happening to the English language?"'[22]

The New English Bible, despite some initial interest, never really took off. Finding that elusive balance between a modern literary style and dignified, religious gravitas had, for its translators, proved just too difficult.

Jewish Bibles

By now, Moses Mendelssohn's German translation no longer stood unchallenged as the only modern Jewish version. Those factors which had persuaded Mendelssohn to translate the Hebrew Bible into German, particularly the desire for Jewish emancipation and social integration, were now tempered by the less welcome reality of assimilation and loss of religious identity.

Samson Raphael Hirsch, the leader of German Jewish orthodoxy, was troubled by conflicting pressures, all of which, he believed, posed a direct threat to the beliefs and practices of the Jewish religion. Apart from the corrosive impact of assimilation, his orthodoxy was burdened by the rise of a new, modernizing movement, with a reformist agenda that uncomfortably challenged the religious status quo. There was also the new academic discipline of Higher Bible Criticism, flying in the face of the traditional Jewish belief that the Pentateuch, or Torah, had been revealed in its entirety to Moses; hypothesizing that it was in fact a composite work constructed from several different, very human, documents.

Hirsch, who notwithstanding his orthodoxy was no dyed-in-the-wool conservative, set out to address these challenges, not by refuting them, but by presenting an alternative worldview. His translation, which was published in stages together with a voluminous commentary between 1867 and 1878, offered an interpretation which reinforced the traditional Jewish understanding of Bible authorship, and promoted his own vision of the positive interaction between traditional religion, contemporary thought and scientific progress. It was a monumental, if intellectual, religious response to modernity.

His work was translated into English in 1956; a rare example of a translation being translated into yet another language; somewhat reminiscent of Wycliffe's fourteenth-century rendering of the Vulgate into English. The difference is that the Vulgate was regarded as a canonical text, whereas Hirsch's work was the product of a scholar whose commentary was as essential for understanding his ideas as was his translation.

Germany was not the only place where Jewish translations were produced. During the course of the nineteenth century, French, Dutch, Russian,

Hungarian, Italian and English versions of the Old Testament appeared. But unlike the vast majority of Christian translations of the period, these translations nearly always appeared alongside the original Hebrew text. For the Jews, the sanctity of the Bible lay in its language; the translations were merely an aid to understanding for those who were not fluent in Hebrew.

Among the Jewish Bibles, most nineteenth-century English versions were based on the Authorized or Revised Versions, with a nod to the Hebrew scholarship of German translators like Mendelssohn and Hirsch. It wasn't until 1892 that the recently formed Jewish Publication Society of America decided that the time had come to start afresh. As was now traditional in Bible translation projects, a committee was established, each member being charged with translating a particular book. The first volumes began to appear in 1903 and the full translation fourteen years later. For most of the twentieth century, it was the pre-eminent English translation of the Bible for Jews. Its supremacy was only seriously challenged when the English language had evolved so far that the translation's conscious aping of the elegant but archaic style of the King James version, with its *thees* and *thous*, *hithers* and *thithers*, began to feel just too antiquated for a religion which, like all twentieth-century faiths, was more anxious than ever to speak to people who lived in the present not the past.

Many, more modern Jewish translations followed, not all of them elegant. In the introduction to his particular contribution to the field, the American scholar Robert Alter noted that in the King James version the problem had been a 'shaky sense of Hebrew' whereas now, in the modern versions, the problem is 'a shaky sense of English'.[23]

Alter's comment throws a spotlight on the tension inherent in any translation, but particularly of a work as old, well known and venerable as the Bible. On the one hand the translator wants to convey the style, rhythm and poetic sense of the original; on the other hand the imperative is to communicate its meaning with clarity and accuracy. It is often a circle that cannot be squared.

The dilemma can be seen clearly in the revised translation that the Jewish Publication Society issued in 1985, which has formed the basis of many more recent editions. When Reuben returns to find his brothers have sold Joseph into slavery he is distraught and declares, in dramatic, alliterative Hebrew, *va'ani ana ani-va.* A literal translation is 'The boy is not and I, where have I come?' which makes sense in classical Hebrew but not in modern English. Understandably the 1985 translators tried to find a more evocative solution. They decided upon 'The boy is gone, now what am I to do?' It's the sort of thing one might say when discovering one's train ticket has disappeared. It scarcely conveys Reuben's despair and it completely misses the poetry and the alliteration.

When it comes down to it, translation is always a matter of choice. One reason why the twentieth century saw so many alternative English versions is the near impossibility of producing an 'ideal' translation.

The Jerusalem Bible

By the middle of the twentieth century, innumerable Protestant editions of the Bible had been published, for an untold number of reasons. Some took account of new manuscript discoveries, others sought to modernize archaic language, to correct perceived inaccuracies or to standardize competing versions. But up to now, this multiplicity of Bible versions had been a Protestant phenomenon. It was not replicated in the Catholic Church, nor to any significant degree within Judaism.

The centralized structure of Catholicism, with ecclesiastical authority vested firmly in the Vatican, meant that any published Bible which did not carry the papal imprimatur could not, by definition, be considered a Catholic version. Significantly, the powers of the Catholic Church to censor works which were doctrinally incorrect, or to prohibit them altogether, proved a powerful disincentive to the production of new Catholic translations.

Since 1582, English-speaking Catholics had used the version originally prepared in Douay in northern France, by refugees fleeing persecution during the reign of Elizabeth I. The version had undergone a substantial revision in 1750 when the Catholic bishop Richard Challoner modernized its unwieldy language, and the language of the New Testament had again been updated in 1941. But from the publication of the Rheims–Douay version onwards, every revision had been based on the Latin Vulgate. This was to change in 1943 when the Pope issued an encyclical letter permitting translation from the Hebrew and Greek.

A group of French Dominicans in Jerusalem were first off the mark, with their 1956 publication of *La Bible de Jérusalem*, an annotated Bible. Like all Catholic Bibles, it included the Apocrypha, books which did not make it into the Jewish scriptures and which were subsequently excluded by Protestants when Luther's emphasis on *sola scriptura*, 'only by Scripture',[24] necessitated a return to the Hebrew Old Testament.

La Bible de Jérusalem was seized upon by English-speaking Catholics anxious for a modern version in their own language. It was soon to be; *The Jerusalem Bible* appeared in 1966, acknowledging its debt to the French version. Cardinal Heenan, the leader of Britain's Catholics, called it 'a genuinely contemporary version of Holy Scripture...a landmark in the evolution of Catholic culture'.[25] The editor, in his foreword, explained that the dual purpose of the new translation was to keep abreast of the times, by recasting the Bible in contemporary language, and to deepen theological thought through annotations and explanations. The notes, he explained, were a direct translation from the French. The English translation was made from the Hebrew and Greek, but cross-referenced against the French version when questions arose. And although the editor acknowledged that it was not his job to impose his own style on the translation, nevertheless literary quality was important. Among those whom he consulted on style was *Lord of the Rings* author J. R. R. Tolkien.

Predictably, the Jerusalem Bible was not universally acclaimed. Not everyone agreed with the editor's assessment that the Jerusalem Bible preserved 'an entirely faithful version of the ancient texts'.[26] A review in the *Westminster Theological Journal* accused the translators of a 'careless, inconsistent, capricious handling of the text of the original'. Although 'attractive in format, vigorous in expression, often felicitous and vital in its wording', its 'cavalier treatment of the Received Text' rendered it 'unsafe for doctrinal study or biblical exposition'.[27]

The public liked it though, even if the original edition with its detailed notes was too scholarly for many tastes. A couple of years after publication the editors brought out a new edition, 'which would bring the modern clarity of the text before the ordinary reader, and open to him the results of modern researches without either justifying them at length in literary and historical notes or linking them with doctrinal studies'.[28] A further revision, incorporating more inclusive language, appeared in 1985 under the title *New Jerusalem Bible*. Edited by Henry Wansbrough it was approved for devotional study but has never received approbation for liturgical use. It nevertheless remains one of the most popular Catholic Bibles.

12

Reworking The Bible

Sexist Language and Gender Politics

The French Jerusalem Bible was revised in 1973 and a dozen years later its English equivalent followed suit. The most noticeable difference between the old and updated versions was the introduction of attempts to deal, to some degree, with the problem of male-orientated language. The ancient Bible, both the Old and New Testaments, was written and compiled in male-centred, patriarchal societies. Both Testaments tend to use the masculine form when speaking of men and women collectively, and both assume the existence of a male deity. For nearly the whole of the Bible's existence nobody gave this much thought, it was just the way things were. But by the latter part of the twentieth century people began to regard this masculine bias as anomalous; society was rapidly tending towards egalitarianism, discrimination on the grounds of gender was recognized as unpalatable and many women were assuming roles that for centuries had been the exclusive domain of men. Yet the Bible, in common with all other ancient, and not so ancient, literature still promoted a male-centric view of the world. The 1985 *New Jerusalem Bible* was one of the first to try to respond to this dilemma.

Had the problem simply been one of translation, if the original Hebrew and Greek had been written in gender-neutral language, matters would have been easily resolved. But the source of the problem was not in the translation, it lay in the original languages, and the issue was wider than just the default use of masculine nouns and pronouns when referring to groups of mixed gender. The vast majority of Bible stories, in both Testaments, are about men; the number of prominent biblical women is small compared to the hordes of men. And since nothing, short of rewriting the Bible, could be done about the dominance of male protagonists, it became all the more urgent for those pressing for a more egalitarian religious environment to argue for something to be done about the unnecessary use of masculine-orientated language, when gender-neutral options were available.

The *New Jerusalem Bible* takes the credit for being the first Bible to try to tackle the issue. In the foreword, the editor stated that considerable effort had been made 'to soften or avoid the inbuilt preference of the English language, a preference now found so offensive by some people, for the masculine'.[1] But despite the considerable efforts, the *New Jerusalem Bible* appears a bit haphazard in the way it deals with masculine language. It does indeed sometimes replace generic references to men with neutral words like 'anyone' but it is just as likely to miss an opportunity. For instance, it treats the false prophet in Deuteronomy 13 as a man, even though it could just as easily have used neutral language; after all, the Old Testament explicitly refers to women who were prophets.[2] Nor is it consistent. In Leviticus it replaces 'a man' with 'anyone' but, inexplicably, in the same verse it introduces the word 'he' as a substitute for the Hebrew's gender-neutral pronoun 'you'.[3]

The *New Jerusalem Bible* pioneered the use of gender-inclusive language, but the 1990 *New Revised Standard Version*, the latest incarnation of the Bible, a page of which had been burned in North Carolina, was far more thorough and systematic in its use of neutral speech. Bruce Metzger, the driving force behind both the *Revised* and *New Revised Standard Versions*, wrote in the preface that one of his committee's considerations was to eliminate masculine language in references to men and women, provided this could be done without altering passages that reflected the historical reality of patriarchal societies.

Metzger, who stands head and shoulders above all others as the Bible historian par excellence as well as a translator, summed up for those who were perplexed by the proliferation of Revised, Standard and Authorized versions, that 'the New Revised Standard Version of the Bible is an authorized revision of the Revised Standard Version, published in 1952, which was a revision of the American Standard Version, published in 1901, which, in turn, embodied earlier revisions of the King James Version, published in 1611. In the course of time, the King James Version came to be regarded as "the Authorized Version". It is as succinct a summary as one is likely to get of the evolution of the English Bible, and its names, in North America.[4]

But even a Bible which set out to eliminate unnecessary, male-orientated language could not hope to free itself of all charges of political incorrectness or sexism. Over the last few decades new, even more politically correct versions have appeared. But of course, as Bible versions depart from the direct and literal meaning of the original text, different techniques of translation are needed to determine the most appropriate renderings. Modern, politically sensitive versions tend to use the technique of 'dynamic equivalence', a theory developed by the linguist and Bible translator Eugene Nida.

Traditional, formal translations look for the closest grammatical and literal match for any particular phrase or word. Dynamic equivalence concentrates more on conveying its sense, style and meaning. The result is a looser translation but one which, the translator hopes, better conveys in a modern world the original intentions of the ancient author.

But while dynamic equivalence is a valid and acceptable contemporary technique, it is susceptible to misinterpretation, by those who don't fully understand it, as 'loose' or free translation. It can be misunderstood as opening the door to polemical or agenda-driven translations, in which the translator is more concerned to make a particular point than to convey the meaning accurately. And if this all sounds as if it is getting a little too technical, it should start to make more sense when we look at one of the most outspoken of all polemical Bible versions, the Queen James Bible.

The Queen James Bible

Much of the Bible's male-centred language can be eliminated by substituting neutral words. The word 'he' when referring to either a man or woman can be replaced by 'one' or, at a pinch, 'they'. The same can be done for more complex phrases, for example Psalm 8.4, which in the King James Version reads: 'What is man, that thou art mindful of him and the son of man, that thou visitest him?'

In Today's New International Version, it became: 'What are mere mortals that you are mindful of them, human beings that you care for them?'[5]

But some things cannot be dealt with through translation techniques alone. The Old Testament contains regulations to control slavery. But it doesn't forbid slavery and modern translations which substitute the word 'servant' for 'slave' don't really solve the problem; all that has changed is that the person who has to sell themselves to pay off their debts, or who is captured in war, is called a servant, not a slave.[6] There are limits to what one can do with translation.

An even more intractable problem looms over homosexuality. The Book of Leviticus[7] prohibits homosexuality between men (but is silent about women). Paul's letter to the Romans[8] also seems to condemn gay sex. This offends many gays who feel that, in the twenty-first century, faith should not discriminate against sexuality. But explicit statements such as these cannot simply be translated away. They can however be excised, if one is not too particular about the integrity of the text or formal translation techniques.

In November 2012 an anonymous group in America published the Queen James Bible. Their stated aim was 'to resolve interpretive ambiguity in the Bible as it pertains to homosexuality'.[9] They identified eight biblical verses which suggest that homosexuality is a sin and set out to rephrase them, to correct what they considered to be the erroneous view of previous translations.

The anonymous editors of the Queen James Bible based their edition on the King James version because they believed it to be the most popular, and because they approved of its poetic and ceremonial style. But crucially, it seems that they made their choice because James I was, in their words, 'a well known bisexual', who was known in his court as 'Queen James'. It's true that rumours of James's sexuality have floated around ever since his reign; he was condemned for his preferences by the eighteenth-century reformer Jeremy Bentham,[10] and more recently David M. Bergeron has published what he calls James's homoerotic correspondence with three of his courtiers.[11] But whether he was actually known, four hundred years ago, as 'Queen James' is another matter.

The editors of the Queen James Bible have worked hard at trying to eliminate the censorious view of homosexuality from the Bible. Their efforts transcend the principles of translation and even of biblical interpretation. In many ways they seem to have tried too hard. Genesis 19.5 has the men of Sodom demanding that Lot bring out his angelic visitors into the street, 'that we may know them'. There is a tradition in both Christian and Jewish interpretation that the word 'know' in this sentence is to be understood sexually, in the same sense as in Genesis 4.1 'and Adam knew his wife Eve'. But this is an interpretation, it is not explicit in the text; and if the verse does refer to homosexual sex, it could just as easily mean it to be consensual as forced. There seems little justification for the Queen James Bible's rendition 'Bring them out unto us, that we may rape and humiliate them'. Rather than achieving their stated aim of editing the Bible to prevent homophobic interpretations, they seem to have exacerbated it.

The editors of the Queen James Bible believed that the biblical references to homosexuality were ambiguous. They set out to resolve these ambiguities. They didn't translate the offending sections of text, they amended them to fit in with their sense of how they should be interpreted. Maybe they should have paid more attention to the work of John J. McNeill. In his seminal work, *The Church and the Homosexual*, he suggests that, when the Bible is read in its original historical and cultural context, its apparent opposition to homosexuality disappears. In the Old Testament, he suggests, homosexuality was condemned because of its use in idolatrous rites; it was proscribed in order to eliminate idolatry. In the New Testament too, McNeill argues, the terminology used suggests an aversion to male prostitution rather than homosexuality itself. McNeill's scholarship is rigorous; his conclusions are as controversial as the subject he tackles.

For all their obvious shortcomings the compilers of the Queen James Bible were sincere in their motives. Their readers can understand them, even if not necessarily agreeing with them. Unlike another Bible, which, in places, took such liberties with the text that it is almost impossible to fathom what was going through its editor's mind. His name is David Stern, he is a well-respected academic theologian. His Bible, which appended his own translation of the New Testament to a reworked version of the 1917 translation issued by the Jewish Publication Society of America, is known as the *Complete Jewish Bible*.

Eccentric Messianic Translations

David Stern is a messianic Jew, one who observes some Jewish practices while believing in the divinity of Jesus. His intention in compiling his *Complete Jewish Bible* was to demonstrate the Jewish provenance and character of the New Testament. One of the ways he did this was to transliterate names into their Hebrew pronunciation, another was to throw in Hebrew words when, presumably, he felt it would sound more authentic. It makes for heavy reading, but there is a logic in his method.

Where his Bible seems to completely lose its way is when Stern interjects Yiddish slang. Yiddish is an amalgam of several languages, mainly Hebrew and German. Its earliest roots are most probably in the tenth century. It wasn't even a twinkle in the eye of a first-century Jewish-Christian. Yet several Yiddishisms crop up in his translation of Luke. In 10.4 the disciples are warned not to *shmoose* on the road; in verse 8 of the next chapter 'importunity' becomes *chutzpah* while the widow in 18.5 is described as a *nudnik*. In John 10.19–20 the Judeans say 'He's *meshugga*! Why do you listen to him?'[12] One gets the impression that, if he could, David Stern would have dressed Jesus and his disciples in *bekishes* and *shtreimels*, the traditional eighteenth-century Polish coats and fur hats worn by many Hassidic Jews.

Far from imparting a Jewish flavour to his translation of the New Testament, Stern seems to have turned it into a comedy routine. When Bruce Metzger, the acclaimed Bible historian, asked Stern why he had included Yiddish words he was told that he wanted to add 'ethnic spice'.[13]

But even Stern's eccentric translation appears conventional when compared to another, which appeared in 2002. Philip Goble's *Orthodox Jewish Bible* is a strange amalgam of transliterated Hebrew words, usually the nouns, and English verbs. When Adam and Eve are expelled from the Garden of Eden the rigours of scratching a living from the soil are described to them, in the King James Version, as 'Thorns also and thistles shall it bring forth to thee; and thou shalt eat the herb of the field'.[14] Goble, who can't resist a transliterated Hebrew noun, prefers '*Kotz* also and *dardar* shall it bring forth to thee and thou shalt eat the *esev* of the *sadeh*'. The archaic English is about the only intelligible part of the sentence.

The translator, in his foreword, suggests that 'those who read the Bible through Gentile spectacles need to take another look'. Unfortunately, unless the reader is fluent in Hebrew and English, or is prepared to spend hours wading through the profusion of notes and references which continually interrupt the text, taking a look is more likely to result in befuddlement than in inspiration.

The Bible Business is Big Business

Wycliffe Bible Translators, named after the fourteenth-century pioneer of the English Bible, are an American missionary and evangelist organization. They specialize in producing Bible translations for missionaries, mainly those working in the Third World. According to *Forbes* magazine, in 2012 Wycliffe ranked at number seventy in the hierarchy of largest American charities, with a revenue of 167 million dollars.[15] Bible translation is big business. As Wycliffe translators have found out, it can also be an extremely troubling enterprise.

Since they were founded in 1942, Wycliffe have taken part in over 700 Bible translation projects. They have produced translations in languages spoken in more than ninety countries. They claim that, in addition to their underlying evangelical agenda, their work can lead to 'better health as a result of access to medical information, economic growth due to the acquisition of marketable skills, and the preservation of culture thanks to a written history'.[16]

For years Wycliffe quietly got on with their work. Despite *Forbes* rating them as one of America's largest charities, very few people beyond the missionary and evangelical world had ever heard of them. That all started to change in 2011.

Their troubles began when they decided to produce a translation of the New Testament for Muslim readers. Acutely aware of Islamic sensitivities, they feared that certain key phrases in the New Testament, such as 'Son of God', might both offend and be misinterpreted; some people may assume that Jesus's birth was the product of a sexual relationship between God and Mary. So for this particular translation they decided to bend their long-established translation rules.

Wherever they felt an ambiguity might be perceived in the text, they resorted to synonyms. They replaced 'Son of God' with phrases like 'beloved son who comes from God'. They found alternatives for 'God the Father' and other potentially misleading attributions.

But this apparently harmless solution quickly had repercussions. As soon as news of their new translation reached the evangelical community, a storm broke out. Wycliffe, and their partner organizations in the field, found themselves accused of falsifying Scripture.

Of course, this could be seen as not so much a case of bending the rules of Bible translation, as of producing effective marketing material. The job of the missionary is, after all, to persuade non-believers to accept the principles of a new religion, of which they probably have little or no knowledge. On the face of it, all the Wycliffe translators were trying to do was to smooth the path of those they were addressing, to bring them to their new faith without putting too many theological obstacles in their way. They weren't the first to take account of the sensibilities of those they were trying to convert; previous translations of the New Testament for Muslims had used the name Allah and, as long ago as 1809, William Carey, a missionary pioneer in India, had substituted the Hindu name Ishwar for that of God in his Bengali translation. There were precedents for culturally sensitive compromise. What Wycliffe did, so it seemed, was little different.

But that's not how some other evangelicals saw it. In their eyes the Bible is not marketing collateral to be translated every which way depending on the proclivities of the audience. The backlash from evangelical churches was fierce, and loud. One missionary reported that 'The reaction of church leaders was violent. We received threats from pastors and Christian leaders.'[17]

The Assemblies of God, a Pentecostal alliance with over sixty million affiliated members, reacted with a mixture of rage and despair. It announced that it would review its relationship with Wycliffe. The Anglican bishop of Tasmania, who seemed to have a much clearer understanding of the disputational implications than the Wycliffe translators, charged that 'Changing fundamental words of Scripture such as "father" and "son" will also fuel the Muslim claim that the Bible is corrupted, full of errors and has been abrogated by the Qur'an and the example of Muhammad.'[18]

The argument raged in evangelical circles until finally, in 2012, Wycliffe, and their associates SIL International, agreed to submit their translation techniques to an external review, to be carried out by the World Evangelical Alliance.

The review panel, an international body comprising some of the world's leading Bible scholars, linguists and missionary experts, reported in April 2013. They recommended, among other things, that whenever the words 'father' or 'son' refer to God or Jesus, they should be translated in such a way that they still suggest the closeness of a familial relationship, without implying a physical one. Modifying adjectives could be used, so that 'father', they suggested, could become heavenly father; son could be preceded by the word 'eternal'. The panel also recommended that the translators used local focus groups to test how a proposed translation might actually be received in practice. Significantly, they also recommended that 'in addition to translating Scripture, translators consider additional ways of communicating the message'[19] to Muslim audiences. In other words, Wycliffe Bible Translators might want to think twice before translating the Bible. Wycliffe translators accepted the report in full.

Two things stand out in this episode. The first is that, however innocuous the process of Bible translation might seem to the outsider, even in the twenty-first century it remains a highly emotive and sensitive business.

The other is that, of all the 700 translation projects across ninety countries that Wycliffe have been involved in, the only time controversy has erupted on this scale is when they produced a text for the benefit of Muslims. It beggars belief that of their vast global audience, Wycliffe Bible Translators believed that only Muslims would have found phrases like 'Son of God' disturbing. Yet this was the only time they felt the need to amend a translation.

One doesn't need to go back to the Crusades to see why Wycliffe thought it important to tread carefully but it does force us to wonder what the real reasons were for their departure from their normal translation practices. It is hardly a surprise that other evangelical churches reacted with anger.

13

The Future for the Translated Bible

The act of translating the Bible really should not be contentious. After all, the Bible is the most famous book ever published; Guinness World Records estimates that five billion copies have been printed since 1815.[1] Not only is it a foundational text of Western culture, the cornerstone of the Judeo-Christian religious tradition, it is also a literary masterpiece in its own right. One need not be religious to read it, and although very few people have ploughed through it all, no one can claim to be well read without having dipped into it. Like any other book, making the Bible available in translation seems to be a perfectly natural and reasonable activity. And yet, as we have seen, translating the Bible has frequently been controversial, even at times murderous.

The controversies have not always been about power. Yes, throughout history religion and power have walked hand in hand. They still do, and not only in contemporary theocracies. Religious lobbies are powerful in many democratic nations; even where there is no formal alliance, those with similar beliefs share vested interests and tend towards political homogeneity. However distasteful we may find it, the conjugality of religion and power explains why in earlier times, a dominant religious faction might have wanted to restrict the availability of the Bible to a particular language or an 'authorized' version. What is harder to understand is the extent to which the medieval Church was prepared to go, the levels of violence and persecution to which they were willing to stoop, to prevent 'unauthorized' versions appearing.

Although perceived challenges to the authority of the medieval Church account for the most dramatic and violent episodes in the translated Bible's history, the majority of controversies have been about authenticity and human emotion. The Septuagint's conflict with the Hebrew Old Testament, Jerome's desire to produce a truly reliable Latin version, arguments between Jewish and Christian theologians over whether Isaiah's *almah* referred to a virgin who would give birth or just a young woman, contemporary striving towards inclusive language; these are all struggles over the authentic reading of the biblical text, its intended meaning and the best way of translating it. It is interesting to consider what might have happened had the Gospel of Matthew been transmitted in Hebrew rather than in Greek; if, rather than translating it as *parthenos*, Matthew's author had used the same word, *almah*, as had Isaiah. Judaism and Christianity would still have differed theologically over Mary's virginity, but translations such as the Revised Standard Version would, presumably, no longer attract censure for translating Isaiah's *almah* in the same way as the Jews do, as a young woman. Rather than burning the offending page from the Revised Standard Version, Pastor Luther Hux would have had to dream up another way of shamelessly grandstanding.

Nor should we discount the emotional element, the irrational discomfort that irks some Bible readers when confronted by an unfamiliar translation. Many of the more recent controversies over the use of modern or ameliorated language owe more to the psychological and emotional attachment that Bible readers have to the particular version they prefer, than to any theological consideration.

It is probably emotion which accounts for the phenomenon known as King James Onlyism. Supporters of the King James Only movement assert that, of all Bible versions, this one alone represents the unchanging divine word. That, without exception, all later translations are either inaccurate, based on corrupt manuscripts or, ominously, are the work of Satan. The synchronic fundamentalism of King James Onlyism has prompted vigorous debate, with dozens of websites dedicated to refuting the arguments of the movement's followers. The underlying question is, to what degree are the King James's acolytes driven by an untroubled belief and conviction, and how much is due to their emotional attachment to its majestic origins and magnificent language? A similar question can, of course, be asked of all religious believers; is your faith driven by personal insight, or is it something so comforting that you cannot but help believe in it?

So what is the future for the translated Bible? For some time now, Bible translations have mainly been attempts to improve or ameliorate versions whose theological battles have already been fought and disposed of. Gender-neutral versions, responding to a perceived need brought about by social change, have been the only significant exception to this drive for perfection. By and large there seems to be no need for any further translations of the Bible, at least until a particular language has evolved to such a degree that the current version appears antiquated.

Good commentaries and interpretations are almost certainly more important today than new translations. Bibles have always been accompanied by explanations; Origen and Jerome were among the first Christian exegetes, with Philo and the rabbis of the first two centuries CE initiating the Jewish interpretative tradition. Bibles like the Queen James may well have proved to be more valuable as a commentary; after all it wasn't really necessary to publish a translation of the whole Bible in order to respond to just eight verses of seemingly homophobic readings. Similarly, David Stern's Jewish New Testament, with its anachronistic yiddishisms, would probably have had more impact as a glossary; indeed Stern is one of the contributors to the recently published *Jewish Annotated New Testament* which, through the use of notes and articles appended to the New Revised Standard Version, draws out the Jewish context within which Christianity emerged.[2]

But, even though the apparent need for them has virtually been eliminated, more translations have been made in the last century than ever before. So the chances are they will probably carry on appearing; sometimes it seems as if nearly every Hebrew and Greek scholar with a personal interest in their religion has the makings of a new Bible translation in their back pocket. King Solomon, regarded in the Jewish tradition as the epitome of wisdom and the author of the book of Ecclesiastes, wrote: 'Of making many books there is no end.'[3] And who would dare argue with him?

Notes

Introduction

1 Nehemiah 8.8; Acts 2.1–11. Neither of these sources explicitly says that the Bible was translated. But that's how they have each been interpreted in their respective traditions.

Chapter 1

1 Canfora, 1987.

2 Canfora, 1987 p. 18, quoting Plutarch, *Short Sayings of Kings and Commanders*.

3 Stothard, 2013.

4 Canfora, 1987 p. 20, quoting the twelfth-century grammarian of the Greek language, John Tzetzes, in his *Prolegomena de Comoedia*.

5 Stothard, 2013.

6 Shutt, 1985; Wasserstein, 2006.

7 Aristeas doesn't mention the name of the island but it is clear from the context, as well as from Philo's later account, that he meant Pharos.

8 Nina Collins challenges the view that Aristeas's account is inaccurate. She places the date of the composition of the Septuagint at 281 BCE (Collins, 2000).

9 Canfora, 1987; Wasserstein, 2006.

10 Metzger, 2001.

11 Philo, *On The Life of Moses II*, 25–44 (V–VII) in both the Yonge and Thackery translations.

12 Metzger, 2001.

13 Philo probably copied from Aristeas. It is possible that both made use of the same common source, but there is no evidence for that.

14 Philo, On *The Life of Moses II*, 37 (VII).

15 Irenaeus, *Against Heresies*, 3, 21, 2–3, trans. Roberts and Donaldson, cited in Kirby, 2001–2013, http://www.earlychristianwritings.com/text/irenaeus-book3.html.

16 Genesis 1.26.

17 Genesis 11.7.

18 Babylonian Talmud Megilla 9a–b and elsewhere. The Talmud lists fifteen changes that the translators made, including Leviticus 11.6 because, according to the Talmud, they feared that the Greek translation of the Hebrew word for hare, *lagos*, sounded like the name of Ptolemy's wife (although *lagos* was actually his grandfather). Not all the divergences listed by the Talmud occur in the version of the Septuagint that we have, and there are many differences between the current version of the Septuagint and the Masoretic text which the Talmud does not list.

Of course, the Talmud does not question the authenticity of the Hebrew text in its day. The fact that some of the 'innovations' in the Alexandrian version also occur in other independent sources, e.g. the Samaritan Pentateuch and Qumran manuscripts, does not enter the Talmud's discussion. There is a huge amount of scholarship on the variant versions of the Bible, but it is beyond the scope of this book. For a brief and concise, if somewhat dated, summary see Bickerman, 1988.

19 Metzger, 2001.

20 Churton, 1861.

21 Bickerman, 1988. p. 101.

22 Wasserstein, 2006.

23 Scholarly opinion is that the Septuagint was not based on the Hebrew text current today. Today's Hebrew Bible, known as the Masoretic text, received its final form over a period of time culminating no later than the eighth century, but beginning much earlier than that. That is not to say that the Septuagint fully reflects the Hebrew text then current; if there was such a thing as a Hebrew 'original' then the Septuagint, the Masoretic text and the many other ancient versions, including the Qumran, the Samaritan and the *Peshitta* all represent divergences from it.

24 Isaiah 7.14. See also below, p. 194.

25 The Greek word *Parthenos* does not necessarily mean virgin; it cannot, for example, in Genesis 34.3, refer to Dinah who has just slept with Shechem. But Matthew clearly understands it in the sense of virgin.

26 Matthew 1.23.

27 Dines, 2004.

28 Trypho was almost certainly not the first-century Jewish sage and olive farmer, Rabbi Tarfon, as the historian Heinrich Graetz believed. Not only do the respective dates of Justin and Tarfon not match up but some of Trypho's arguments fly in the face of rabbinic opinion in Tarfon's time. See Ben Zion Bokser, *The Jewish Quarterly Review*

New Series, 64(2) (Oct. 1973) pp. 97–122 and the article by the same author in the *Encyclopedia Judaica* s.v. 'Justin Martyr'.

29 *Dialogue with Trypho,* Chapter 71, trans. Roberts and Donaldson from Kirby, 'Historical Jesus Theories', *Early Christian Writings,* cited in Kirby, 2001–2013.

30 Dines, 2004.

31 Justin, *Hortatory Address to the Greeks,* 13, trans. Roberts and Donaldson from Kirby, 'Historical Jesus Theories', *Early Christian Writings,* cited in Kirby, 2001–2013, http://www.earlychristianwritings.com/text/justinmartyr-hortatory.html.

32 Soferim 1.7.

33 Scholion to Megillat Ta'anit s.v. Tevet. The sources in this and the previous note are quite late but, as is often the case with rabbinic works, are likely to reflect earlier teachings still in circulation. Conversely a case can be made for arguing that the views themselves were indeed late and were expressed by people looking back on the historical consequences for the Jews of the Septuagint's adoption by the Church.

34 *Faith, Fact & Fantasy,* C. F. D. Moule, HarperCollins: London, 1964, p. 106.

35 Although these were Jewish translations, those fragments which have survived were transmitted mainly through Christian channels. One reason is that the Jews nearly always spoke in the vernacular of the lands in which they lived. A Greek translation was only useful for Greek-speaking Jews, who became progressively fewer as global Greek influence diminished. However, Greek, as the language of the New Testament, remained important for Christians for far longer. Another reason is that as a result of the insecure and volatile conditions in which the Jews lived, the only written materials they preserved were those in everyday use, i.e. mainstream, rabbinic texts which were invariably written in Hebrew sprinkled with Aramaic.

36 For a thorough but unconvincing attempt to equate Aquila with Onkelos see Silverstone, 1931.

37 Silverstone, 1931.

38 Hayward, 1995.

39 Salvesen, 1991.

40 Salvesen, 1991.

41 Salvesen, 1991.

42 Epiphanius of Salamis, 'De Mensuris et Ponderibus', 15–17, http://www.tertullian.org/fathers/epiphanius_weights_03_text.htm.

43 Babylonian Talmud Yevamot 72a.

44 Kelly, 1998.

45 Dines, 2004.

46 Augustine of Hippo, *On Christian Doctrine*, 2.1, 5.22 (Schaff, 1890).

47 Rajak, 2009.

48 Matthew 19.12.

49 Eusebius Pamphilus, *Church History* 6.8, in *A Select Library of the Nicene and Post-Nicene Fathers of the Christian Church*, Second Series, Vol. 1, P. Schaff, 1890 (Christian Classics Ethereal Library), http://www.ccel.org/ccel/schaff/npnf201.iii.xi.viii.html.

50 McGuckin, 2004.

51 Metzger, 2001.

52 McGuckin, 2004.

Chapter 2

1 Eusebius Pamphilus, *Church History* 1.13, in *A Select Library of the Nicene and Post-Nicene Fathers of the Christian Church*, Second Series, Vol. 1, P. Schaff, 1890 (Christian Classics Ethereal Library), http://www.ccel.org/ccel/schaff/npnf201.iii.vi.xiii.html.

2 Liebermann, 1942.

3 Mishnah Yoma 3.10. In the Mishnah, Izates's name is Monbaz. The biblical passage is Numbers 5.11–31.

4 Sabar, 2013. The Syrian Christian village of Maaloula was possibly the last place where Aramaic was spoken as a first language. At the time of writing its Christian population had fled because of the Syrian civil war and the future of Aramaic as a living language may be coming to an end.

5 Weitzman, 1999a. Evidence from within the text itself, e.g. 1 Chronicles 29.19 which reflects anti-gnostic phraseology in the Kaddish, suggests a date no earlier than the third century, while quotations from the *Peshitta* by the Syrian Church Father Aphrahat set the end date at 344.

6 E.g. 2 Chronicles 15.5–7, quoted in Weitzman, 1999b, p. 7.

7 Bickerman, 1988.

8 In Tosefta Shabbat 14.2 (compiled in the third century) Rabbi Halafta recalls a *Targum* of Job being brought to Rabban Gamaliel who was sitting on a step on the Temple mount.

9 There are suggestions that in some Greek-speaking Jewish communities the weekly reading was made from one of the Greek translations. See Charles Perrot, 'The Reading of the Bible in the Ancient Synagogue', *Mikra: Text, Translation, Reading and Interpretation of the Hebrew Bible in Ancient Judaism and Early Christianity*, ed. Martin Jan Muldar and Harry Sysling, Philadelphia: Fortress Press, 1988, pp. 137–59.

Perrot adduces M. Megillah 1.8 and 2.1, M. Yad 4.5 and particularly T. Megillah 3.13 (4.13) to suggest that Greek was 'surely' read in Jerusalem's Hellenistic synagogues (p. 155). But T. Megillah only refers to 'foreign-speaking synagogues' where not enough people can read Hebrew; the implication is that this was unusual. See also Meir Bar-Ilan, *Writing in Ancient Israel and Early Judaism*, Part Two, in the same volume, who extends the idea to suggest that the Torah was also read in various communities in Egyptian, Elamite or the language of the Medes.

10 Nehemiah 8.8. The word that we have translated as 'with an interpretation' is often rendered as 'clearly' or 'distinctly'. But that suggests that they articulated well, whereas the context and the usual meaning of the Hebrew is about explaining, not articulating.

11 Babylonian Talmud Megillah 3a.

12 The liturgical role of a translator is also found in the early Church. A report by a Christian pilgrim in the fourth century mentions a Greek-speaking bishop in Jerusalem who, when preaching, had a presbyter standing alongside him, to translate his sermon into Aramaic. Griffith, 2013, citing John Wilkinson (trans.), *Egeria's Travels to the Holy Land: Newly Translated with Supporting Documents and Notes* (Jerusalem: Ariel Publishing House, 1981), p. 46.

13 Alexander, 1988.

14 Babylonian Talmud Gittin 56b.

15 Dio Cassius, 67.14. Flavius Clemens is often equated with the Apostolic Father, Clement of Rome, but the earliest sources suggest otherwise (Lampe, 2006).

16 Mishnah Megillah 4.10. The priestly blessing (Numbers 6.22–27) was also not to be translated, not because it was ignominious but because it was prefaced by the words '*thus* you shall bless', i.e. in these exact, Hebrew words.

17 Jerusalem Talmud Megillah 4.1 (74d).

18 When reading from the prophets, three consecutive sentences could be delivered before pausing for the translator.

19 See for example *Targum* Pseudo-Jonathan on Exodus 22.19 and Ch. Albeck's comments in '*Halacha Hitzona b'Targumei Eretz Yisrael uv'Aggada*', B. M. Lewin Jubilee Volume, ed. J. L. Fishman (Jerusalem, 1940), pp. 95–6.

20 S. A. Kaufman, '*Targum* Pseudo Jonathan and Late Jewish Literary Aramaic', in M. Asher et al., eds, *Moshe Goshen-Gottstein: In Memoriam*, Studies in Bible and Exegesis 3, Bar Ilan University Press, Ramat Gan, 1993; E. M. Cook, *Rewriting the Bible: The Text and Language of the Pseudo-Jonathan Targum* (PhD Dissertation, University of California, Los Angeles, 1986).

21 Isaac Casaubon, a sixteenth-century Christian scholar, records hearing the *Targum* read in the synagogue in Frankfurt in 1590 (Grafton & Weinberg, 2011).

22 McNamara, 2010.

23 Moore, 1927. p. 176.

24 An excellent account of the discovery of the Genizah, and of the roles of Mrs Lewis and Mrs Smith in its discovery, is in Soskice, 2009.

25 I think it preferable to follow Sokoloff and translate *Memra* in this way, rather than adopting McNamara's translation of *Memra* as Word, which of course predetermines the point he is trying to make. Michael Sokoloff, *A Dictionary of Jewish Palestinian Aramaic*, Bar Ilan University Press, Ramat Gan, 1990.

26 *Targum* Pseudo-Jonathan to Genesis 2,8.

27 For a discussion of Logos in a targumic context, with reference to *Memra*, see McNamara, 2010.

28 (Flesher, 2011). The *Targum* in question is Pseudo-Jonathan, an interesting but relatively unimportant *Targum* in the grand scale of things, which was unknown until the thirteenth century and which happens to have a high profile because a medieval printer decided to include in it his compendium of Bible commentaries. It is still printed in what are known as 'rabbinic bibles' (*mikraot gedolot*) today.

Chapter 3

1 E.g. *Talita Kumi* (Mark 5.41); *Eli, Eli, lama sabachthani* (Matthew 27.46, Mark 15.34); *Mammon* (Matthew 6.24, Luke 16.13); *Korban* (Mark 7.11); *Raca* (Matthew 5.22).

2 This Aramaic layer is most visible in parts of the Gospel of Mark, and in a theoretical gospel called 'Q', which is thought to be the original basis of both Matthew and Luke. Martin McNamara writes that it is clear that 'an Aramaic substratum has to be reckoned with, at least as far as the Gospels and parts of the Acts of the Apostles are concerned' (McNamara, 2010) p. 247.

3 The Greek words οφειληματα and αμαρτιας in Matthew 6.12 and Luke 11.4 respectively both derive from the Aramaic חויב. The Aramaic word for sin is חטא. The King James translation of Matthew 6.12 is 'And forgive us our debts, as we forgive our debtors' and of Luke 11.4 is 'And forgive us our sins; for we also forgive every one that is indebted to us.' Yet the underlying Aramaic oral text would have been identical.

4 See, for example, Younan, 2000.

5 Tatian, *Oratio ad Grecos*, 42, quoted in Williams, 2012, p. 144.

6 Schmid, 2012. Sebastian Brock points out that if Tatian composed the *Diatessaron* while he was in Rome its original language is likely to have been Greek. If however he wrote it after he returned home he is likely to have used Syriac (Brock, 1997).

7 Soskice, 2009.

8 'Curzon's Visits to Monasteries in the Levant', *The Ecclesiologist*, Series 7, Volume 10, August 1849.

9 W. Cureton, *Remains of a Very Antient Recension of the Four Gospels in Syriac*, London: John Murray, 1858, p. ii.

10 W. Cureton, *Remains of a Very Antient Recension of the Four Gospels in Syriac*, London: John Murray, 1858, dedication page.

11 I have to confess that when writing my book *The Talmud: A Biography* I recounted the well-known tale that Mrs Smith and Mrs Gibson had rescued the manuscripts from the monastery's dining hall, where they were being used as butter dishes! I have since read Janet Soskice's excellent *Sisters of Sinai: How Two Lady Adventurers Found the Hidden Gospels* (London: Chatto & Windus, 2009), which comprehensively and convincingly refutes this account as nothing more than apocryphal. As Ecclesiastes might have said: Of researching books there is no end...'

12 Williams, 2012.

13 W. H. P. Hatch, 'The Subscription of the Chester Beatty Manuscript of the Harclean Gospels', *Harvard Theological Review*, 30 (1937), pp. 141–55, quoted in Parpulov, 2012, p. 309.

14 Kiraz, 2001.

15 Jerome, *Letter to Chromatius, Jovinus, and Eusebius*, 5, quoted in Rebenich, 2002.

16 Sutcliffe, 1975. p. 81.

17 Nirenberg, 2013.

18 Quoted in Rebenich, 2002, p. 15. The disagreement reflected the schism over the consubstantial doctrine that was dividing the Church in Antioch.

19 Rebenich, 2002.

20 Sutcliffe, 1975.

21 Metzger, 2001.

22 Jerome, 'Preface to the Four Gospels', in Jerome, *The Principal Works of St. Jerome*, ed. Philip Schaff, Grand Rapids, MI: Christian Classics Ethereal Library, 1893, p. 488, http://www.ccel.org/ccel/schaff/npnf206.vii.ii.viii.html.

23 Jerome, *Epistle* 57.5, in *Nicene and Post-Nicene Fathers*, Second Series, Vol. 6, ed. Philip Schaff and Henry Wace, trans. W. H. Fremantle, G. Lewis and W. G. Martley Buffalo, NY: Christian Literature Publishing Co., 1893), http://www.newadvent.org/fathers/3001057.htm.

24 Metzger, 2001. p. 33.

25 Rebenich, 2002.

26 Rebenich, 2002. p. 53.

27 Rebenich, 2002 p. 34, quoting Jerome's *Epistle* 22.17.

28 Op. cit., pp. 36–7, quoting Jerome's *Epistle* 22.16.

29 Jerome, 'Introduction to Book of Job', in *The Principal Works of St. Jerome*, ed. Philip Schaff, Grand Rapids, MI: Christian Classics Ethereal Library, 1893, p. 491, http://www.ccel.org/ccel/schaff/npnf206.vii.iii.viii.html.

30 Jerome, 'Preface to the Book of Hebrew Questions', in Jerome, *The Principal Works of St. Jerome*, ed. Philip Schaff, Grand Rapids, MI: Christian Classics Ethereal Library, 1893, p. 486, http://www.ccel.org/ccel/schaff/npnf206.vii.ii.v.html.

31 Jerome, 'Introduction to Book of Job, in Jerome, *The Principal Works of St. Jerome*, ed. Philip Schaff, Grand Rapids, MI: Christian Classics Ethereal Library, 1893, p. 492, http://www.ccel.org/ccel/schaff/npnf206.vii.iii.viii.html.

32 Loewe, 1975.

33 Metzger, 2001.

34 Heather and Matthews, 1991. Images of the codex can be found at http://app.ub.uu.se/arv/codex/faksimiledition/contents.html.

35 *Epitome of The Ecclesiastical History of Philostorgius, Compiled By Photius, Patriarch Of Constantinople*, trans. Edward Walford, London, 1855.

36 Wace, 1911.

37 Heather and Matthews, 1991.

38 Rebenich, 2002.

39 Metzger, 2001.

40 Henri Van Hoof, 'Traduction biblique et genèse linguistique', *Babel*, 36(1), 1990, pp. 38–43.

41 *Epitome of The Ecclesiastical History of Philostorgius, Compiled by Photius, Patriarch of Constantinople*, trans. Edward Walford, London, 1855, Book 2, Ch. 5.

42 Heather and Matthews, 1991.

43 Nersessian, 2001.

44 Delisle and Woodsworth, 1995.

45 Holland, 2012.

Chapter 4

1 Griffith, 2013. p. 2.

2 Qur'an, *Al Baqarah* 2:285.

3   Griffith, 2013.

4   Qur'an, *Al Baqarah* 2:136.

5   Griffith, 2013. Griffith mentions only Christian homiletical collections such as those complied by Jacob of Serug and Ephrem the Syrian. But Jewish works such as Pirkei d' Rabbi Eliezer, a post-Islamic 'interpreted' Bible written in Hebrew, suggest that similar tracts could have been composed for Arabic-speaking Jews.

6   Tritton, 1930.

7   Griffith, 2013.

8   Griffith, 2013. See also 'H. Kachouch, The Arabic Versions of the Gospels: A Case Study of John 1:1 and 1:18', in David Thomas (ed.), *The Bible in Arab Christianity* (The History of Christian–Muslim Relations, Vol. 6; Leiden: Brill, 2007), referenced in Griffith, 2013.

9   Bennison, 2009.

10 Gutas, 1998.

11 Griffith, 2013, citing Richard Steiner, *A Biblical Translation in the Making: The Evolution and Impact of Saadia Gaon's Tafsīr*, Cambridge, MA: Harvard University Press, 2010.

12 'Hunayn Ibn Ishaq: A Forgotten Legend', Samir Johna, *American Foundation For Syriac Studies*, July 2011 http://www.syriacstudies.com/2011/07/13_hunayn_ibn_ishaq_a_forgotten_legend_samir_johna/

13 For a biography of Saadia Gaon see Malter, 1921.

14 Exodus 35.3.

15 Schur, 1995.

16 Even though the city of Babylon had ceased to exist many centuries earlier, the name remained. For a history of the Babylonian Talmud and the story of its evolution in the academies of Babylon see my book *The Talmud: A Biography* (Freedman, 2014).

17 Stern, 2001.

18 Steiner, 2011.

19 Steiner, 2011. However Henry Malter believes Saadia wrote his first translation in Egypt (Malter, 1921).

20 Saadia translated the Pentateuch, Isaiah, Psalms, Proverbs, Job, Lamentations, Esther and Daniel (Griffith, 2013).

21 Steiner, 2011.

22 Griffith, 2013.

23 Preface to the *Tafsir*, translated in Steiner, 2011, p. 1.

24 Schaff, 1882a. p. 62.

25 Lockwood, 1969.

26 Goldberg, 2006.

27 Metzger, 2001.

28 Berend, 2007 (Goldberg, 2006).

Chapter 5

1 Brown, 2003.

2 The Lindisfarne Gospels can be viewed on the British Library's website, http://www.bl.uk/turning-the-pages/?id=fdbcc772-3e21-468d-8ca1-9c192f0f939c&type=book.

3 Griffith, 2013.

4 Mellinkoff, 1970.

5 Exodus 35.34, Hebrew קרן. The Septuagint chooses δεδόξασται, which Sir Lancelot C. L. Brenton in his 1851 translation renders as 'glorified'. See also Mellinkoff, 1970, p. 142, note 4.

6 Mellinkoff, 1970. p. 21.

7 Michelangelo's Moses is in Rome's San Pietro In Vincoli.

8 Levine, 2006.

9 Thomsett, 2011.

10 A description of the Lyon manuscript can be found in Anne Brenon, 'Cathars and the Representation of the Divine: Christians of the Invisible', *Iconoclasm and Iconoclash: Struggle for Religious Identity*, ed. Willem J. van Asselt, Paul Van Geest and Daniela Muller, Leiden: Brill, 2007 pp. 247–61.

11 O'Shea, 2001.

12 The true figure is unknown but as Zoe Oldenbourg points out, it could not have reached the one million mark as has been suggested (Oldenbourg, 1961).

13 Sneddon, 2012.

14 Lambert, 1992.

15 O'Shea, 2001.

16 Lerner, 1972.

17 Lichtmann, 1997.

18 Lerner, 1972.

19 Lichtmann, 1997 p. 67, translating from Paul Verdeyen, SJ, 'Le Proces D'Inquisition contre Marguertie Porete et Guiard de Cressonessart (1309–1310)', *Revue d'Histoire Ecclesiastique*, 81 (1986), pp. 47–94.

20 Ibid.

21 Schaff, 1882b. p. 261.

22 Thomsett, 2011. p. 113.

23 Schaff, 1882b. p. 261.

24 Schaff, 1882b. p. 262.

25 Bruce, 1984.

26 Knighton, 1995. p. 242.

27 Daniell, 2001. p. 57.

28 Knighton, 1995. p. 245.

29 Schaff, 1882d. p. 192.

30 See Rosalyn Rossignol, *Critical Companion to Chaucer: A Literary Reference to His Life and Work,* New York: Infobase Publishing, 2006, s.v. John Wycliffe.

31 Neville Chamberlain, BBC Radio broadcast, 27 September 1938.

32 Fudge, 2010.

33 Fudge, 2010. p. 48.

34 Fudge, 2013.

35 Quoted in Richard Rolt and Richard Houston, *The Lives of the Principal Reformers, Both Englishmen and Foreigners: Comprehending the General History of the Reformation; from Its Beginning, in 1360, by Dr. John Wickliffe, to Its Establishment, in 1600, Under Queen Elizabeth: With an Introduction; Wherein the Reformation is Amply Vindicated, and Its Necessity Fully Shewn, from the Degeneracy of the Clergy, and the Tyranny of the Popes.* Published by E. Bakewell et al., London, 1759.

36 Other inventions (few of which were manufactured due to the technical limitations of the time) include a device for measuring the speed of the wind, a parachute, a giant crossbow and a diving suit (DaVinci Inventions, 2008).

37 Arnold, 2011. p. 5.

38 Letter printed in the first edition of the first six books of the Annals of Tacitus, 1515, quoted in Schaff, 1882b, p. 328.

39 Arnold, 2011.

40 Pico Della Mirandola, *Oration on the Dignity of Man: A New Translation and Commentary*, Cambridge: Cambridge University Press, 2012.

41 Idel, 2011.

42 Martines, 2006.

43 Arnold, 2011.

44 Freedman, 2014.

45 G. Lloyd Jones, Introduction in (Reuchlin, 1983).

46 Psalms 6.32, 38, 51, 102, 130 and 143, which Reuchlin published in 1512 under the title *In Septem Psalmos Poenitentiales*.

47 Arnold, 2011.

48 Smith, 1911. p. 29.

49 Arnold, 2011.

50 Martines, 2006.

51 Holborn, 1982.

52 Quoted in Schaff, 1882b, p. 429.

53 Martin Luther, *Address to the Nobility of the German Nation*, quoted in Bainton, 1963, p. 1.

54 Martin Luther, *Luther's Works*, American Edition, ed. Jaroslav Pelikan, St. Louis: Concordia Publishing House, 1958, 4;351, quoted in (Ages, 1967) p. 66.

55 Gritsch, 2003.

56 Ellingworth, 2007.

57 Gritsch, 2003.

58 Volz, 1963.

59 Romans 3.28.

60 Schaff, 1882c.

61 Gritsch, 2012. p. 140.

62 Gritsch, 2012.

63 Gritsch, 2003.

64 Sheehan, 2005.

65 The twelfth-century Jewish Bible interpreter and grammarian David Kimchi considers the Hebrew word to imply that the mountain is to be distinguished by its height. His equally erudite predecessor, Abraham Ibn Ezra, associates it with a root word in Leviticus 21.20 meaning rounded or humped.

Chapter 6

1   Daniell, 2001 p. 3. David Daniell, the William Tyndale scholar par excellence, is the principal source for the account that follows of Tyndale's life and work.

2   Moynahan, 2002.

3   (Daniell, 2001) p. 103, quoting John Foxe, *The Acts and Monuments of John Foxe*, Vol. IV, ed. S. R. Cattley and J. Pratt, London: Religious Tract Society, 1877, pp. 617–18.

4   William Tyndale, *Prologue to the Book of Genesis*.

5   Preface to *The Parable of the Wicked Mammon*, William Tyndale, 1528, reproduced in *The Works of the English Reformers: William Tyndale and John Frith*, Vol.1, ed. Thomas Russell, London: Ebenezer Palmer, 1831, p. 79. Tyndale calls Strasbourg by its medieval name, Argentine.

6   Daniell, 2001. p. 147.

7   *Practice of Prelates*, William Tyndale, 1530, reproduced in *The Works of the English Reformers: William Tyndale and John Frith, Volume 1*, ed. Thomas Russell, London: Ebenezer Palmer, 1831, p. 483.

8   Edward Hall, *The Union of Two Noble and Illustre Families of Lancaster and York* (1548), cited in McGrath, 2001.

9   Daniell, 2001.

10   Genesis 1.3; Wycliffe's verb 'made' is not in the original Hebrew.

11   Matthew 22.21. Caesar is in the original Greek text. Wycliffe's '*those things*' is a translator's interpolation, Tyndale condenses it to '*that*'.

12   (Teems, 2012) p. 268ff. includes a list of words that first appeared in Tyndale's translation.

13   Exodus 12.27: 'It is the sacrifice of the Lord's Passover which passed over the houses of the Children of Israel in Egypt.' Wycliffe renders this: 'It is the sacrifice of the passing of the Lord...'

14   Moynahan, 2002.

15   For example, changing Tyndale's highly accurate rendering of Genesis 46.34 'For an abomination unto the Egyptians are all that feed sheep' to 'For the Egyptians abhor all shepherds'. For further examples see Daniell, 2001, pp. 336ff.

16   Daniell, 2001.

17   Bruce, 1961.

18   Metzger, 2001.

Chapter 7

1 Jenkins and Preston, 2007.

2 Yaacob Dweck, *The Scandal of Kabbalah: Leon Modena, Jewish Mysticism, Early Modern Venice*, Princeton, NJ: Princeton University Press, 2011.

3 Foster, 1963.

4 Jenkins and Preston, 2007.

5 'Rhetoric and Politics in Italian Humanism', Delio Cantimori, trans. Frances A. Yates, *Journal of the Warburg Institute*, 1(2) (Oct. 1937), pp. 83–102.

6 Foster, 1963.

7 Brown, 1891. The book was Christoforo Marcello's *Universalis Anima Traditionis*.

8 Montaigne, *Of Prayers*, 1580, in *Essays of Michel de Montaigne*, trans. Charles Cotton, 1877; Project Gutenberg 2006, https://www.gutenberg.org/files/3600/3600-h/3600-h.htm#link2HCH0056.

9 E.g. Reuben's speech in Genesis 37.21–22, where his attempt to save Joseph from the pit becomes a lecture in morality; see Bainton, 1963, p. 27.

10 Genesis 46.27; Acts 7.14.

11 Bainton, 1963. p. 8.

12 Arnold, 2011. The three Marys are the prostitute in Luke 7, Mary Magdalen of Luke 8 and John 22, and the sister of Martha in John 11 and Luke 10.

13 Wait, 2001.

14 Sayce, 1963.

15 Conerly, 1993.

16 Morreale, 1969.

17 Details of the facsimile edition, and a further history of the Bible, can be found at http://www.facsimile-editions.com/en/ab/.

18 Kamen, 1997. p. 112.

19 Roth, 1948.

20 Roth, 1948. p. 74.

21 Elyada, 2012.

22 Teter & Fram, 2006.

23 Quoted in Elyada, 2012, p. 158.

24 Elyada, 2012.

25 Reck-Malleczewen and Friedrich Percyval, *Bockelson: Geschichte eines Massenwahns*, 1937, Berlin: Schützen-Verlag.

26 *Diary of a Man in Despair*, Fritz Reck-Malleczewen, London: Duck Editions, 2000. Quoted in Jason Cowley, 'Hating the Mob', *New Statesman*, 6 March 2000, http://www.newstatesman.com/node/137057.

27 Von der Lippe & Reck-Malleczewen, 2008 p. xv.

28 Gray, 2007.

29 Leviticus 26.8.

30 The above account is taken from Norman Cohn's *The Pursuit of the Millennium* (Cohn, 1957). There are many other accounts of the events in Münster, some of which vary in their details. It remains, and probably always will be, a very confused time.

Chapter 8

1 D. Gillard (2011), *Education in England: A Brief History*, www.educationengland.org.uk/history.

2 David Cressy, *Literacy and the Social Order: Reading and Writing in Tudor and Stuart England*, Cambridge: Cambridge University Press, 1980.

3 Chitty, 2004.

4 Lewis Carroll, *Through the Looking Glass*, London: Macmillan, 1872, Ch. 6.

5 (Nicolson, 2003). The word at issue is the Greek *tupoi,* which Augustine translates as 'archetype', Doauy as 'figure' and KJB as 'example'.

6 John Milton, *Of Reformation Touching Church Discipline*, in *John Milton: Selected Prose*, ed. C. A. Patrides, Columbia, MO: University of Missouri Press, 1985, p. 78.

7 Nicolson, 2003.

8 E.g. Joshua 10.3: 'Tyrants take for themselves glorious names, when indeed they are the very enemies of God and all justice.' Genesis 33.6: 'Jacob and his family are the image of the Church under the yoke of tyrants who out of fear are brought to subjection.' Exodus 1.22: 'When tyrants cannot prevail by deceit, they burst into open rage.'

9 Jeremiah 8.22. 'Treacle' in the Bishops' Bible is spelt 'tryacle'.

10 McGrath, 2001.

11 *The Church History of Britain: From the Birth of Jesus Christ Until the Year 1648, Volume 5*, Thomas Fuller, ed. J. S. Brewer, Oxford University Press, 1845, p. 285.

12 McGrath, 2001. p. 164.

13 Norton, 2004. p. 4.

14 Nicolson, 2003.

15 The 1611 first edition of the King James Bible, 'The translators to the reader', Section *The purpose of the Translators, with their number, furniture, care, &c.* Quoted in Norton, 2004, p. 3. English modernized.

16 Nicolson, 2003.

17 Genesis 8.6–9.

18 Norton, 2004.

19 Norton, 2004. p. 8.

20 Daiches, 1941.

21 Nicolson, 2003.

22 Norton, 2004.

23 Bodleian Library Bibl. Eng. 1602 b. 1.

24 Norton, 2004.

Chapter 9

1   Altmann, 1973.

2   *Korban Ha-Edah* (Dessau and Berlin) 1743–1762.

3   Sorkin, 1996.

4   Altmann, 1973.

Chapter 10

1   Haraszti, 1956.

2   Daniell, 2003.

3   'More Bible Curiosities and Mistranslations', Gabriel A. Sivan, *Jewish Bible Quarterly*, October 2006, 34(4), pp. 211–17.

4   Winship, 1945. p. 68.

5   Idem, p. 172.

6   Idem, p. 176.

7   Harley, 1900.

8   Harley, 1900. p. 161.

9   Harley, 1900.

10 Genesis 3.22.

11 Psalm 23.5. For the Septuagint I have used Albert Pietersma's translation in *A New English Translation of the Septuagint*, Oxford: Oxford University Press, 2009. Note that the change of ownership of the cup (from *my* to *your*) is the Septuagint's and not Thomson's.

12 Lepore, 2012 p. 111.

13 Cassedy, 2014. p. 229.

14 Thomas Jefferson to James Madison, 12 August 1801, in *The Writings of Thomas Jefferson*, ed. Paul Leicester Ford (New York: Putnams, 1892–99), 8:81, quoted in (Lepore, 2012) p. 119.

15 Noah Webster, *Preface to The Webster Bible*, New Haven, 1833.

16 1 Samuel 25.22, 25.34; 1 Kings 14.10; 16.11; 21.21; 2 Kings 9.8.

17 E.g. John 11.39, where Webster uses the verb 'offensive' to describe Lazarus's body, which in the King James Version 'stinketh'.

18 Noah Webster, *Introduction to The Webster Bible*, New Haven, 1833.

19 Daniell, 2003. p. 651.

20 Sampson, 2006.

21 Hynes, 2013.

22 Sampson, 2006. p. 96.

23 Sampson, 2006. p. 97.

24 Genesis 8.5.

25 *The Boston Post*, 22 January 1874, quoted in Hynes, 2013, p. 31.

26 Abby & Julia Smith, letter to unnamed correspondent, 20 July 1875, quoted in Sampson, 2006, p. 57.

27 Julia Smith, quoted in Sampson, 2006, p. 154.

28 (Housley, 1993).

Chapter 11

1   Soskice, 2009.

2   *Hints for an Improved Translation of the New Testament*, Revd James Scholefield, London, 1832, pp. v–vi.

3 *Notes on the Proposed Amendment of the Authorised Version*, William Selwyn, Cambridge, 1856.

4 Metzger, 2001.

5 Browne, 1859. p. 6.

6 Batalden, 2013.

7 Batalden, 2013.

8 Batalden, 1988.

9 Freeze, 1983.

10 Batalden, 1988.

11 (Freeze, 1983) p. 45, quoting Bishop Innokentii in N. M. Vostokov, *Innokentii arkhiepiskop Khersonskii*, Russkaia Starina 24 (1879), p. 661.

12 Above, page 184.

13 *Evangelical Repository and Bible Teacher*, 58 (October 1881), 153; cited by Thuesen, 1999, p. 55.

14 Price, 2006.

15 *Addresses on the Revised Version of Holy Scripture*, C. J. Ellicott, Society for Promoting Christian Knowledge, London, 1901, p. 121.

16 *The life of Philip Schaff: in part autobiographical*, David S. Schaff, New York: C. Scribner's Sons, 1897, p. 386.

17 Isaiah 7.14.

18 E.g. the Septuagint translates the Hebrew עלמה as νεανίς in Exodus 2.8, as νεάνιδες in Song of Songs 1,3 but as παρθένος in the contentious Isaiah passage. See above page 16.

19 Quoted in Thuesen, 1999, p. 97.

20 'Air Force Manuals', *CQ Almanac 1960*, 16th edn, Washington: Congressional Quarterly, 1960, 11–52. *CQ Almanac Online Edition*, Web, 4 Feb. 2015.

21 Ebor, 1961.

22 T. S. Eliot, Review of New English Bible, *Sunday Telegraph*, 16 December 1962.

23 Alter, 2004.

24 See above, page 97.

25 *Pittsburgh Post-Gazette*, 21 October 1966 p. 2.

26 *The Jerusalem Bible*, Editor's Foreword by Alexander Jones, London: Darton, Longman and Todd, 1966.

27 Gleason Archer, 'The Old Testament of The Jerusalem Bible', *Westminster Theological Journal*, 33 (May 1971), pp. 191–4.

28 *The Jerusalem Bible Reader's Edition*, Editor's Foreword by Alexander Jones, New York: Doubleday, 1968, p. v.

Chapter 12

1 Henry Wansbrough, Editor's Foreword, *New Jerusalem Bible*, New York: Doubleday, 1990, p. vi.

2 Miriam in Exodus 15.20 and Deborah in Judges 4.4 are both described as prophets.

3 Leviticus 1.2: '*A man among you who brings an offering...from the cattle...you will bring your offering*', is transformed into '*When any of you brings an offering...he can offer an animal...*'

4 Bruce Metzger, 'To The Reader', *New Revised Standard Version*, New York: Oxford University Press, 1989, p. xi.

5 *Today's New International Version* was published in 2005 as a gender-neutral revision to the *New International Version*, which was intended as an interdenominational alternative to the *Revised Standard Version*.

6 E.g. Deuteronomy 15.12; 21.11.

7 Leviticus 18.22; 20.13.

8 Romans 1.24–27.

9 Queen James, 2012. p. 1.

10 Jeremy Bentham: Offences against Oneself (c.1785) republished in *Journal of Homosexuality*, 3(4) (1978), pp. 389–405; continued in 4(1) (1978).

11 David M. Bergeron, *King James and Letters of Homoerotic Desire*, Iowa City: University of Iowa Press, 1999.

12 *Shmoose* means to converse, *chutzpah* – which has found its way into English slang and might, just, be allowable in a Bible translation – means insolence, or audacity; a *nudnik* is a particularly irritating sort of idiot and *meshugga* means mad.

13 Metzger, 2001. p. 148.

14 Genesis 3.18.

15 http://www.forbes.com/companies/wycliffe-bible-translators.

16 http://www.wycliffe.org/About/Whatwedo.aspx.

17 'The Son and the Crescent', *Christianity Today*, 4 February 2011, http://www.christianitytoday.com/ct/2011/february/soncrescent.html.

18 'Wycliffe Bible Translation Criticized over Trinity Word Substitution in Muslim Countries', Tom Breen, *Huffington Post*, 26 April 2012; http://www.huffingtonpost.com/2012/04/26/bible-translator-trinity_n_1455982.html.

19 The WEA Global Review Panel, *Report to World Evangelical Alliance for Conveyance to Wycliffe Global Alliance and Sil International*, 26 April 2013.

Chapter 13

1 Guinness World Records, *Best Selling Work of Non-Fiction*, http://www.guinnessworldrecords.com/world-records/best-selling-book-of-non-fiction.

2 Levine and Brettler, 2011.

3 Ecclesiastes 12.12.

Bibliography

Ages, A., 1967. 'Luther and the Rabbis'. *Jewish Quarterly Review*, 58(1), pp. 63–8.

Alexander, P., 1988. 'Jewish Aramaic Translations of Hebrew Scriptures'. In Mubler, M.J. and Sysling, H., eds, *Mikra*. Philadelphia: s.n.

Alter, R., 2004. *The Five Books of Moses: A Translation with Commentary*. New York: W. W. Norton & Co.

Altmann, A., 1973. *Moses Mendelssohn: A Biographical Study*. Tuscaloosa, AL: University of Alabama Press.

Arkush, A., 1994. *Moses Mendelssohn and the Enlightenment*. Albany, NY: State University of New York Press.

Arnold, J., 2011. *The Great Humanists: European Thought on the Eve of the Reformation*. London: I.B.Tauris.

Bainton, R. H., 1963. 'The Bible in the Reformation'. In S. Greenslade, ed., *The Cambridge History of the Bible: The West from the Reformation to the Present Day*. Cambridge: Cambridge University Press.

Batalden, S. K., 1988. 'Gerasim Pavskii's Clandestine Old Testament: The Politics of Nineteenth-Century Russian Biblical Translation'. *Church History*, 57(4), pp. 486–98.

Batalden, S. K., 2013. *Russian Bible Wars: Modern Scriptural Translation and Cultural Authority*. Cambridge: Cambridge University Press.

Bennison, A. K., 2009. *The Great Caliphs: The Golden Age of the 'Abbasid Empire*. London: I.B.Tauris.

Berend, N., ed., 2007. *Christianization and the Rise of Christian Monarchy: Scandinavia, Central Europe and Rus' c.900–1200*. Cambridge: Cambridge University Press.

Bickerman, E. J., 1988. *The Jews in the Greek Age*. Cambridge, MA: Harvard University Press.

Brock, S., 1997. *A Brief Outline of Syriac Literature*. Kottayam, India: St Ephrem Ecumenical Research Institute.

Brown, H. F., 1891. *The Venetian Printing Press: An Historical Study Based on Documents for the Most Part Hitherto Unpublished*. New York: Putnam's.

Brown, M. P., 2003. *The Lindisfarne Gospels: Society, Spirituality and the Scribe*. London: British Library Publishing Division.

Browne, G., 1859. *History of the British and Foreign Bible Society from its institution in 1804, to the close of its jubilee in 1854: compiled at the request of the jubilee committee*. London: The Society's House.

Bruce, F. F., 1961. *History of the Bible in English*. Cambridge: James Clarke & Co.

Bruce, F. F., 1984. 'John Wycliffe and the English Bible'. *Churchman*, 98(4), pp. 294–306.

Canfora, L., 1987. *The Vanished Library*. Berkeley: University of California Press.

Casey, M., 2002. *An Aramaic Approach to Q: Sources for the Gospels of Matthew and Luke*. Cambridge: Cambridge University Press.

Cassedy, T., 2014. 'A Dictionary Which We Do Not Want: Defining America against Noah Webster, 1783–1810'. *The William and Mary Quarterly*, 71(2), pp. 229–54.

Chitty, C., 2004. *Education Policy in Britain (Contemporary Political Studies)*. Basingstoke: Palgrave Macmillan.

Churton, W. R., 1861. *The Influence of the Septuagint Version of the Old Testament upon the Progress of Christianity*. London: Macmillan.

Cohen, M. R., 1994. *Under Crescent and Cross: The Jews in the Midle Ages*. Princeton, NJ: Princeton University Press.

Cohn, N., 1957. *The Pursuit of the Millennium*. Oxford: Oxford University Press.

Collins, N., 2000. *The Library in Alexandria and the Bible in Greek*. Leiden: Brill.

Conerly, P., 1993. 'Bible in Vulgar Translation'. In G. Bleiberg, M. Ihrie & J. Pérez, eds, *Dictionary of the Literature of the Iberian Peninsula, Volume 1*. Westport, CT: Greenwood Publishing Group, pp. 202–5.

Daiches, D., 1941. *The King James Version of the English Bible: An Account of the Development and Sources of the English Bible of 1611 with Special Reference to the Hebrew Tradition*. Chicago: University of Chicago Press.

Daniell, D., 1992. *Tyndale's Old Testament: Being the Pentateuch of 1530, Joshua to 2 Chronicles of 1537, and Jonah*. New Haven: Yale University Press.

Daniell, D., 2001. *William Tyndale: A Biography*. New Haven: Yale University Press.

Daniell, D., 2003. *The Bible in English: Its History and Influence*. New Haven: Yale University Press.

DaVinci Inventions, 2008. *Leonardo da Vinci Inventions*. [Online] Available at: http://www.da-vinci-inventions.com/ [accessed 3 August 2013].

Delisle, J. and Woodsworth, J., 1995. *Translators Through History*. Amsterdam: John Benjamins Publishing.

Dines, J. M., 2004. *The Septuagint*. London: T&T Clark.

Ebor, D., 1961. Preface to the New English Bible. In *New English Bible*. Oxford: Oxford University Press, Cambridge University Press.

Ellingworth, P., 2007. 'From Martin Luther to the English Revised Version' In P. A. Noss, ed., *A History of Bible Translation*. Rome: Edizioni di storia e letteratura, pp. 105–39.

Elyada, A., 2012. *A Goy Who Speaks Yiddish: Christians and the Jewish Language in Early Modern Germany*. Stanford, CA: Stanford University Press.

Feiner, S., 2010. *Moses Mendelssohn: Sage of Modernity*. New Haven: Yale University Press.

Flesher, P. V., 2011. *The Targums: A Critical Introduction*. Leiden: Brill.

Foster, K., 1963. 'Continental Versions to 1600: Italian'. In S. Greenslade, ed., *The Cambridge History of the Bible: The West from the Reformation to the Present Day*. Cambridge: Cambridge University Press, pp. 110–12.

Freedman, H., 2014. *The Talmud: A Biography*. London: Bloomsbury Press.

Freeze, G. L., 1983. *The Parish Clergy in Nineteenth-Century Russia: Crisis, Reform, Counter-Reform*. Princeton, NJ: Princeton University Press.

Fudge, T. A., 2010. *Jan Hus: Religious Reform and Social Revolution in Bohemia*. London: I.B.Tauris.

Fudge, T. A., 2013. *The Trial of Jan Hus: Medieval Heresy and Criminal Procedure*. Oxford: Oxford University Press.

Goldberg, E. J., 2006. *Struggle for Empire: Kingship and Conflict Under Louis the German, 817–876*. Ithaca: Cornell University Press.

Grafton, A. & Weinberg, J., 2011. *I Have Always Loved the Holy Tongue*. Cambridge, MA: Belknap Press of Harvard University Press.

Gray, J., 2007. *Black Mass: Apocalyptic Religion and the Death of Utopia*. London: Allen Lane.

Greenslade, S.L., 1963. English Versions 1525–1611. In S.L. Greendslade, ed., *The Cambridge History of the Bible: The West from the Reformation to the Present Day*. Cambridge: Cambridge University Press.

Griffith, S. H., 2013. *The Bible in Arabic: The Scriptures of the 'People of the Book' in the Language of Islam*. Princeton, NJ: Princeton Universty Press.

Gritsch, E. W., 2003. 'Luther as Bible Translator'. In D. K. Kim, ed., *The Cambridge Companion to Martin Luther*. Cambridge: Cambridge University Press, pp. 62–72.

Gritsch, E. W., 2012. *Martin Luther's Anti-Semitism: Against His Better Judgement*. Grand Rapids, MI: Wm B. Eerdmans.

Gutas, D., 1998. *Greek Thought, Arabic Culture: The Graeco-Arabic Translation Movement in Baghdad and Early Abbasid Society (2nd–4th/5th–10th c.)*. Abingdon, Oxon: Routledge.

Haraszti, Z., 1956. *The Enigma of the Bay Psalm Book*. Chicago: University of Chicago Press.

Harley, L. R., 1900. *The life of Charles Thomson, secretary of the Continental congress and translator of the Bible from the Greek*. Philadelphia: George W. Jacobs & Co.

Hayward, C. T. R., 1995. *Saint Jerome's Hebrew Questions on Genesis*. Oxford: Clarendon Press.

Heather, P. & Matthews, J., 1991. *The Goths in the Fourth Century*. Liverpool: Liverpool University Press.

Holborn, H., 1982. *A History of Modern Germany: The Reformation*. Princeton, NJ: Princeton University Press.

Holder, R. W., 2009. *Crisis and Renewal: The Era of the Reformations*. Louisville, KY: Westminster John Knox Press.

Holland, T., 2012. *In the Shadow of the Sword*. New York: Doubleday.

Housley, K., 1993. *The Letter Kills but the Spirit Gives Life: The Smiths – Abolitionists, Suffragists, Bible Translators*. Glastonbury, CT: Historical Society of Glastonbury, CT.

Hynes, J., 2013. 'The 1870s Tax Resistance of Julia and Abby Smith: From Natural Rights to Expediency in the Shadow of Separate Spheres'. *Tennessee Journal of Race, Gender, & Social Justice*, 2(2), pp. 1–36.

Idel, M., 2011. *Kabbalah in Italy 1280–1510: A Survey*. New Haven: Yale University Press.

Jenkins, A. K. & Preston, P., 2007. *Biblical Scholarship and the Church: A Sixteenth-century Crisis of Authority*. Aldershot: Ashgate.

Kamen, H., 1997. *The Spanish Inquisition: A Historical Revision*. London: Weidenfeld & Nicolson.

Kaplan, D., 2011. *Beyond Expulsion: Jews, Christians, and Reformation Strasbourg*. Stanford, CA: Stanford University Press.

Katz, J., 1998. *Out of the Ghetto: The Social Background of Jewish Emancipation, 1770–1870*. Syracuse, NY: Syracuse University Press.

Kelly, J., 1998. *Golden Mouth: The Story of John Chrysostom – Ascetic, Preacher, Bishop*. Ithaca: Cornell University Press.

Kiraz, G., 2001. *Syriac Orthodox Resources*. [Online] Available at: http://sor.cua.edu/Bible/Peshitto.html [accessed 18 November 2013].

Kirby, P., 2001–2013. *Early Christian Writings*. [Online] Available at: http://www.earlychristianwritings.com [accessed 10 October 2013].

Knighton, H., 1995. *Knighton's Chronicle 1337–1396*. Oxford: Clarendon Press.

Lambert, M., 1992. *Medieval Heresy: Popular Movements from the Gregorian Reform to the Reformation*. Oxford: Wiley-Blackwell.

Lampe, P., 2006. *Christians at Rome in the First Two Centuries: From Paul to Valentinus*. London: Continuum.

Lepore, J., 2012. *The Story of America: Essays on Origins*. Princeton, NJ: Princeton University Press.

Lerner, R. E., 1972. *The Heresy of the Free Spirit in the Later Middle Ages*. Berkeley: University of California Press.

Levine, A.-J., 2006. *The Misunderstood Jew: The Church and the Scandal of the Jewish Jesus*. New York: HarperCollins.

Levine, A.-J. and Brettler, M. Z. eds, 2011. *The Jewish Annotated New Testament*. New York: Oxford University Press.

Lichtmann, M., 1997. 'Marguerite Porete and Meister Eckhart: The Mirror of Simple Souls Mirrored'. In *Meister Eckhart and the Beguine Mystics: Hadewijch of Brabant, Mechthild of Magdeburg, and Marguerite Porete*. London: Bloomsbury.

Liebermann, S., 1942. *Greek in Jewish Palestine: Studies in the Life and Manners of Jewish Palestine in the II–IV Centuries C.E.*. New York: Jewish Theological Society of America.

Lockwood, W., 1969. 'Vernacular Scriptures in Germany and the Low Countries before 1500'. In G. W. H, Lampe, ed., '*The Cambridge History of the Bible, Volume 2: The West from the Fathers to the Reformation*. Cambridge: Cambridge University Press.

Loewe, R., 1975. 'The Medieval History of the Latin Vulgate'. In G. W. H. Lampe and P. R. Ackroyd, eds, *The Cambridge History of the Bible, Volume 2: The West from the Fathers to the Reformation*. Cambridge: Cambridge University Press, pp. 102–54.

Malter, H., 1921. *Saadia Gaon: His Life and Works*. Philadelphia: Jewish Publication Society of America.

Martines, L., 2006. *Fire in the City: Savonarola and the Struggle for the Soul of Renaissance Florence*. Oxford: Oxford University Press.

McGrath, A., 2001. *In the Beginning: The Story of the King James Bible and How it Changed a Nation, a Language and a Culture*. New York: Doubleday.

McGuckin, J. A., ed., 2004. *The Westminster Handbook to Origen*. Louisville, KY: Westminster John Knox Press,.

McNamara, R., 2010. *Targum and Testament Revisited: Aramaic Paraphrases of the Hebrew Bible*. 2nd edn. Grand Rapids, MI: Wm B. Eerdmans.

Mellinkoff, R., 1970. *The Horned Moses in Medieval Art and Thought*. Berkeley: University of California Press.

Metzger, B. M., 2001. *The Bible in Translation: Ancient and English Versions*. Grand Rapids, MI: Baker Academic.

Moore, G. F., 1927. *Judaism in the First Centuries of the Christian Era, Vol. 1, The Age of the Tannaim.* Hendrickson Publishers' Edition, March 1997. Harvard: Harvard University Press.

Morreale, M., 1969. 'Vernacular Scriptures in Spain'. In G. Lampe, ed., '*The Cambridge History of The Bible, Volume 2: The West from the Fathers to the Reformation.* Cambridge: Cambridge University Press, pp. 465–91.

Moynahan, B., 2002. *Book of Fire: William Tyndale, Thomas More and the Bloody Birth of the English Bible.* London: Hachette.

Nersessian, V., 2001. *The Bible in the Armenian Tradition.* London: British Library.

Nicolson, A., 2003. *When God Spoke English: The Making of the King James Bible.* London: HarperCollins.

Nirenberg, D., 2013. *Anti-Judaism: The History of a Way of Thinking.* New York: W. W. Norton & Co. Inc..

Norton, D., 2004. *A Textual History of the King James Bible.* Cambridge: Cambridge University Press.

Oldenbourg, Z., 1961. *Massacre at Montségur: A History of the Albigensian Crusade.* London: Weidenfeld & Nicolson.

O'Shea, S., 2001. *The Perfect Heresy: The Revolutionary Life and Death of the Medieval Cathars.* London: Profile Books.

Parpulov, G. R., 2012. 'The Bibles of the Christian East'. In R. Marsden and E. A. Matter, eds, *The New Cambridge History of the Bible: Volume 2: From 600 to 1450.* Cambridge: Cambridge University Press, pp. 309–24.

Pastor, J., Stern, P. and Mor, M., 2011. *Flavius Josephus.* Leiden: Brill.

Price, J. D., 2006. *King James Onlyism: A New Sect.* Singapore: self-published.

Queen James, 2012. The Queen James Bible: www.QueenJames.com

Rajak, T., 2009. *Translation and Survival: The Greek Bible of the Ancient Jewish Diaspora.* Oxford: Oxford University Press.

Rebenich, S., 2002. *Jerome.* London: Routledge.

Reuchlin, J., 1983. *On the Art of the Kabbalah: De Arte Cabalistica.* Norwalk, CT: Abaris Books.

Roth, C., 1948. *The House of Nasi: Doña Gracia.* Philadelphia: Jewish Publication Society of America.

Sabar, A., 2013. 'How to Save a Dying Language'. *Smithsonian Magazine,* February.

Salvesen, A., 1991. *Symmachus in the Pentateuch.* Manchester: Victoria University of Manchester.

Sampson, E., 2006. *With Her Own Eyes: The Story of Julia Smith, Her Life, and Her Bible.* Knoxville: University of Tennessee Press.

Sayce, R., 1963. 'Continental Versions to 1600: French'. In S. Greenslade, ed., *The Cambridge History of The Bible: The West from the Reformation to the Present Day.* Cambridge: Cambridge University Press, pp. 113–21.

Schaff, P., 1882a. *History of the Christian Church, Volume IV: Mediaeval Christianity. A.D. 590–1073.* Grand Rapids, MI: Christian Classics Ethereal Library.

Schaff, P., 1882b. *History of the Christian Church, Volume VI: The Middle Ages. A.D. 1294–1517.* Grand Rapids, MI: Christian Classics Ethereal Library.

Schaff, P., 1882c. *History of the Christian Church, Volume VII: Modern Christianity. The German Reformation.* Grand Rapids, MI: Christian Classics Ethereal Library.

Schaff, P., 1882d. *History of the Christian Church, Volume VI: The Middle Ages. A.D. 1294–1517*. Grand Rapids, MI: Christian Ethereal Library.

Schaff, P., 1890. *St Augustine's City of God and Christian Doctrine*. [Online] Available at: http://www.ccel.org/ccel/schaff/npnf102 [accessed 10 October 2013].

Schmid, U. B., 2012. 'The Diatessaron of Tatian'. In B. D. Ehrman and M. W. Holmes, eds, *The Text of the New Testament in Contemporary Research: Essays on the Status Quaestionis*. Leiden: Brill.

Schur, N., 1995. *The Karaite Encyclopedia*. Frankfurt: Peter Lang.

Sheehan, J., 2005. *The Enlightenment Bible: Translation, Scholarship, Culture*. Princeton, NJ: Princeton University Press.

Shutt, R., 1985. 'Letter of Aristeas: A New Translation and Introduction'. In J. H. Charlesworth, ed., *The Old Testament Pseudepigrapha*. New York: Doubleday.

Silverstone, A., 1931. *Aquila and Onkelos*. Manchester: Manchester University Press.

Simpson, J., 2007. *Burning to Read: English Fundamentalism and its Reformation Opponents*. Cambridge, MA: Harvard University Press.

Smith, P., 1911. *The Life and Letters of Martin Luther*. Boston: Houghton Mifflin Company.

Sneddon, C. R., 2012. 'The Bible in French'. In *New Cambridge History of the Bible*. Cambridge: Cambridge University Press, pp. 251–67.

Sorkin, D., 1996. *Moses Mendelssohn and the Religious Enlightenment*. London: Halban.

Soskice, J., 2009. *Sisters of Sinai: How Two Lady Adventurers Found the Hidden Gospels*. London: Chatto & Windus.

Steiner, R. C., 2011. *A Biblical Translation in the Making: The Evolution and Impact of Saadia Gaon's Tafsir*. Harvard, MA: Harvard University Press.

Stern, S., 2001. *Calendar and Community; A History of the Jewish Calendar*. Oxford: Oxford University Press.

Stothard, P., 2013. *Alexandria: The Last Nights of Cleopatra*. London: Granta.

Sutcliffe, F. E., 1975. 'Jerome'. In G. W. H. Lampe and P. R. Ackroyd, eds, *The Cambridge History of the Bible, Volume 2: The West from the Fathers to the Reformation*. Cambridge: Cambridge University Press.

Teems, D., 2012. *Tyndale: The Man who Gave God an English Voice*. Nashville: Thomas Nelson.

Teter, M. and Fram, E., 2006. 'Apostasy, Fraud and the Beginnings of Hebrew Printing in Cracow'. *AJS Review*, 30(1), pp. 31–66.

Thomsett, M., 2011. *Heresy in the Roman Catholic Church*. Jefferson, NC: McFarland & Co.

Thuesen, P. J., 1999. *In Discordance with the Scriptures: American Protestant Battles over Translating the Bible*. Oxford: Oxford University Press.

Tritton, A., 1930. *Caliphs and Their Non-Muslim Subjects: A Critical Study of the Covenant of 'Umar*. Oxford: Oxford University Press.

Volz, H., 1963. 'Continental Versions to c.1600'. In S. Greenslade, ed., *The Cambridge History of the Bible, The West from the Reformation to the Present Day*. Cambridge: Cambridge University Press, pp. 94–109.

von der Lippe, G. and Reck-Malleczewen, V., 2008. *A History of the Münster Anabaptists: Inner Emigration and the Third Reich: A Critical Edition of Friedrich Reck-Malleczewen's Bockelson: A Tale of Mass Insanity*. New York: Palgrave Macmillan.

Wace, H., 1911. *Dictionary of Christian Biography and Literature to the End of the Sixth Century A.D., with an Account of the Principal Sects and Heresies.* London: John Murray.

Wait, E. M., 2001. *Great Challenges of Reformation Europe.* Huntington, NY: Nova Science Publishers.

Wasserstein, A., 2006. *The Legend of the Septuagint: From Classical Antiquity to Today.* Cambridge: Cambridge University Press.

Weitzman, M., 1999a. *The Syriac Version of the Old Testament.* Cambridge: Cambridge University Press.

Weitzman, M., 1999b. 'From Judaism to Christianity: The Syriac Version of the Hebrew Bible'. In A. Rapoport-Albert and G. Greenberg, eds, *From Judaism to Christianity: Journal of Semitic Studies Supplement 8.* Oxford: Oxford University Press, pp. 3–29.

Williams, P. J., 2012. 'The Syriac Versions of the New Testament'. In: B. D. Ehrman and M. W. Holmes, eds, *The Text of the New Testament in Contemporary Research: Essays on the Status Quaestionis.* Leiden: Brill.

Winship, G. P., 1945. *The Cambridge Press, 1638–1692: A Reexamination of the Evidence concerning the Bay Psalm Book and the Eliot Indian Bible as Well as Other Contemporary Books and People.* Philadelphia: University of Pennsylvania Press.

Index